One-Yard WONDERS

Look How Much You Can Make with Just One Yard of Fabric!

Rebecca Yaker and Patricia Hoskins

Photography by John Gruen

Photo styling by Raina Kattelson

Storey Publishing

The mission of Storey Publishing is to serve our customers by publishing practical information that encourages personal independence in harmony with the environment.

Edited by Deborah Balmuth and Nancy D. Wood
Art direction and book design by Jessica Armstrong

Photography by © John Gruen, except for authors' photo by © Gene Pittman
Photo styling by Raina Kattelson
Illustrations by Missy Shepler/Shepler Studios

For information on the fabrics used in this book, see page 294.

Indexed by Nancy D. Wood

Storey Publishing
210 MASS MoCA Way
North Adams, MA 01247
www.storey.com

Printed in China by R.R. Donnelley
10 9 8 7 6 5 4 3 2 1

LIBRARY OF CONGRESS CATALOGING-IN-PUBLICATION DATA

Yaker, Rebecca.
  One-yard wonders / Rebecca Yaker and Patricia Hoskins.
    p. cm.
  Includes index.
  ISBN 978-1-60342-449-3 (pbk. : alk. paper)
  1. Machine sewing. 2. Clothing and dress. 3. House furnishings.
  I. Hoskins, Patricia. II. Title.
TT713.y35 2009
646.2—dc22
                    2009023721

CONTENTS

CHAPTER 1

Sewing Fundamentals

What do you see when you open the closet of your sewing room? Is it filled to the brim with fabrics that you just had to have but didn't have any plans for? Do you sometimes feel overwhelmed trying to find coordinates, or do you need ideas for small projects? Don't be ashamed any longer! After all, what fabricaholic hasn't bought a yard of this and a yard of that, always hoping to find that perfect use — only to see those yards pile up, just waiting for inspiration to be transformed into something stunning and useful?

In Your Own Back Yardage

Maybe you're like us and stockpile fabric until you realize that there is no more room and you must put those pretty goods to good use. Well, here's your chance — raid that stash and get ready to work some one-yard magic! This book contains dozens of delightful projects all requiring a mere 36 inches of a single cut of fabric, plus a few odds and ends you probably already have.

So, prewash and iron your favorite yard of fabric and let's get to work creating the perfect shopping tote, gardening apron, accent pillows, collar and leash for Fifi — 101 great projects in all. Once you crack open this book, you'll no longer feel the guilt of those previously unused yards weighing upon your conscience (and pocketbook). This is your opportunity to create something just right for you from your beloved yardage.

The main supplies you will need to complete all these projects are your one-yard piece of fabric, thread, and your sewing machine. Some projects may also require basic notions and embellishments, but we'll be sure to let you know before you get started. Take a quick pass through this chapter for some sewing tips and reminders — and it's not a bad idea to read through the illustrated glossary at the back of the book. Then let's get sewing!

Your Sewing Pantry

Here's a list of the 40 essentials we think you'll want to have on hand, not just to complete your projects, but to ensure a frustration-free sewing experience every time! Just as you wouldn't attempt to cook a fabulous recipe without your essential cooking utensils, and just as you keep your kitchen stocked with a smattering of basic ingredients, so you must keep your sewing pantry stocked with some fundamental sewing necessities.

25 Equipment Must-Haves

1. Sewing machine and assorted feet: zigzag, zipper, and walking feet are definitely at the top of the list. A magnetic seam guide and other machine accessories are handy, too — especially long tweezers, a small screwdriver, a brush, and oil.
2. Sewing machine needles for various fabric weights
3. Seam ripper
4. 60" tape measure
5. Point turner (knitting needle or chopstick can be used in a pinch)
6. Fabric shears (7" to 9" blade)
7. Pinking shears
8. Trimming scissors (4" blade)
9. Rotary cutter (go wild and get a pinking blade!)
10. Cutting mat
11. Clear quilter's ruler (3" × 18" is great, or 5" × 24")
12. Hand-sewing needles (assorted, including embroidery needles)
13. Tailor's chalk and/or fabric marker
14. Carbon paper and tracing wheel
15. Tissue, tracing paper, or other pattern-making paper
16. Paper scissors
17. Transparent tape
18. Straight pins (dressmaker's, quilter's, or similar)
19. Safety pins
20. Iron and ironing board
21. Curved ruler (French curve)
22. Bodkin (used to feed elastic and ribbon through casings — you can also use a large safety pin)
23. Lighter (used to prevent fraying on polyester webbing, cordura, and other man-made materials)
24. Pincushion (wrist-strap and magnetic versions make cleaning up spilled pins a cinch)
25. Thimble (metal, leather, plastic — experiment to find the most comfortable option for you)

15 Necessary Notions

1. Spools and prewound bobbins of thread in assorted colors
2. Elastic in various widths: ¼", ½", ¾", 1"
3. Zippers in assorted lengths: metal, polyester, invisible
4. Interfacing: sew-in and fusible, including double-sided fusible
5. Various closures, such as buttons, hooks and eyes, snaps, buckles, D-rings
6. Velcro
7. Twill tape
8. Rickrack
9. Bias tape (homemade or store-bought): single-fold and double-fold
10. Ribbons and trims in assorted widths
11. Embroidery floss
12. Decorative buttons
13. Fabric scraps
14. Webbing
15. Liquid fabric sealant (such as FrayCheck)

Fabric Facts

What makes fabric so fun to work with is that it comes in such a wide variety of patterns, textures, styles, and weights. From handsome, durable duck twills to more delicate cotton voiles, there's a suitable fabric for anything you can imagine making. Given all these choices, it's important to match the fabric to the project so you get useful and pleasing results. Here are some factors to consider when choosing the material for your projects, and some important notes about fabric preparation, cutting, and care.

Weight

Fabrics come in a variety of weights, which can sometimes be a bit confusing. If a project requires a specific fabric weight, we mention it in the materials list for that project.

Quilting-weight cotton may also be called sheeting weight. This fabric is soft and drapes nicely but is not see-through. It is appropriate for a wide variety of projects, from apparel to quilts to curtains to bags and more. You may often see interfacing or linings required with this weight of fabric. When lightweight fabric is called for, that may mean quilting weight or, depending on the context, even lighter fabrics such as voile, rayon, or silk, to name a few.

Home-decor weight is a bit heavier; it still drapes nicely but is sturdier than quilting weight. Its applications range from drapes and pillows to sturdier apparel projects, bags (again), and lighter-use upholstery projects. Depending on the context, both home-decor and quilting-weight fabrics may be referred to as medium-weight. In these instances, either weight would be fine to get the job done.

Upholstery or **heavyweight** fabrics are sturdier yet, with far less draping. Such fabrics are perfect for heavy-duty upholstery projects, stiff and structured bags, and other projects that require a lot of structure and shape.

Content

Most projects in this book call for 100 percent cotton or cotton-blend fabrics. That said, don't limit yourself! Feel free to experiment with silks, polyesters, wools, linens, or blended fabrics — as long as they are in the same basic weight category the project calls for, we're sure your finished results will be stunning!

Knit vs. woven. Nearly all projects in this book call for woven fabrics. Woven fabrics are produced by interlacing threads in two directions (resulting in the grainline and crossgrain designations you will see later in the book). Unless they contain spandex or a similar elastic fiber, woven fabrics tend not to stretch, except along the bias (or diagonal). Knit fabrics are made of a series of interlocking loops. The result is a fabric that typically can be stretched and manipulated in a variety of directions. If you are having trouble distinguishing between knit or woven fabric, pull a thread from one crosswise edge. If you see fringe, it's a woven fabric; if you see a row of loops, it's a knit.

Care. Most cotton fabrics can be machine washed and dried, but don't necessarily assume so. Sometimes fabrics may be specially treated to give them extra texture and/or shine. If you are working with something extra special, it's always a good idea to note the care instructions that are often included on the bolt end at the fabric store. When in doubt, ask the sales associate.

Cutting Your Fabric

Find a clean, flat, smooth, large surface for laying out and cutting your fabric. If you don't have a table reserved for this purpose, your dining room table may be the next best location. There's nothing wrong with laying your fabric out on the floor, as long as it's not on carpet! In any case, you may choose to use a cutting mat to help protect your work surface.

Always lay out all of your pattern pieces before cutting. You don't want to run out of fabric, do you? Many of the projects in this book, and, heck, just about any sewing pattern, will provide a pattern-piece layout guide to get the maximum use out of your fabric yardage. Paying special attention to pattern layout is strongly advised.

Grainline is the direction of the fabric that runs parallel to the selvage edge. Woven fabrics typically do not have give (stretch) in the direction of the grain. Sewing patterns usually have a double-ended arrow printed directly on the pattern piece to indicate where the grainline should run. When laying out your pattern pieces, make sure that you are placing your pattern pieces truly straight along the grainline. This is definitely a case for measuring twice and cutting once. If you cut your pieces crooked, you will feel it on your body. The grainline is your buddy – embrace it!

Pay special attention to pattern-piece anatomy. Are there actual pattern pieces for the project, or are there simply directions and measurements for cutting? How many of each pattern piece do you need to cut and from what material? Does it need to be cut on the fold? Be sure to note the grainline and any special notches and dots, which will be necessary for fabric placement later. All these little details will help you get the job done!

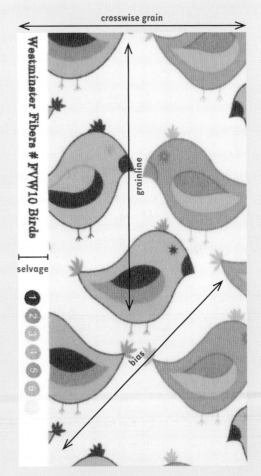

Take note of the print on your actual fabric. Does the design point in one direction (unidirectional), two directions (bidirectional), or is it a tossed print (non-directional)? Take special care to ensure that all the pattern pieces point in the appropriate direction of the fabric design – you wouldn't want to end up with an upside-down skirt or purse! Throughout the projects in this book, we have called out when projects would not be suitable for unidirectional prints.

Although rarely specified as the tools to use in the upcoming projects, a rotary cutter, cutting mat, and quilter's ruler may help make cutting go much faster in many projects, especially when cutting square or rectangular pieces. It is generally not advisable to use a rotary cutter to cut a curved edge.

MORE THAN JUST A PRETTY FACING

Interfacing comes in a variety of types, primarily sew-in and fusible, with various weights of each. The main purpose of interfacing is to provide shape and support in your projects, for instance in collars, cuffs, lapels, waistbands, and bags, to name a few.

Choosing between fusible or sew-in interfacing is really a matter of personal preference, although one type may be specifically called for in a pattern. Generally speaking, fusibles are more common for apparel and provide slightly crisper results. Sew-ins can be a little heavier and are choice for tailored lapels and various handbag and tote patterns. Be sure to follow the manufacturer's instructions for the best results. It's a good idea to test the fusible interfacing on a scrap of fabric to make sure you achieve the results you want.

Making & Using Patterns

Patterns turn up in this book in two ways:

* You'll be told to look for a full-sized pattern in the pattern inserts in the front pocket of the book.

* You'll be given instructions for drafting your own pattern from a set of measurements. You may do this directly onto the wrong side of the fabric or play it safe and draft it first on pattern-making or tissue paper. When drafting your pattern pieces, use a ruler for straight edges and a curved ruler for curved and rounded edges. In general, take care that your lines are neat and tidy to ensure worry-free construction.

When cutting pattern pieces, take note of the notch locations along the edges. You may choose to either clip out from the seam allowance or slightly clip into the seam allowance to ensure the notch placements remain visible when working with your cut fabric pieces.

Note the use of various notations on the pattern pieces, such as notches, darts, tucks, and pleats. All marks should be transferred to the wrong side of your cut fabric pieces *before* removing the paper pattern piece. To complete this task, use tailor's chalk, a fabric marker, or carbon paper and tracing wheel, but whatever you do, make sure these marks don't bleed through to the right side of your fabric!

We've got a sneaky trick to help you mark dots. Use a paper punch to punch out holes in your paper pattern pieces where marked dots appear. You can then easily mark the fabric at the center of the punched-out circle while the pattern template is still placed on your fabric.

Best Sewing Practices

* **Pay close attention to the thread you select** for your sewing project. Threads vary by weight, luster, and content, and all of these will affect the look of the stitches and the thread tension of your sewing machine. Experiment to determine what works best for your project. It's always a good idea to do a little test sewing on a swatch of the actual project fabric to determine the right thread tension. Getting these details right ahead of time will ensure your results are not clumsy!

* **Always pin while you sew.** We know, it seems tedious, but you will be absolutely amazed by the professional results you'll achieve when you pin your projects as you sew them. Just remember to remove the pins along the way; otherwise, there will be that rare instance when you break your needle on a pin, and that's a drag.

* **Don't pull your fabric while sewing.** Your sewing machine has been designed to move your fabric along as you stitch – the feed dogs and presser foot work together to make this happen. Pulling your fabric as you stitch will result in uneven stitches, screwy tension, and an unhappy sewing machine. If the fabric does not feed through easily, it may be time for a service call.

* **Always backstitch** (*see* Stitch Terminology *on page* 13) at the beginning and end of every seam to lock your stitches: ⅛" to ¼" of backstitching should be enough to do the trick!

* **When stitching 90-degree angles** (corners), as you stitch to the corner, stop with your needle in the down position one seam-allowance width before reaching the raw edge. Lift the presser foot and pivot on the needle. Lower the presser foot and resume stitching. This will guarantee neat corners and save both time and thread while stitching.

* **Notch and clip the seam allowance around curves** and trim corners to ease fullness (*see* Clipping and Notching *on page 17*). One quick solution is to also use pinking shears to remove some of that excess fabric. But whatever you do, *don't* clip through your stitching line.

* **Press as you stitch** – the success of your project depends on it. Not doing so will make your projects look "homemade" as opposed to "handcrafted." You might hate ironing, but know that pressing is something different entirely. Ironing is done on a finished garment, while pressing is done as you create it, to mold and shape your work in progress. Keeping all your seams neat, even, and tidy as you work will definitely pay off. Invest in an iron with a nice steam button – you won't be sorry.

Sewing-Machine Help

We can't overemphasize the helpfulness of having at least one great vintage sewing reference book at hand to answer all those questions you never even knew you had. We're partial to Singer (pick a year, any year — we chose ours for the illustrations); but there are lots of other great handbooks to be found at garage sales, thrift stores, and online. Stock up! It's always great to have a vintage sewing library right at your fingertips! Below are some other good sewing-machine practices.

* It's a good idea to change your needle with every new project you start. Pay close attention to the needle size in relation to your fabric. You'll thank yourself later.

* Speaking of needles, check to make sure you're using the right one for the job. Ballpoint needles are perfect for sewing with knits, as they're designed to slip through, not pierce, the fabric fibers. Universal needles, typically used for wovens, come in different sizes, for lightweight on up to very heavyweight fabrics. Using an inappropriate needle may result in breaking the needle and/or snagging or tearing your fabric needlessly.

* If your machine has trouble with multiple layers of heavy fabric, you may want to use a "Jean-a-ma-Jig" (a product designed to help your machine handle heavyweight fabrics) or a folded scrap of heavy fabric to keep your presser foot level when stitching over bulky seams and hems.

* Take the time to familiarize yourself with tension settings — top needle tension and, if applicable, bobbin tension as well. Learn and note what settings work best on your machine for different stitches and different fabrics. This information will be found in your sewing-machine manual.

* There are almost as many sewing-machine presser feet as there are sewing situations. If you struggle with invisible zippers, binding, piping, or something else entirely, check out your sewing-machine manufacturer's website and see what special feet are available for your machine. Chances are there's a special-purpose foot that, while not magic, will alleviate many of the aches and pains you've experienced with sewing tricky stuff.

* Please don't neglect basic do-it-yourself sewing-machine maintenance. Regular cleaning and delinting in the bobbin and needle areas can rectify (and prevent) many a sewing headache! And don't forget the sewing-machine oil — check your manual to determine the right way to keep your machine lubed.

* Finally, take your faithful friend in for regular tune-ups. You shouldn't skip your annual physical, and your machine is no different!

Stitch Terminology

As you make your way through the projects, you'll see different words and phrases used to describe various kinds of sewing and stitching. Read on to refresh your memory (or to learn a thing or two!) so you'll know exactly which stitches each project is calling for.

Machine Stitches

Select your sewing-machine stitch length according to your fabric and project. Don't forget to check your stitch length, width, and type before each project and at each step within the project to ensure that it's appropriate for the task at hand. Here are a few pointers and reminders:

*   **Straight stitch** is the most commonly used stitch for constructing your projects. Construction seams are generally sewn at a shorter stitch length (up to 2.5mm) to ensure longevity and stability.

*   **Basting** is used to hold two or more pieces of fabric together temporarily and is not intended to be used structurally. Machine-baste by using a straight stitch on the longest stitch length available. The longer stitch length allows you to easily remove the basting if necessary. Typically, you do not back-stitch at the beginning and end of machine basting, as this stitch is meant to be temporary.

*   **A gathering basting stitch** is as it sounds – a long stitch used to gather an edge of the fabric. When using a gathering basting stitch, do not backstitch and leave the beginning and ending tails long. You will use these loose threads to draw up the fabric and create a gathered effect.

*   **Backstitching** is used to secure and reinforce your stitching at the beginning and end of a seam to keep it from unraveling. Most, if not all, modern sewing machines have a backstitch function or button. When you start stitching a seam, backstitch for about ¼" (or 3 to 4 stitches), stitch your seam, and repeat at the end. Taking the time to backstitch will certainly pay off in your finished product.

*   A **staystitch** is most often used when a fabric piece is cut on the bias or on a curve. It is a single stitch line on a single layer of fabric. Typically, a line of longer stitches is made at or just within the seam allowance, and helps to stabilize the fabric to prevent it from becoming stretched or distorted later when attached to another piece.

*   **Topstitching** is not a special stitch; it is simply a stitching line that is stitched on the right side of your project. We like it because a nice, even, clean topstitch gives your finished work a detail-oriented, professional appearance. Topstitching can be purely decorative or it can provide reinforcement, create pockets, or serve other functions. It could be a single straight stitch, a double stitch using a twin needle, a shell stitch, or a zigzag. If sewn with a straight stitch, we think it looks best with a slightly longer stitch length than the one used for seams. Take the time to experiment with your sewing machine and see what you think works and looks best. After all, the finishing touches are all up to you!

✳ An **edgestitch** is a type of topstitch that is typically stitched ⅛" away from an edge, with a stitch length a bit longer than that you might use for your structural seams. Edgestitching may be used to close an open seam after turning, or may simply be a decorative touch.

✳ The accommodating **zigzag stitch** can be varied in length and width. A very close zigzag stitch may be called a satin stitch and can be used for buttonholes. Zigzag stitches within a seam allowance can also be used to finish seams when no serger is on hand and are also frequently used to provide a bit of reinforcement at a seam that will see lots of use and pulling. The zigzag stitch is also used for sewing stretch knits.

✳ **Stitching in the ditch** is used to stitch through multiple layers of fabric when you don't want your topstitching to show. On the right side of the fabric, stitch through all layers in the "ditch" of an existing seamline. Be precise!

✳ A **box stitch** is often used to secure handles and straps to bags and hardware. To make one, stitch a square or rectangle, typically 1" or 1½" in size, then stitch an X from corner to corner.

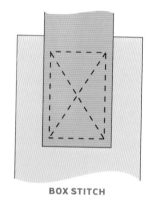

BOX STITCH

Hand Stitches

A sewing machine can't do everything! Hand sewing is often the only way to stitch a button or other closure onto a completed item or to ensure that you only go through one layer of fabric. A few other finishing techniques, such as slip- and whipstitches, can only be accomplished by hand.

✳ A **slipstitch** (sometimes called a blindstitch) joins two pieces of fabric together without the stitches showing. With your hand-sewing needle coming out of one fabric, pierce the other fabric and run the needle under the fabric about ¼". Come out and repeat for the other fabric layer. You will only move down the stitching line when you are underneath the fabric layers. Where you cross from one fabric to another, you cross over on the same vertical, so to speak. After a few stitches, pull the thread gently to tighten and hide the stitches.

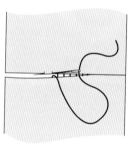

SLIPSTITCH

✳ **Whipstitch.** Unlike a slipstitch, a whipstitch is not invisible but is used similarly to stitch two pieces of fabric together. In a whipstitch you always come out of the same fabric and stitch in the same direction into the second fabric. If used at a raw edge, it will overcast that edge.

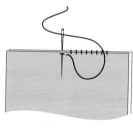

WHIPSTITCH

Key Techniques

Having some basic cutting and sewing skills under your belt can make your project's process easier and the results more ravishing. Take a moment to review these techniques and familiarize yourself with the terminology and methodology you'll need as you go along.

Seam Savvy

The seam allowance is the distance between the seam line (stitching line) that joins two or more pieces of fabric together and the cut edge of the fabric. Traditionally, standard seam allowances are ⅝" wide, but it is becoming increasingly common for seam allowances to be ½" wide. Sometimes seam allowances can be as narrow as ⅛" on items such as doll clothes, so be sure to pay attention to the pattern instructions, as the seam allowance is always indicated. Most projects in this book call for a ½" or ¼" seam allowance.

To stitch a scant ¼" seam, measure where you would place the fabric for a regular ¼" seam and move your fabric over just a teensy bit to stitch a slightly smaller seam (somewhere between ¼" and ⅛"). Scant seams are often called for to reinforce a seam, such as an armhole. They are also used in various other seam finishing techniques such as French seams. Don't worry, project instructions will specify when this type of seam is required.

There is an abundance of ways to finish your seam allowances when creating an unlined project. A serger would be the simplest method of finishing seam allowances, but you have plenty of other options, with or without a special sewing machine. If you have pinking shears, simply pink the seam allowances for a 1950s flair! Otherwise, your sewing machine may have an overcast or zigzag stitch that will do the job in a jiffy. Here are some other possible seam-finishing options:

* **Lapped seam**. This type of seam is most frequently used for leather and other nonfraying materials. Use a disappearing marker or chalk to mark seam lines on both fabric pieces. Trim the upper fabric back to the seam line. With both right sides facing up, overlap the upper and lower fabrics, aligning the raw edge of the upper fabric with the marked seam allowance of the lower fabric. Pin and

---

THE QUESTION OF BUTTONHOLES

Buttonholes can be very tricky and can make or break your finished piece. They can be made either by hand or by sewing machine. Most commonly, sewing machines create buttonholes in either a one-step or three-step method (consult your manual). Buttonhole orientation is either horizontal or vertical and length is determined by measuring the button width (across the widest part) plus button thickness. Practice and practice on a scrap piece of fabric before making the buttonhole on your finished piece. If you rarely have luck creating buttonholes, go make a friend at your local corner tailor and pay to have them done professionally. Depending on the project, it may be worth it!

LAPPED SEAM

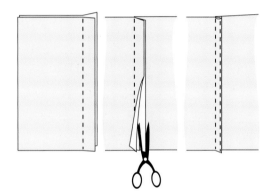

MAKING A FLAT FELLED SEAM

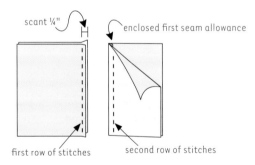

scant ¼"

enclosed first seam allowance

first row of stitches

second row of stitches

FRENCH SEAM

topstitch the layers together very close to the raw edge of the upper fabric. Stitch again close to the raw edge of the lower fabric. For fabrics that fray, instead of trimming the upper fabric, you may instead fold the seam allowance under to the wrong side.

✳ **Flat felled seam.** A very strong seam, often seen on jeans and other heavy-duty applications, flat felled seams, like French seams, hide raw edges and are sewn in multiple steps. First, stitch a ½" or ⅝" seam with right sides out (wrong sides together). Trim one layer of the seam allowance in half, to ¼". Fold and press the longer seam allowance in half, encasing the other, trimmed allowance. Topstitch close to folded edge to secure allowance to fabric. The finished project will have two parallel topstitching lines on both sides of the seam allowance.

✳ **French seam.** Often used for durability and tidiness, this seam hides raw edges in unlined projects. French seams are made by first stitching a scant ¼" seam with wrong sides together. You then turn the fabrics wrong side out (right sides together) at the seam and stitch another ¼" seam to enclose the raw edges (total finished seam allowance equals ½"). To stitch a scant ¼" seam, see instructions in Seam Savvy, page 15. This tiny bit of extra fabric lets you turn the seam around without using a bigger seam allowance.

Clipping and Notching

Speaking of seam allowances, curves and corners will often need special attention to reduce bulk and lie flat. Here are some commonly used techniques.

* **Clipping curves**. Clipping is used to reduce tension on concave seams (inward curves). Clip within the seam allowance to, but not through, the stitching line. Sharper curves require more clipping, and corners are typically clipped at a 45-degree angle. (*For outer curves, see* Notching.)

* **Notching**. Notching is used to make convex seams (outward curves) lie flat. Cut notches at regular intervals within the seam allowance to, but not through, the stitching line. Sharper curves require more notches.

* **Trimming corners**. Cut corner seam allowances at a 45-degree angle close to where two stitching lines meet. This will ensure a sharp corner once the fabric is turned right side out.

CLIPPING AN INNER CURVE

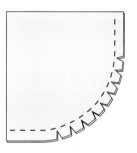

NOTCHING OUTER CURVES

TRIMMING CORNERS

Making and Using Bias Tape

Another great way to finish raw edges is to use bias tape, also called binding. Bias tape is made from a strip of fabric that has been cut along the bias. You can buy it prepackaged with a single or double fold. Both types come in a variety of widths and colors.

* **Single-fold bias tape** is often used to finish neck-line and armhole edges.

* **Double-fold bias tape** is often used to encase raw edges. You will notice that double-fold bias tape is slightly off center, making one side a little wider than the other. This is for ease of application; the narrower edge always lies on top of the fabric, facing you as you sew, so that when you stitch close to the edge of the tape, you are virtually guaranteed to catch the back side of the tape on the other side of the fabric.

HOW TO MAKE BIAS TAPE

To make your own double-fold bias binding, follow the steps below. These instructions also work for making drawstrings or ties.

1 To find the bias of your fabric, place your fabric wrong side up and align the 45-degree angle line of your quilting ruler along the selvage edge of your fabric. Using your fabric pen, draw a straight line along the edge of your ruler to mark the bias. Draw a second parallel line that is four times the desired finished width of your finished bias tape. For example, your lines would be 2" apart to create ½" bias tape. Determine how many strips to cut based on the length of bias tape required.

2 With right sides together, stitch two short ends together to make one long strip. Press the seam open.

3 With wrong sides together, fold the bias strip in half lengthwise, align the raw edges, and press.

4 Open the strip and press the raw edges on both sides in to the crease. (If you want finished ends for a belt or tie, press both short ends under ½".)

5 Refold along the original foldline and press.

6 Use for binding the raw edges of a project, or topstitch closed to use as a belt, drawstring, or tie.

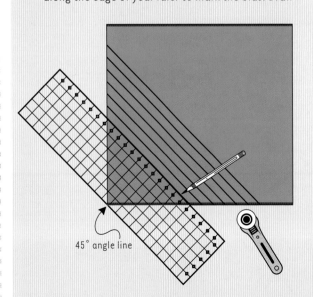

45° angle line

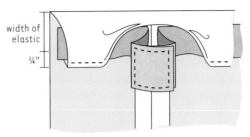

CASING WITH ELASTIC

Making Hems

The hem is a finished fabric edge, usually turned under; for instance, the bottom edge of a skirt or pair of pants. Hems, however, are not limited to clothing or bottom edges. Pocket edges and sleeves can be hemmed. There are many sizes and ways to hem, so pay attention to your pattern, as the hem height is typically indicated.

The double-fold hem is an easy and standard way to completely hide raw edges. Fold or press under the raw edge to the wrong side of the fabric (typically ¼"), then fold or press under again (anywhere from ¼" up to 1" or more). Topstitch close to the first fold. (You could also use a slipstitch or a blindstitch to finish the hem.) A narrow ¼" double-fold hem is folded twice at ¼".

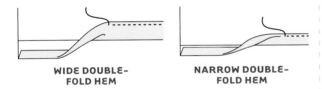

WIDE DOUBLE-FOLD HEM   **NARROW DOUBLE-FOLD HEM**

Casings for Elastic and Drawstrings

A casing is a channel sewn through two layers of fabric to allow elastic, cording, ribbon, or other material to pass through. Casings are the standard technique used for elastic and drawstrings. Here's how you make one (in this example, we will show how to insert elastic):

* Press under the top edge of the piece ¼".
* Determine how much room you need for the elastic or drawstring. Typically you would add ⅛" to ¼" to the width of the elastic, to allow for stitching and a bit of wiggle room. For drawstrings it's nice to have about an inch to spare so the fabric gathers nicely. (Most patterns will specify exact casing height.) Press under the top edge again to this width.

* Edgestitch the casing in place, leaving a 1" opening at a side seam.
* Measure and cut elastic for your project, adding 1" for overlap.
* Insert the elastic into the casing (using a bodkin or large safety pin), securing the opposite end of the elastic to the piece with a safety or straight pin before you begin pulling the elastic through.
* Overlap the ends of the elastic by ½" and stitch together securely, making sure the elastic is not twisted. A little box, as shown, holds things in place very nicely.
* Tuck the stitched ends of the elastic back inside the casing and stitch the casing opening closed.

Darts and Pintucks

Darts are most commonly used in clothing projects to take in fullness and add shaping. They are usually wide at the seam edge and taper to a point. You will find them used in various projects throughout the book including, but not limited to, toys, apparel, and bags.

Often decorative and sometimes used for shaping, pintucks are formed by matching two lines,

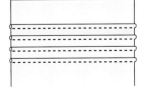

PINTUCKS

wrong sides together, stitching close to the fold, thereby creating a folded tuck. Most commonly, tucks are stitched along the grainline and are equal distances apart.

Making Gathers

Gathers are used decoratively and functionally. When trying to fit and adjust gathers evenly on a long piece of fabric, mark off the halfway, quarter-length, and even eighth-length distances on both the main fabric (to which the gathered piece will eventually be attached) and the piece that is to be gathered before beginning the gathering process. The piece to be gathered is typically twice as long as the main fabric, so these marks will be farther apart on the gathering piece.

To create gathers, use a basting stitch within the seam allowance on the piece to be gathered. Do not backstitch at the beginning and end of the basting seam and be sure to leave long tails at both ends. Use these tails to gather the fabric. If you are gathering heavyweight or upholstery fabrics, you may want to use two parallel rows of basting stitches for strength, ⅛" apart. Take care that your basting lines do not cross one another.

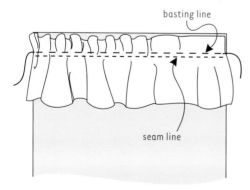

basting line

seam line

MAKING GATHERS

After gathering, pin the two pieces together at their respective marked lines and you're pretty much guaranteed to have even gathers. When joining a gathered piece and a nongathered piece, it is best to stitch with the gathered piece on top to help control the fullness. Sometimes you may need to adjust gathers as you stitch the seam so that the gathered folds lie nicely and evenly.

Piping

Piping is a decorative detail inserted between two seams. One edge has welting, while the other has a raw edge to attach, called a flange. You can buy prepackaged piping, although color choices may be limited. In this book, piping always refers to a trim being sandwiched between two seams.

You can make your own piping with a bias strip of fabric and small cording. First, determine the appropriate bias strip width, which is your seam allowance times two, plus the circumference of your cording. Follow the bias tape instructions for how to cut and attach the individual bias strips (*see page* 18). Fold the bias strip in half lengthwise, with wrong sides together, and insert the cording inside the fold. Use a long stitch length and your zipper foot to stitch along the edge of the cording to secure it. When attaching the piping to your project, align all raw edges. In a pinch, a folded bit of wide ribbon can substitute wonderfully for bias tape!

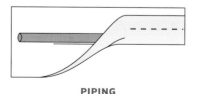

PIPING

CHAPTER 2

DWELL REDUX

We know what it's like to shop for hours and hours to find just the perfect accent for your home. Well, quit spending all that time at the mall and make something perfectly unique for you and only YOU! In this chapter you will find accent pieces for some of the most important rooms in your home. Use these ideas to domesticate your office, dress up your bedroom, revive your living room, and even brighten your bathroom.

FRAMED TACK BOARD

Designed by Bethany Nixon

Here's the perfect way to showcase your favorite cloth. Use the board for to-do lists, family photos, love notes, or whatever favorite mementos you want to display. Do you wear a lot of jewelry? Hanging it here will turn your beads and bangles into wall art, while keeping your favorites close at hand.

MATERIALS

* 1 yard of 44/45" fabric (any weight will do)
* 1 spool of coordinating thread
* Old frame from the thrift store
* Corkboard or cork bulletin board, at least as large as your selected frame
* Box cutter
* Cutting mat to protect your work surface
* Household stapler or staple gun
* Large decorative pushpins
* Hanging hardware (if not already on the frame)

Finished dimensions – will vary according to the frame you select

① Prep the Frame and Corkboard

First, remove the artwork from the frame. Using the artwork as a template, cut the corkboard to size with a box cutter. (If the frame you're using is empty, trace the back opening onto the corkboard.) Use a cutting mat to protect your work surface. Set the corkboard in the frame to check the fit.

② Position the Fabric

Lay the fabric over the front of the corkboard and center the fabric – this is how it will look inside the frame. If you have a bold graphic or would like the pattern to lie a certain way, this is your opportunity to position it. Once you have it just the way you like it, hold the fabric in place while flipping the corkboard and fabric upside down.

③ Finalize Fabric Placement

Using scissors, trim the fabric at least 2" longer than the edge of the corkboard on all four sides. Fold this extra fabric over the edges and onto the back of the corkboard. Pull it taut and staple it on all four sides.

④ Reassemble the Frame

Lay the covered corkboard back into the frame and secure it in place using the existing hardware on the frame. If necessary, you may want to supplement with new hanging hardware.

LineD BOOKCase

Designed by Danielle Wilson

Although this project doesn't involve sewing, it perfectly fits the idea of "what to do with that one coveted yard of fabric" because it puts your lovely fabric on display to enjoy all the time. This no-sew project can also be taken apart so you can reuse the fabric or change your look. Expand this concept to other furniture in your home, like a small china hutch.

MATERIALS

* 1 yard of 44/45" fabric (any weight will do)
* All-purpose spray adhesive
* Double-sided poster tape
* Posterboard (enough to cover the back of the bookcase; you may need to use more than one piece)
* Small bookcase (we used the 31½" × 41¾" Billy Bookcase from Ikea)
* Clear tape
* Paper scissors

Finished dimensions – will vary according to the bookcase you select. Keep in mind not to select one taller than 32".

❶ Make the Posterboard Insert

Remove the shelves and lay the bookcase flat on its back. Measure the inside height and width of the bookcase and cut your poster-board to fit. Depending on the interior dimensions, you may need to cut more than one piece of posterboard to fit precisely in your bookcase. If so, determine how many pieces of posterboard you will need, align them, and use clear tape to overlap all edges to secure them to each other. You will want this insert to be neat and precise so it will fit perfectly.

❷ Measure and Cut

Cut your fabric 4" larger than your posterboard. For example, if your posterboard measures 26" × 30", you will cut your fabric to 30" × 34". These extra 4" will allow for overlap around the edges.

❸ Adhere the Fabric to the Posterboard

Working in a well-ventilated area, place the posterboard on a flat surface. Starting at one end, and working in small sections, apply spray adhesive to the posterboard *only*. Carefully lay the fabric on, right side up so that it is smooth and taut, until the entire insert is covered. If your fabric shifts or wrinkles, simply lift it off the posterboard and reposition it. Turn the insert over so the fabric side is face down, and then fold the overhanging fabric around the edges of the posterboard and tape it securely with clear tape, working your way around the entire piece.

❹ Position the Fabric in the Bookcase

Place a small piece of double-sided poster tape in each corner on the wrong side of the posterboard and at several places around the edges and in the center for good adhesion. Carefully place the insert, fabric side up, into the inside back of your bookcase, making sure the corners are aligned. Press firmly so that the poster tape adheres. Stand bookcase upright, replace shelves, and fill as desired.

FOLDING CHAIR PINAFORE SLIPCOVER

Designed by Angie Knowles

Who would have thought that dressing up an old card-table folding chair could be so simple? Better yet, who knew that an icky folding metal chair could be so stylish? This is the perfect project to spruce up those chairs for a party — personalize them for each of your guests or change them according to the season.

MATERIALS

* 1 yard of 54/60" fabric (nondirectional home-decor weight)
* 1 spool of coordinating thread
* 2½ yards of ¼" grosgrain ribbon

Finished dimensions – will accommodate all standard folding card-table chairs

Seam allowance – ½" unless otherwise specified

① Measure, Mark, and Cut

With your fabric in a single layer, wrong side facing up, follow the layout to measure and mark the pattern pieces directly onto the wrong side of your fabric, then cut them out:

* **Chair back** 19½" wide × 12½" tall (cut 2)
* **Pinafore pleat** 28½" wide × 4" tall (cut 2)
* **Seat** 17" wide × 22" tall (cut 1)
* **Seat skirt** 5" wide × 33¾" tall (cut 1)

NOTE: *Place "tall" dimensions along the grainline of your fabric.*

② Make the Pinafore Ruffle

With right sides together, align the raw edges of the pinafore pleat pieces and stitch one short end, connecting both pieces. Press the seam open.

With right sides together, fold the strip in half lengthwise and stitch the short ends. Clip the corners, turn the strip right side out, and press.

To make 1" pleats, mark every 1" along the raw edge. Fold the pleats per the diagram, starting from the left side and moving toward the

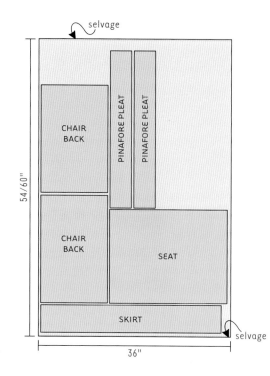

CUTTING LAYOUT

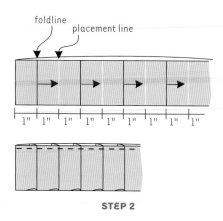

foldline
placement line

1" 1" 1" 1" 1" 1" 1" 1" 1"

STEP 2

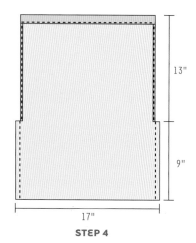

13"

9"

17"

STEP 4

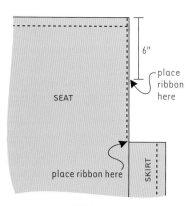

6"

place ribbon here

SEAT

place ribbon here

SKIRT

STEP 6

right. When you have finished, your 55" piece will measure 18" pleated. Baste though all pleated layers along raw edge to hold pleats in place.

❸ Complete the Chair Back

Center the pinafore pleat along the top edge on the right side of one of the chair backs, ¾" from each edge, aligning raw edges. Pin and baste in place. With right sides together, line up the raw edges of the second chair back piece with raw edges of the first, sandwiching the pleated piece in between. Stitch around both sides and the top, leaving the bottom edge open. Clip the corners, turn, and press. Make a 1" double-fold hem along the bottom edge (*see page* 19).

❹ Prepare the Seat

Staystitch along both long sides of the seat. Position fabric so that front edge is at the bottom. Measure 9" from the bottom short end of the seat on both long sides. At the 9" mark, clip to (but not through) the stitching line. Above the clip line, press under the side raw edges ¼", then press under another ¼" and topstitch. On the top edge, make a 1" double-fold hem in the same way.

❺ Make the Skirt

On both short ends of the skirt piece, press under a ¼" seam allowance, then press under another ¼" and topstitch. Make a 1" double-fold hem along the bottom raw edge of the skirt in the same way. Pin the skirt to the seat, right sides together, on the sides and front, aligning raw edges. Start stitching at one 9" notch and down the side, across the bottom and up to the opposite 9" notch, pivoting at the corners. Clip the corners and press.

❻ Add the Ties

Cut 4 pieces of 20" grosgrain ribbon. Find the center of each piece of ribbon, and stitch them in place, 6" from the back seam and at the corner where the skirt and seat meet. Tie them to the chair supports and enjoy your new customized chair!

DRESSER ORGANIZER & CHARGING STATION

Designed by Elizabeth Hartman

Use this handy basket to gather essentials on your dresser or desktop. It has an opening in the back for your phone's (or other small electronic items') charging cord. So, gather your change, your cell phone, and all the other various sundries you have scattered on your dresser. Place them in your basket and marvel at the new, stylishly organized you!

MATERIALS

* 1 yard of fabric (any weight or width)
* ½ yard of lightweight fusible interfacing
* ½ yard of fusible fleece
* ¼ yard of heavyweight interfacing, such as Peltex or Timtex
* 1 spool of coordinating thread
* 24" × 6" clear quilter's ruler
* Sewing-machine walking foot (optional)

Finished dimensions – 8" square by 3½" high
Seam allowance – ½" unless otherwise specified

① Measure, Mark, and Cut

Measure and mark the following pattern pieces directly onto the wrong side of your fabric, then cut them out:

* **Basket** 15" wide × 15" tall (cut 2)
* **Bias strip** 2½" wide × 33½" long (cut 1 on the bias of the fabric)

Cut from fusible fleece:

* **Basket** 15" wide × 15" tall (cut 1)

Cut from lightweight fusible interfacing:

* **Basket** 15" wide × 15" tall (cut 2)

* **Cord opening reinforcement**
  2" wide × 5" tall (cut 2)

Cut from heavyweight interfacing:

* **Basket base** 7¾" wide × 7¾" tall (cut 1)

NOTE: *Place "tall" dimensions along the grainline of your fabric.*

② Quilt the Interior Panel

Iron the fusible fleece onto the wrong side of *one* of your fabric squares, following manufacturer's instructions; this will become the interior of your organizer. Decoratively quilt this piece as desired by marking your choice of quilting lines with a fabric pen (you could try a diagonal grid with 1¼" spaces between lines). Follow the lines to machine-quilt each piece. You may want to use a walking foot, if you have one.

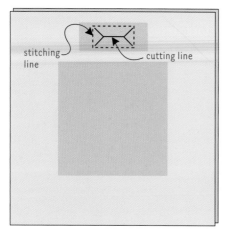

STEP 4

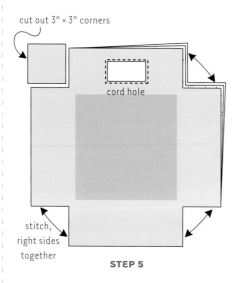

STEP 5

❸ Make the Exterior Panel

Iron one piece of lightweight fusible interfacing onto the wrong side of the remaining 15" fabric square. Draw a line 3½" parallel to each edge on the interfaced side of the panel. These lines will create an 8" square in the center of the panel.

Center and place the heavyweight interfacing in this marked square and cover it with your second square of lightweight fusible interfacing with the fusible side facing down. Iron the fusible interfacing to secure the smaller piece of heavyweight interfacing in place.

❹ Make the Cord Opening

On the interfaced side of the exterior panel, draw a guideline ¾" above the top of one side of the center square. Center a 2" × 5" strip of fusible interfacing along this line and press in place. Repeat with the second strip of interfacing, overlapping the first for extra stability.

Place the quilted interior panel and exterior panel right sides together with the exterior panel on top. Draw a 1½" × 3" rectangle centered on the 2" × 5" interfacing strip. This rectangle will be your cord opening. Pin around this rectangle, through all layers, securing both panels together. Stitch along the lines, following the edges of the rectangle exactly. Using sharp scissors, cut a line through all layers in the center of the rectangle. Make angular cuts toward each of the four corners; be very careful to clip right up to, but not through, your stitching line.

Gently pull one panel through the opening you have made until both panels are turned right side out with wrong sides together. Press the pieces and topstitch around the cord opening.

❺ Form the Basket Shape

Cut out a 3" square from each of the four corners of the exterior piece. Repeat this process for the interior piece. Stitch the exterior into a box shape by matching the right sides of each cut-out corner and stitching them closed. Your stitching should come close to —

but not through — the centered heavy-weight interfacing. Press the seams open and adjust the interior and exterior so they form a basket shape.

6 Bind the Top Edge

* Press under both short ends of your bias strip ½". Press one long edge over ½" to the wrong side.
* Pin the unpressed raw edge of the bias tape around the entire top exterior of your basket with a slight overlap at the end. Stitch through all layers around the entire perimeter of the basket top.
* Fold the bias tape to the inside of the basket and carefully press in place. Use a zigzag stitch around the top of the basket, stitching through all layers and encasing the raw edges at the top of the basket in the binding.

Mailbag Pocket Duo

Designed by Cara Angelotta and Mark Cesarik

If you need a pretty and very stylish set of receptacles to help you organize your post-office deliveries, have we got a project for you! Use the two bags to help sort things out: catalogs vs. bills; in vs. out; whatever. The best part? You can customize these bags to fit your needs precisely.

MATERIALS

* 1 yard of fabric (any weight and/or width)
* 1 spool of coordinating thread
* Coordinating ribbon or hooks to hang your mailbags when complete

Finished dimensions – each mailbag is 12" wide × 10" tall
Seam allowance – ½" unless otherwise specified

➊ Measure, Mark, and Cut

Place your fabric in a single layer with wrong side facing up. Measure and mark the following pieces directly on the wrong side of your fabric, then cut them out:

* **Exterior** 13" wide × 11" tall (cut 4)
* **Lining** 13" wide × 11" tall (cut 4)
* **Hanging loop** 3½" wide × 5½" tall (cut 6)

NOTE: *Place "tall" dimensions along the grainline of your fabric.*

➋ Stitch the Exteriors

With right sides facing, pin two exterior fabric pieces together and stitch around two (short) sides and the bottom edge, leaving the top of the bag open. Press under the raw edge ½", then turn the pieces right side out. Do the same with the two remaining exterior pieces.

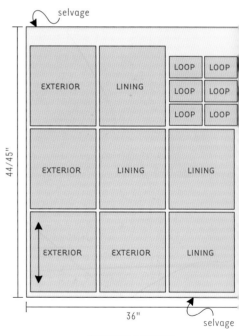

CUTTING LAYOUT

❸ Stitch the Linings

As with the exteriors, pin two lining pieces together with right sides facing. Stitch around two (short) sides and the bottom edge, leaving the top of the bag open. Press under the raw edge ½", but do not turn right side out. Do the same with the two remaining lining pieces.

❹ Make the Loops

With right sides together, fold a loop piece in half lengthwise. Stitch a ½" seam to form a tube. Turn the tube right side out and press. Do the same with the five remaining loop pieces. Then fold each tube in half (width-wise), aligning the unfinished edges, and press.

❺ Attach the Loops

Pin three loops to the wrong side of the fabric on one side of a lining section; this will become the back of the mailbag. Place one loop directly in the center, lining up the bottom edges of the loops with the hem pressed under in step 3. Place the other two loops ½" from each of the side seams. Secure the loops by edgestitching a scant ¼" seam. You may want to reverse the stitch a few times to secure the loops to the lining, because this part of the mailbag will get the most stress, especially if you have a lot of mail. Attach the remaining loops to the second lining in the same manner.

❻ Assemble the Mailbags

With wrong sides together, place a lining inside an exterior bag, aligning the top folded edges and side seams. Edgestitch ¼" around the top edge. Use ribbon to hang your mailbags from nails or pretty hooks on the wall.

ORGANIZED BED POCKET

Designed by Amanda Anderson

Do you love your bed for all its softness and coziness but find that it becomes cluttered with the book you've been reading, eyeglasses, a water bottle? If you are without a bedside table to manage these necessities, or just need the extra space, then this is the perfect project. The organizer slips between the mattress and box spring to hold the little things you need to keep close, and thanks to a clever strip of nonskid material, it won't be pulled out by the weight of even the heaviest books.

MATERIALS

* 1 yard of 44/45" fabric (any weight will do)
* 1 spool of coordinating thread
* 1 package of ½" double-fold bias tape (3½ yards)
* 1 rubberized shelf liner or other nonskid material, at least 20" × 10"

Finished dimensions – 20" wide × 15" tall (not including what is tucked under the mattress)

Seam allowance – ½" unless otherwise specified

① Measure, Mark, and Cut

With right sides together, fold your fabric in half lengthwise, aligning the selvages. Measure and mark the following pattern pieces directly onto the wrong side of your fabric, then cut them out:

* **Backing** 20" wide × 15" tall (cut 2)
* **Pocket** 20" wide × 9" tall (cut 2)

NOTE: *Place "tall" dimensions along the grainline of your fabric.*

② Layer the Pieces

With wrong sides facing, pin the two pocket pieces together. Finish the top raw edges by encasing them with double-fold bias tape. Stitch in place.

With wrong sides facing, pin the two backing pieces together. Pin the pocket on top of the backing, aligning all bottom edges. Baste the four pieces together at the side seams with a scant ¼" seam allowance.

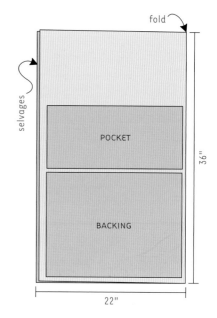

CUTTING LAYOUT

❸ **Make the Pocket**

The number of pocket compartments, and
their width, is up to you. Decide how you
want to divide up the pocket by measuring
the items you intend to store (a flashlight,
eyeglasses, magazines) and marking where
the seams need to be. To make the divisions,
cut a 9½" length of bias tape and turn the
top raw edge ½" to the wrong side. Pin the
bias strip over the marked vertical seam line
and stitch through all four layers of fabric.

❹ **Finish the Edges**

To create the curved corners on the lower
edge of your bed pocket, place a standard
drinking glass upside down on one bottom
corner and trace the portion of glass that
falls within the seam allowance. Trim away
the excess fabric. Repeat this step in the
opposite bottom corner. Enclose the sides
and bottom raw edges with bias tape, and
stitch (*see page* 18).

❺ **Add the Liner**

Pin a 20" × 10" piece of rubberized shelf
liner along the top edge of the organizer,
placing the bottom edge of the liner piece
behind the pocket so that it overlaps it
½". Pin the remaining length of bias tape
on top of both pieces, along the overlap,
concealing the raw edge. Stitch through all
three layers. Slip the rubberized section
between your mattress and box spring and
load it up!

RUFFLED café CURTain

Designed by Patricia Hoskins

Want a bit of privacy, but still crave sunlight? These café curtains lend a festive retro touch to any room! One yard of fabric is perfect for a typical kitchen or bathroom window or to jazz up any other smallish window in your home.

MATERIALS

* 1 yard of 44/45" or 54/60" fabric (quilting or home-decor weight)
* 1 spool of coordinating thread
* Curtain rods to fit window

Finished dimensions – 44/45" fabric will fit the bottom half of a window up to 60" high × 30" wide; 54/60" fabric will fit the bottom half of a window up to 60" high × 40" wide

Seam allowance – ½" unless otherwise specified

① Measure, Mark, and Cut

Place your fabric in a single layer with wrong side facing up. Trim the selvages from the fabric. Mark the following piece directly on the wrong side, along one 44/45" edge of your fabric (to leave plenty of room for the curtain panels), and cut it out:

* **Ruffle** 44" wide × 4" tall (cut 2)

To make two curtain panels, with right sides together, fold the remaining curtain fabric in half lengthwise, aligning raw edges. Press a crease along the fold. Open the fabric and cut it in half along the crease to make the panels. If using 44/45" fabric, the finished cut dimensions will be 22" wide × 32" tall.

On the wrong side of each curtain panel, along the bottom raw edge, mark center points and quarter points (for a 22"-wide panel, marks would fall at 5½", 11", and 16½" from the left-side raw edge).

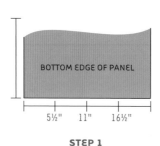

STEP 1
Marking the curtain panel

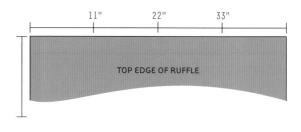

STEP 1
Marking the ruffle

Do the same along the top raw edge of both ruffle pieces (for a 44"-wide ruffle, marks would fall at 11", 22", and 33" from the left side raw edge).

❷ Gather the Ruffles

At the bottom raw edge of each ruffle, press under a narrow ¼" double-fold hem and topstitch in place (*see page* 19). Use a basting stitch to gather the top raw edge of each ruffle (*see page* 13). With right sides together and raw edges even, pin each ruffle to a curtain panel, matching side raw edges and all quarter and center marks. Adjust the ruffle gathers evenly to fit, pinning as you work the gathers. Stitch in place and press both seams toward the curtain panel.

❸ Hem the Sides

Press under a narrow ¼" double-fold hem on both sides of each curtain panel and ruffle. Topstitch in place.

❹ Make the Rod Casing

Measure your window to determine the desired finished height of the curtain. Measure that distance up from the bottom of the ruffle and add 2" for making the curtain-rod casing. (Adjust the 2" measurement if necessary to fit diameter of your curtain rod.) Cut off any extra length. Press under the top raw edge of each curtain panel ½", then press under another 2". Topstitch the hem to form the casing. Hang your curtain in the window and enjoy!

smocked pillow in the round

Designed by Welmoed Sisson

Add the perfect accent to your decor with this detailed pillow. To complete this fabulous project, you'll need to use some very basic smocking techniques. If that's new to you, then this pillow is the perfect way to learn a smattering about smocking. Even better, you'll end up with a great addition to a couch, chair, or bed. The pleating is done on a grid pattern, and the thickness of the finished pillow is determined by the total number of pleats.

MATERIALS

* 1 yard of 44/45" fabric (quilting weight)
* 1 yard of Pellon Tru-Grid (available 44/45" wide, a 1" graph for scaling up, duplicating, or altering patterns)
* One 14" square pillow (that's right – you're going to turn a square pillow into a round one)
* Two 1½" cloth-covered shank buttons (purchased or you can cover your own)
* 1 spool of coordinating thread
* Tufting needle

Finished dimensions – creates a 12" round pillow
Seam allowance – ½" unless otherwise specified

❶ Prepare the Smocking Grid

Cut a piece of Tru-Grid into an 18" × 44" rectangle. Pierce a small hole every 1½" across the entire piece of Tru-Grid, until you have a grid pattern that is 11 rows wide and 29 rows long.

❷ Position and Mark the Grid

Place your yard of fabric wrong side up. Mark the center along both selvages and position the Tru-Grid on top, aligning the centerline of the grid with the center of the fabric. Pin the Tru-Grid in a few places to secure it to the fabric. Using a washable fabric pen or tailor's chalk, make a dot at each hole in the grid. Once all dots have been clearly marked, remove the Tru-Grid. In order not to lose your place during the smocking process, it is necessary to mark all diagonal "connecting dots" as shown in the diagram. With right sides together, align the selvage edges. In order to hide the side seam in the finished pillow, place the seam right on a line of dots and ensure that the pattern lines up continuously (see diagram). Stitch the side seam, press it open, and re-mark the dots and connections along the seam, if necessary.

STEP 1
Marking the grid

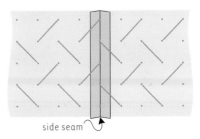

side seam

STEP 2
Handling the seam

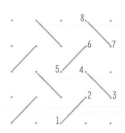

STEP 3

The smocking process

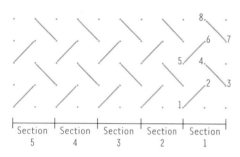

| Section 5 | Section 4 | Section 3 | Section 2 | Section 1 |

STEP 3

Smocking in sections

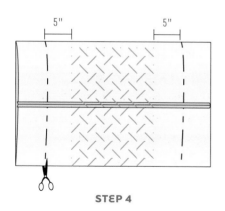

STEP 4

❸ Smock the Fabric

Begin the smocking process anywhere along the fabric. You may find it easiest to start at the right and work toward the left; you will need to experiment to see which direction is most comfortable for you. Working from the wrong side of the fabric, pinch the fabric together at dot #1 and dot #2. Handstitch the two points together, joining them with a few stitches. Knot the stitch securely, and do *not* clip the thread.

Move horizontally to dot #3. Pinch dots #3 and #4 together and join with a few stitches. Be sure to leave an extra length of thread between each joining stitch as it is much quicker to leave a length of thread connecting each stitch as opposed to clipping and re-knotting at each new connection. (It is important to leave the thread between the points rather loose, as this will give the final piece flexibility.) Repeat this process until you have smocked the entire circumference to meet your first stitch. Move over one row, and smock the next round. Ultimately, there are five smocked rounds; continue until all have been completed.

❹ Finish the Pillow

Mark a line 5" from each side of the finished smocked section. Trim away excess fabric 1" beyond this marked line. Turn right side out.

Using a hand-sewing needle and thread, make long running stitches along the 5" line, each stitch approximately 1" in length. Pull the thread to tightly gather the end of the pillow, tucking the raw edges to the wrong side as you tighten the gathers. Knot the thread securely. Stuff the pillow form into the pillow, gently stretching the smocked area to accommodate it. Gather the other end of the pillow in the same manner, encasing the pillow form. Place two covered buttons at the center of each gathered end, using a tufting needle to stitch the buttons in place. Knot threads securely.

BaTHROOM MaKeOVeR

Designed by June Scroggin

Are you ready to revitalize your bathroom? Here are a few ways to add some fresh decorative details to a weary WC without breaking the bank. Making all four of these bathing beauties from one yard of fabric is not only super efficient, it also helps to create a unifying aesthetic.

MATERIALS

* * 1 yard of 44/45" or 54/60" fabric (any weight will do)
* * 1 spool of coordinating thread

Seam allowance – ½" unless otherwise specified

NOTE: *Keep in mind that all projects in Bathroom Makeover will be cut from the same yard of fabric. Take care to place your project pattern pieces economically. It might also be a good idea to draw all pattern pieces on the wrong side of your fabric before you start cutting.*

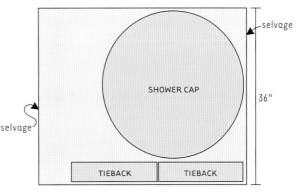

CUTTING LAYOUT

Shower Cap

ADDITIONAL MATERIALS

* * Super-thin vinyl
* * ¼" elastic, cut to length that is 1½" less than the circumference of your head

Finished dimensions – 28½" diameter

❶ Measure, Mark, and Cut

Measure and mark the following piece directly onto the wrong side of your fabric, then cut it out. Also cut the same shape from the vinyl.

* * 30" diameter circle

❷ Attach the Pieces

Place the vinyl circle on the wrong side of your fabric and baste the edges together. This will keep it from sliding as you work.

❸ Make the Elastic Casing

Press under the fabric and vinyl raw edges ¼". (To keep the vinyl from becoming a melted mess, keep your iron on a low setting, and don't allow it to come into contact with the vinyl.) Press under another ½" and stitch close to the folded edge, leaving a 2" opening. Thread the elastic through the casing, overlap the ends of the elastic ½", and stitch together securely. Stitch the casing opening closed (*see page* 19).

Curtain Tiebacks

ADDITIONAL MATERIALS

* Four 2" rings (bamboo, metal, your choice)

Finished dimensions — each tie is 1½" × 17"

① Measure, Mark, and Cut

Measure and mark the following pieces directly onto the wrong side of your cotton fabric, and cut them out:

* **Tiebacks** 18" wide × 4" tall (cut 2)

NOTE: *Place "tall" dimensions along the grainline of your fabric.*

② Make the Ties

Press under the short edges ½". Fold and press two ties in the same way as you would to make bias tape (*see page* 18). Edgestitch along the three folded sides on both ties.

③ Attach the Rings

Fold each end of the tieback over a ring and stitch in place. Do the same for the other tieback.

Towel Trimming Set

ADDITIONAL MATERIALS

* Set of two each: large bath towels, hand towels, and washcloths

Finished dimensions — will vary according to your preferred towel-banding widths

① Determine Fabric Dimensions

Measure the width and length of the area where you wish to trim your various towels and washcloths. Add 1" to each measurement. Measure and mark the required pieces directly on the wrong side of your cotton fabric and cut them out.

② Place the Fabric

Press under the raw edges on the long sides ½". Carefully center this prepared trim piece over the section of the towel you wish to embellish, leaving ½" extra hanging off each side. Topstitch close to the edge on each long side. Turn the unfinished short edges of the trim to the back side of the towel, and stitch in place.

③ Complete the Set

Repeat step 2 for the rest of the towels in your set.

Bathroom Scale

ADDITIONAL MATERIALS

* Dial bathroom scale
* Paper (to make the pattern piece)
* Paper-cutting scissors
* Lightweight fusible interfacing
* Liquid seam sealant (such as Dritz FrayCheck)
* Decoupage gel-medium, in a semiglossy finish (such as Mod Podge Gloss-Lustre)
* Clear acrylic sealer (brush-on preferred)
* Disposable foam paintbrushes
* Wax paper

Finished dimensions — will vary according to your scale

❶ Measure, Mark, and Cut

Place the paper on top of your scale. Trace the sections you want to cover onto paper and cut out the pattern template using paper scissors. (One easy way to do this would be to run your fingernail around the edge of the areas to be covered. This makes a nice, sharp crease on the paper.) Pin the pattern template to your fabric and, using fabric scissors, cut the pieces out. Use the same template to cut the same pieces from your fusible interfacing.

❷ Interface the Pieces

Iron the interfacing to the wrong side of your fabric as directed by the manufacturer.

❸ Attach the Pieces

Place each interfaced fabric piece on wax paper with the fabric's right side up (the wax paper will help protect your work surface). Treat the edges with liquid seam sealant and allow to dry.

❹ Coat the Pieces

Use a foam paintbrush to apply a coat of gel-medium to the fabric. Let dry completely. Then apply a second coat of gel-medium; let this second coat dry completely.

❺ Attach the Pieces to the Scale

Flip your pieces over and apply a coat of gel-medium to the interfaced side of the fabric. Immediately apply a coat of gel-medium to the scale right where you will be placing the fabric. While both are still wet, quickly place the fabric pieces right side up in place on your scale. Press firmly in place and let dry overnight. Coat each fabric section, including the edges where the fabric meets the scale, with two more layers of gel-medium, allowing the adhesive to dry completely between coats.

❻ Finish Up

Apply a finishing coat of acrylic sealer, allowing it to dry completely. Climb aboard your new, improved scale!

TWO-DRAWER FILE CABINET COVER

Designed by Sharon Madsen

Get organized without having to stare at an unsightly file cabinet. If your file cabinet sits in a highly visible place in your home, this project creates the perfect camouflage — that old metal cabinet now becomes a delightful detail rather than a distracting eyesore. This cover is designed to cover the top, sides, and front of a two-drawer file cabinet; the back is left uncovered and is best placed against a wall.

MATERIALS

* 1 yard of 54/60" fabric (home-decor weight)
* 1 spool of coordinating thread
* Six 1½" buttons (purchased or cover your own using a button-covering kit)
* Approximately 10 yards of ½" double-fold bias tape (purchased or make your own, *see page* 18)

Finished dimensions — 15" wide × 19" deep × 26½" tall
Seam allowance — ½" unless otherwise specified

NOTE: *Ties can be substituted for the button and button loops.*

1 Measure, Mark, and Cut

Most two-drawer filing cabinets have very similar dimensions, but there can be slight variations in size. With that in mind we recommend you measure your cabinet before starting the project to guarantee accuracy and a perfect fit. Take the following measurements of your actual cabinet:

* **Cabinet height = A**
* **Cabinet depth (from back to front) = B**
* **Cabinet width (across the front) = C**

Once you have your measurements, determine your required pattern pieces as follows:

* **Side/top panel** B wide × (A + half of C + ½") tall
* **Front panel** C wide × (A + ½") tall

Lay out your fabric in a single layer with the wrong side facing up. Follow the layout to measure and mark the pattern pieces directly onto the wrong side of your fabric, then cut them out.

NOTE: *Place "tall" dimensions along the grainline of your fabric.*

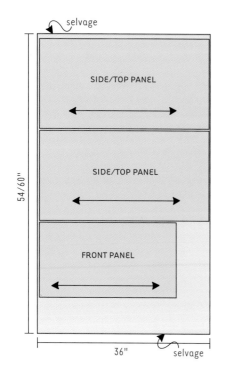

selvage

SIDE/TOP PANEL

SIDE/TOP PANEL

FRONT PANEL

54/60"

36"   selvage

CUTTING LAYOUT

② Prepare the Front Panel

Bind three edges of the front panel (the two long edges and the bottom short edge) with bias tape (*see page* 18).

③ Make the Top and Side Panels

Stitch the two side/top panels, right sides together, along the top short edge; this seam will sit on top of the cabinet. Press the seam open, and on the right side, cover this seam decoratively with bias tape by stitching close to each edge of the bias tape.

④ Attach All the Panels

With wrong sides together, pin the front panel to the side panels, aligning the top center of the front panel with the bias-tape seam. Stitch these pieces together along the top short edge of the front panel only. Don't worry about this seam showing, as it will be covered in the next step.

⑤ Bind the Edges

Bind one long edge and both short bottom edges of the side/top panels with bias tape, fully encasing the seam from step 4. Hem the remaining long edge of the side/top panel with a narrow ½" hem (this edge will be at the back of the file cabinet).

⑥ Make Button Loops

On both side edges of the side/top panels, place marks at 7", 14", and 21" from the bottom for button loop placement. Edgestitch along the entire length of a 48" piece of bias tape. Cut six pieces measuring 8" each, and fold each piece in half to create a loop. Pin the loops to the wrong side of the fabric at the 7", 14", and 21" markings. Stitch securely in place.

⑦ Button It Up

On the right side of the front panel, place your buttons 2½" in from the edge at the 7", 14", and 21" positions. Sew the buttons at these markings. Slip the cover over your file cabinet and button it in place.

CHAPTER 3

HOUSEHOLD AFFAIRS

Daily chores can be so mundane and uninteresting, but when you have beautiful handmade projects to get you through your laundry, cooking, and cleaning, you'll suddenly look forward to getting the job done. This chapter is full of useful (and snazzy) household accessories, so get out your recently revved-up ironing board, and get ready to tie on your new, favorite apron. Or use a just-sewn set of hot-looking hot pads to create the most out-of-this-world meal — and then carry it to that special potluck party in a handcrafted casserole-dish cover.

HANGING LAUNDRY BAG

Designed by Rae Hoekstra

Need a neat, out-of-the-way place to store your dirty clothes? This laundry bag fits the bill, as it hangs inside your closet: door closed, problem solved! Tight on closet space? Try hanging it on the back of a door with two over-the-door hooks. This project would also be perfect for a kid's room, where it can be used to store toys and other treasures.

MATERIALS

* 1 yard of 44/45" (home-decor weight, or oilcloth would also work well)
* 1 spool of coordinating thread
* 5 size-16 snaps (you can use sew-in snaps, or pronged snaps and a snap press)
* 2 packages of ½" double-fold bias tape

* Dinner plate, 10"–12" diameter (for template)
* 2 pieces of 9" × 12" craft felt squares for appliqué letters (optional)

Finished dimensions – 21" × 31"
Seam allowance – ½" unless otherwise specified

① Measure, Mark, and Cut

Place your fabric in a single layer with the wrong side facing up. Measure and mark the following pattern pieces directly on the wrong side of your fabric, and cut them out:

* **Upper back** 22" wide × 28" tall (cut 1)
* **Lower back** 22" wide × 8" tall (cut 1)
* **Front** 22" wide × 32" tall (cut 1)
* **Straps** 11" wide × 4" tall (cut 2)

NOTE: *Place "tall" dimensions along the grainline of your fabric.*

② Make the Back Flap Opening

Encase the upper raw edge of the lower back piece with bias tape, using a zigzag stitch. Repeat this step with the lower raw edge of the upper back piece. Position the two back pieces, right sides up, so that the lower piece overlaps the upper piece by 2." Baste together along the side seams at a scant ¼" seam allowance. Attach three pairs of snaps onto the upper and lower back pieces to fasten this overlapped opening.

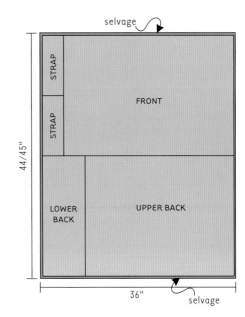

CUTTING LAYOUT

❸ Make the Laundry Opening

Using a dinner plate as a template, place it in the top center of the front piece, 3" from the top of the bag. Trace around the plate and cut out. Stitch bias tape around the opening using a zigzag stitch, fully encasing the raw edge.

❹ Make and Attach the Straps

* On one short end of each strap piece, press under ½". Fold, press, and stitch straps (as if making double-fold bias tape, *see page* 18).

* Place one strap in the top corner of the front piece, aligning the raw edges. Repeat with the second strap in the opposite top corner. Align and pin the front and back pieces, right sides together, sandwiching the straps between the two pieces. Stitch across the top of the bag. Turn right side out and press. Topstitch along the top edge of bag.

❺ Make Rounded Bottom Corners

Place a standard drinking glass upside down on one bottom corner and trace the portion of glass that falls within the seam allowance using a fabric pen. Trim away the excess fabric. Repeat this step in the opposite bottom corner.

❻ Bind the Exterior of the Bag

Starting at the top edge of the strap on the right side, tuck the end of the bias tape into the opening of the strap. Stitch the bias tape over the raw edge of the strap using a zigzag stitch, encasing the seam. Continue working your way around the entire outside raw edge of the bag, ending at the left strap, encasing the entire seam. Once you reach the top of the left strap, tuck the end of the bias tape into the open end of the strap. Stitch across the ends of each strap to close.

❼ Snap the Straps

Attach a pair of snaps to each of the straps. Place one half of the snap on each strap 1" above the top of the bag and the other 1" from the end of each strap.

❽ Add Letters (optional)

Using a bold graphic font, print out the letters "WASH ME," each approximately 4" tall. Cut the letters from the printer paper to use as pattern pieces. Pin to felt and cut out letters.

Determine placement of the letters in the circular opening of the bag and stitch them in place with a zigzag stitch.

GRANNY'S CLOTHESPIN APRON

Designed by Elorie Bechtel

It's such a treat to be able to hang your laundry out on the line during the warm months of summer. Not only do you save energy, but you also get to enjoy that clean summer scent on your sheets. It's all going to be so much easier now that you have a clothespin apron – you can finally say goodbye to that old coffee can you've been using to store your clothespins!

MATERIALS

* Locate the pattern in the front pocket (sheet #2)
* 1 yard of 44/45" fabric (quilting-weight cotton)
* 1 spool of coordinating thread

Finished dimensions – 16" × 9"

Seam allowance – ½" unless otherwise specified

① Measure, Mark, and Cut

With right sides together, fold your fabric in half lengthwise, aligning the selvages. Place the pattern pieces as shown on the cutting layout. Also measure and mark the additional pieces. Cut out the pieces and transfer the notches from the pattern pieces to the wrong side of the fabric.

* **Apron back** (cut 1 on fold)
* **Apron front** (cut 1 on fold)
* **Apron tie** 3" wide × 32" long (cut 4)
* **Waistband** 17½" wide × 4" tall (cut 1 on fold)
* **Pocket binding** 9½" × 2" (cut 2 on bias)
* **Apron trim** 6½" × 2" (cut 2 on bias)

NOTE: *Place pattern pieces along the grainline of your fabric as shown.*

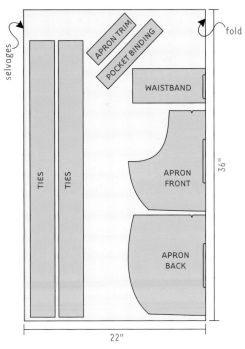

CUTTING LAYOUT

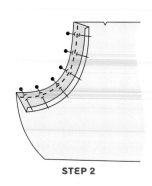

STEP 2

❷ Attach Binding to Front Pockets

Press one long edge of the pocket binding ½" to the wrong side. With right sides together, align the raw edge of the pocket binding (not the one you just pressed) and one of the raw concave edges of the apron front pocket. Stitch the binding in place, as shown in the diagram. Fold the bias tape to the reverse side of the pocket fabric. Press and pin. Stitch in the ditch (*see page* 14) from the front side, making sure to catch the folded edge of the bias trim on the reverse. Repeat for the second pocket edge.

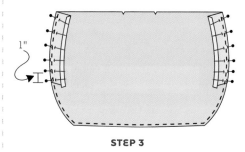

STEP 3

❸ Join the Apron Front and Back

Place the apron front on top of the apron back with both wrong sides facing up, matching the notches at the top edge. Press one long edge of apron trim ½" to the wrong side. With wrong sides facing up, align the raw edges of the apron trim and the side of the apron back (note that the trim will overlap the apron front by 1", per diagram). Stitch through all layers around the curved edge of the apron, leaving the top notched edge open.

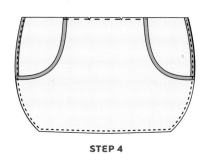

STEP 4

❹ Finish the Edges of the Apron

Clip to but not through the seam along the rounded corners to ease fullness. Turn the apron right side out. Fold the apron trim to the front. Press and pin. Topstitch around the apron, making sure to catch the edges of the apron trim. Match notches at the top edge of the apron and baste in place using a scant ¼" seam from pocket edge to pocket edge.

STEP 5

❺ Make the Waistband

Turn both short edges of the waistband under ½" to the wrong side and press.

⑥ Attach the Waistband

Turn one long side of the waistband under ½" to the wrong side and press. With right sides together, align the raw edge of the waistband to the top raw edge of the apron, matching notches. Stitch in place. Fold the waistband in half lengthwise, wrong sides together, with the turned-under edge just overlapping the back of the apron, and press. Stitch in the ditch from the front side, making sure to catch the turned-under edge of the waistband on the reverse. Leave waistband ends open.

STEP 6

⑦ Make the Ties

To make pointed ends, pin two ties right sides together. Measure and mark 1½" from the top right corner. Draw a line from this mark to the lower right corner and cut along this line. Repeat with the remaining two ties. Stitch three sides of each tie, as shown. Clip the corners, turn the apron ties right side out, and press. Topstitch close to the edges on all three finished sides. You will have two ties that are 2" wide.

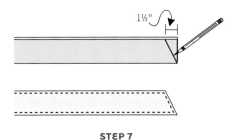

STEP 7

⑧ Attach the Ties

Slip at least ½" of the raw end of each tie into the waistband opening and stitch through all layers close to the folded edge of the waistband.

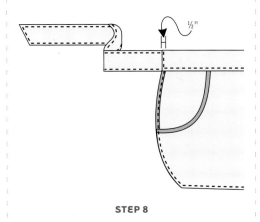

STEP 8

TABLETOP IRONING-BOARD COVER

Designed by City Chic Country Mouse

Few think of ironing as fun, but with a snazzy new ironing-board cover for your tabletop ironing board, this humdrum household chore suddenly has a whole new appeal. Not to mention the fact that you can now make your ironing board coordinate with your decor – how lovely!

MATERIALS

* 1 yard of fabric (any weight or width will do)
* 1 spool of coordinating thread
* 2½ yards of cotton or polyester cording
* 1 cord lock (optional)
* Wrapping paper, freezer paper, or paper bags, cut and taped together to measure 18" × 36"
* Paper-cutting scissors

Finished dimensions – will fit a 12" × 30" tabletop ironing board

① Measure, Mark, and Cut

Position your ironing board upside down on the paper and trace it to create a pattern template. To make the cutting line, measure and mark 2½" from the traced edge all the way around the outline. Cut out the pattern with paper-cutting scissors, then pin it to your fabric. Using fabric scissors, cut the cover from the fabric. Mark the center of the wide end of this fabric piece.

NOTE: *If you have a directional fabric, cut the fabric so that the design appears upright when the ironing board is standing on end.*

② Make the Casing

Press under the raw edge ¼" and zigzag the edge in place all the way around. Press under another ½" and topstitch close to the zigzag folded edge, leaving a 1" opening at the center of the wide end for inserting the drawstring (*see page* 19). As you turn the sharp corners, you will need to make some tucks to eliminate fullness.

③ Insert the Cording

Thread the cording through the entire length of the casing. Attach a cord lock or tie a knot in the cord ends.

④ Cover the Ironing Board

Place the cover on your ironing board, pulling the drawstring tight while smoothing out the gathers. Trim any excess cord, if necessary. Now, stoke up your iron and get ready to use your beautiful new ironing-board cover!

KITSCHY KITCHEN APRON

Designed by Mother's Apron Strings

Feel free to preheat the oven while you make this flirty half-apron. No need to sacrifice style the next time you are in the kitchen! Now go get baking!

MATERIALS

* 1 yard of 44/45" fabric (any weight will do)
* 1 spool of coordinating thread
* 2 funky, vintage, and/or coordinating buttons, any size (optional)

Finished dimensions – approximately 22" wide × 20" long, not including ties
Seam allowance – ½" unless otherwise specified

① Measure, Mark, and Cut

Place your fabric in a single layer with the wrong side facing up. Measure and mark the following pattern pieces directly on the wrong side of your fabric as shown, then cut them out:

* **Ruffle** 36" wide × 5" tall (cut 1)
* **Apron ties** 4" wide × 31" tall (cut 2)
* **Waistband** 22" wide × 4" tall (cut 1)
* **Apron** 22" on the top, 27" on the bottom, 20" from top to bottom (cut 1)

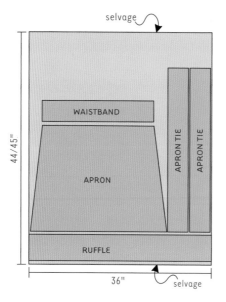

CUTTING LAYOUT

② Hem the Apron

Make a narrow ¼" double-fold hem along both angled sides and the bottom edge of the apron (*see page* 19). Topstitch along all three edges.

③ Make the Apron Ties

Press one short end of each apron tie ½" toward the wrong side. Fold in half lengthwise, with right sides together, aligning raw edges. Stitch along the unfolded end and the long side of each piece, leaving the pressed edge open. Clip the corners, turn right side out, and press. Topstitch close to the edges on all four sides.

④ Make the Ruffle

Create a ¼" double-fold hem on one long and two short sides of the ruffle. Use a basting stitch to gather the top raw edge of the ruffle piece to a finished, gathered length of 21" (*see page* 13). With right sides facing up, place the ruffle along the top unfinished edge of the apron, aligning the raw edges. Adjust ruffles so they are evenly distributed along the width of apron's top edge (*see page* 37). Baste the pieces together with a scant ¼" seam allowance.

⑤ Attach the Waistband

Press one long raw edge of the waistband under ½" to the wrong side of the fabric. With right sides together, align the raw edge of the waistband to the raw edge of the apron/ruffle, and stitch. Press seam allowances toward the waistband. With right sides together, fold the waistband in half lengthwise, and stitch across the short ends. Clip the corners, turn the waistband right side out, and press. Topstitch around all four sides of the waistband on the right side.

⑥ Attach the Apron Ties

Pin one apron tie on the back side of the waistband, overlapping the edge 1½". Stitch in place. Do the same with the other apron tie. For a little extra pizzazz, attach a vintage button on each side of the waistband where the tie attaches.

COTTAGE APRON

Designed by Charlot Meyer

Move over, butcher's apron, there's a feminine version in town! The Cottage Apron has just the right amount of flounce, yet does the job of keeping you clean while you're getting busy in the kitchen.

MATERIALS

* Locate the pattern in the front pocket (sheet #3)
* 1 yard of 44/45" fabric (quilting-weight cotton)
* 1 spool of coordinating thread
* 2 coordinating ½" buttons
* 4 yards of ¼" or ½" double-fold bias tape
* 3 yards of 2"-wide coordinating ribbon
* ½ yard eyelet trim

Finished dimensions – approximately 30" wide × 33" long
Seam allowance – ½" unless otherwise specified

❶ Measure, Mark, and Cut

With right sides together, fold your fabric in half lengthwise, aligning the selvages. Cut out the apron pattern and pocket as listed below. Transfer markings from the apron pattern to the wrong side of the fabric.

* **Apron** (cut 1 on fold)
* **Pocket** 6½" × 6½" (cut 2)

❷ Prep the Apron

Staystitch the side edges of the apron.

STEP 2

➌ Make and Place the Pockets

Encase the upper edge of each pocket in bias tape and stitch. Press under the sides and lower edges of the pockets ¼". Pin the pockets on the apron along the placement lines and attach by topstitching close to the side and lower edges.

➍ Make the Darts

Cut along the line indicated on the pattern. With right sides together, fold the apron along the dart lines, aligning the dots, and stitch. Press darts outward.

Baste along the gathering line. Pinning as you go, gather between the small dots until the outer edges of the apron's bottom line up with the outer edges of the top. (*For more on gathering, see page* 13.) With the right sides facing, pin the top and bottom sections together and stitch.

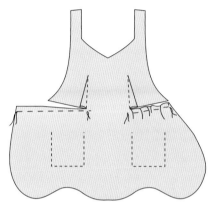

STEP 4

➎ Add Bias Tape

Starting at the outer edge of one strap, encase the raw edges of the entire outer edge of the apron with bias tape and stitch. Do the same for the neck edge. Stitch eyelet trim to the neckline, behind the bias tape on the wrong side.

➏ Make the Straps

Cut two 32" pieces of ribbon for the waist ties. Fold one end ½" to the wrong side and pin the ribbon at the bottom edge of the vertical dart, covering the gathering line on the right side of the apron as shown. Edgestitch the ribbon to the apron along both edges.

For the shoulder straps, cut two ribbons long enough to cross your back and reach the waist ties. With right sides together, stitch the ribbons to each shoulder. Make a buttonhole in the free end of each shoulder strap. Sew a button on the wrong side of the apron, behind the waist tie, to fasten the shoulder straps.

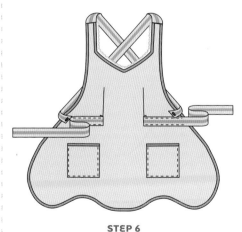

STEP 6

picnic-tastic Lunch Mats

Designed by Rebecca Yaker

Prepare to enjoy a lovely outdoor meal on these very stylish picnic-ready placemats! They're perfectly portable – just slip your utensils right into the pocket. And don't worry about losing your napkin on those breezy days, because there's a handy spot for that, too!

MATERIALS

* 1 yard of 44/45" fabric
* 1 spool of coordinating thread

Finished dimensions – each placemat is 11" × 15" (1 yard of fabric makes 4)

Seam allowance – ½" unless otherwise specified

1 Measure, Mark, and Cut

With right sides together, fold your fabric in half lengthwise, aligning the selvages. Measure and mark the following pattern pieces directly on the wrong side of your fabric, then cut them out:

* **Placemat** 22" wide × 16" tall (cut 4)
* **Pocket** 7" wide × 4" tall (cut 4)
* **Napkin holder** 2" wide × 4" tall (cut 4)

NOTE: *Place "tall" dimensions along the grainline of your fabric.*

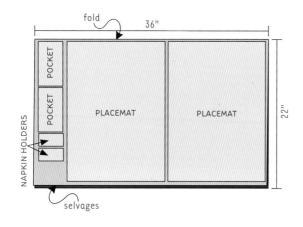

CUTTING LAYOUT

2 Make the Placemats

With right sides together, fold a placemat in half, matching short ends. Stitch around all three raw edges, leaving a 4½" opening along long edge for turning. Clip the corners and turn right side out. Neatly turn the raw edges at the opening to the inside; press. Topstitch around all four sides of placemat, stitching the turning opening closed as you go. Do the same for the three remaining placemats.

3 Make the Pockets

On the top edge of a pocket piece, make a narrow ¼" double-fold hem (*see page* 19). Topstitch.

Fold and press the napkin holders as you would to make double-fold bias tape (*see page* 18). Topstitch along both long edges.

Position napkin holder on pocket, 2" down from the top hemmed edge, aligning raw edges. Baste in place along sides. Press the three raw edges of the pocket (and attached napkin holder) ½" to the wrong side. Place on the right side of placemat, 1" from edge, and 1" up from the bottom. Topstitch around bottom and side edges, leaving top open to insert utensils.

Repeat these steps for remaining three placemats.

oven mitt & hot pads

Designed by Lelia Thell

It can be so difficult to find jazzy hot pads that speak to your style. Well, look no further, because with this pattern you can make yourself the perfect retro (or mod, or classic, or whatever) set of oven mitts and hot pads.

MATERIALS

* Locate the pattern in the front pocket (sheet #3)
* 1 yard of 44/45" cotton fabric (any weight will do)
* 1 spool of coordinating thread
* ½ yard of insulated batting
* Quilter's safety pins
* Sewing-machine walking foot, optional

Finished dimensions – mitt is 10" × 13", and the pads are 8" square

Seam allowance – ½" unless otherwise specified

① Measure, Mark, and Cut

Measure and mark all pieces directly on the wrong side of your fabric, then cut them out. For the mitt, you will not be cutting out the pattern yet, as you need to quilt the fabric first. The binding strips do not need to be cut on the bias, although you can do so if you wish.

* **Oven mitt** 10" wide × 14" tall (cut 4)
* **Mitt hanging loop** 1¼" wide × 6" tall (cut 1)
* **Mitt binding strip** 2¼" wide × 14" tall (cut 1)
* **Pads** 9" wide × 9" tall (cut 4)
* **Pad hanging loop** 1¼" wide × 6" tall (cut 2)

* **Pad binding strip** 2½" wide × 36" tall (cut 2)

Cut from insulated batting:

* **Oven mitt** 10" wide × 14" tall (cut 2)
* **Pads** 9" wide × 9" tall (cut 2)

NOTE: *Place "tall" dimensions along the grainline of your fabric.*

② Quilt the Fabric

* For the mitt: Put two mitt pieces with wrong sides together, and place a layer of batting between them. Pin through all three layers with quilter's pins, and use a disappearing fabric marker or tailor's chalk to mark the fabric with your choice of quilting lines (you could try diagonal 1½" squares). Machine-quilt the layers together following the lines. You may want to use a walking foot if you have one.
* Do the same with the fabric for the hot pads.

③ Cut Out the Mitt

Use the pattern piece provided to cut two front/back shapes from the quilted fabric.

④ Stitch the Mitt

Pin the front and back right sides together, aligning the raw edges. Leaving the bottom straight edge open, stitch all around the curved edge, pivoting at the point between the thumb and fingers. Notch the seam allowance around the curved edges. Snip to, but not through, the stitching line at the pivot point. Turn the mitt right side out.

⑤ Make the Hanging Loops

For both the mitt and hot pads, press and fold the loop strips in the same way that you'd make double-fold bias tape (*see page* 18). Topstitch along the folded edge. Make the loop by folding the strip and matching up the ends.

⑥ Attach the Loops

✳ **For the mitt:** Pin these ends on the right side of the mitt side seam, opposite the thumb, aligning raw edges. Stitch in place. Don't worry about the raw edges showing, as these will be covered with binding in step 8.

✳ **For the hot pads:** Align one raw edge of a loop with the raw edge of a hot pad, 1" from a corner, and stitch in place with a scant ¼" seam allowance. Align the other end of the same loop on the other side of the same corner — make sure your loop is not twisted — and stitch in place. Repeat for the second hot pad.

⑦ Make the Binding

Make bias tape from all the binding strips (*see page* 18).

⑧ Bind the Mitt

Open up the binding strip, fold under one short end ½" and press. Starting with this finished end, enclose the raw edge of the oven mitt in binding tape, ending where you started and tucking the unfinished short end under the pressed end (note that the raw edges of the loop from step 6 will have been caught in between the mitt and the binding strip). Fold the binding strip to the inside of the mitt and stitch it in place, making sure to catch the back edge of the tape when topstitching the front.

⑨ Bind the Pads

Open up the binding strip, fold under one short end ½", and press. Starting with this finished end, line up one long raw edge of the binding strip with the raw edge of the hot pad, starting at the center of one side.

Begin stitching at the folded edge of the binding. When you get near the first corner, stop stitching ¼" from it. Backstitch. Remove the hot pad from the machine and cut the threads.

Fold the binding at a 45-degree angle just before the corner and again right after, so that when the binding tape is flipped over the edge of the hot pad, the folds will lie flat and look the way you would like them to. Pin these folds in place. Start stitching again, using a few back-stitches at the beginning. Repeat with the 3 remaining corners.

When nearing your starting point, trim excess binding, and tuck unfinished short end under pressed end.

Turn the binding to the back of the hot pad, encasing the raw edges. On the front of the hot pad, stitch in the ditch around the edge, making sure to catch the back of the binding in the seam. Repeat for the second hot pad.

HEY, HOT DISH

Designed by Natalya Kremenetskaya

*Casseroles are a staple at potlucks and family gatherings. Because every-
one loves a nice hearty hot dish, you need a way to keep your specialty
warm en route to the festivities. This hot-dish caddy is the perfect solution.
Everyone will love your hot tuna noodle surprise — and the chic wrap your
casserole arrived in!*

MATERIALS

* 1 yard of 44/45" fabric
* 1 spool of coordinating thread
* 1 yard of insulated batting
* 1 package of ½" double-fold bias
  tape (or 2 yards if you choose to
  make your own)
* 1 package of ⅞" double-fold bias tape (or
  2½ yards if you choose to make your own)
* 1 yard of cording (to use as drawstring)

Finished dimensions – 17" diameter
Seam allowance – ½" unless otherwise specified

① Measure, Mark, and Cut

With right sides together, fold your fabric in half lengthwise, aligning the selvages. Measure and mark the following pattern pieces
directly on the wrong side of your fabric, then cut them out:

* **Top and bottom** 17" diameter circle (cut 4)
* **Handles** 3" wide × 17" tall (cut 4)

Cut from insulated batting:

* **Top and bottom** 17" diameter circle (cut 2)
* **Handles** 3" wide × 17" tall (cut 2)

NOTE: *Place "tall" dimensions along the grainline of your fabric.*

② Insulate the Pieces

Lay two fabric circles with wrong sides together, then place a layer
of batting between them. Baste all three layers together with a
scant ¼" seam allowance. Do the same for the remaining two fabric
circles. Insulate two handles in the same way.

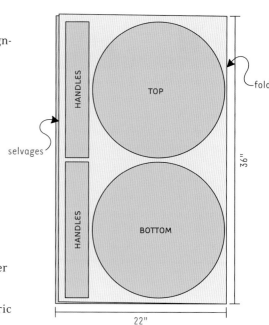

CUTTING LAYOUT

MAKING IT FIT

This casserole caddy has been designed to accommodate a 2½-quart round, square, or oval casserole dish. You can revise the proportions if your dish is larger. Simply measure the diameter of your dish plus the height. Add 3" to this measurement to determine the diameter of the pattern circles. Cut the length of your handles to match.

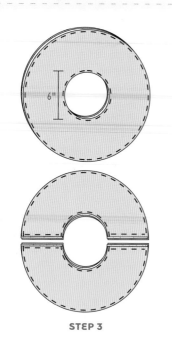

STEP 3

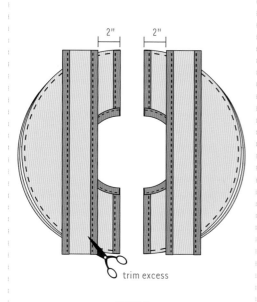

2" 2"

trim excess

STEP 5

③ Make the Top

Cut a 6" diameter hole in the center of one circle piece, creating a donut shape. Baste around this edge with a scant ¼" seam allowance. Cut the donut in half to create the two top pieces of the casserole caddy and baste along the straight edges.

④ Bind the Handles and Inside Top

Using the ½" double-fold bias tape, bind both long edges of the handles (*See page* 18). Also bind the straight edges of the top pieces.

Using the ⅞" bias tape, turn and press one end ½" to the wrong side. Carefully bind the inner half-circle of both front pieces. As you approach the end, cut the bias tape, turn the end to the wrong side, and continue stitching to the end to create a clean finish. Leave both ends open, as this will function as the opening of the drawstring casing.

⑤ Layer the Pieces

Place the two top pieces on top of the bottom circle, aligning all raw edges. Position the handles parallel to the center opening, leaving about 2" on either side. Trim the overhanging handle ends as shown. Pin all pieces together and baste in place with a scant ¼" seam allowance.

⑥ Bind the Outer Edge

Use the remaining ⅞" bias tape to bind the outside edge of the casserole caddy. As you approach the end, cut the bias tape, turn the end to the wrong side, overlap the ends by ½", and stitch to create a clean finished end. Thread the drawstring through the casing, knotting the ends to prevent fraying. Now you can tuck your favorite round casserole dish inside the top flaps, pull the string tight for a snug (and heat-preserving) fit, and enjoy keeping your favorite hot dish hot!

tea cozy

Designed by Sarah Hunter

Make haste and get that teakettle boiling! Pick your favorite tea and brew yourself a pot. And once you have this handy tea cozy close by, you don't need to worry about drinking it all at once! So, enjoy – and relax!

MATERIALS

* 1 yard of 44/45" fabric (preferably flannel)
* 1 spool of coordinating thread
* 1 yard of ⅝" coordinating decorative ribbon

Finished dimensions – approximately 7" × 11"
Seam allowance – ½" unless otherwise specified

1 Measure, Mark, and Cut

Measure and mark the following pattern pieces directly on the wrong side of your fabric, and cut them out.

* **Exterior and lining** 13½" wide × 9" tall (cut 4)
* **Tab top** 3" wide × 4" tall (cut 1)

NOTE: *Place "tall" dimensions along the grainline of your fabric.*

2 Make the Tab Top

Fold and press the tab piece as you would to make double-fold bias tape (*see page* 18). Topstitch the folded edge. Pin a 4" piece of ribbon to one side of the tab and stitch it in place along both edges. Fold the tab in half with the ribbon facing out. Set aside.

3 Make the Lining

Pin two lining pieces with right sides together. Stitch the sides and top, leaving the bottom edge open.

CUSTOM COZY

Since teapots come in all shapes and sizes, measure your pot before you start, to make sure this cozy will fit. For the width, measure your teapot from the spout to the handle; for the height, measure from top to bottom. Add 2" to both measurements to allow for seam allowances. If your numbers don't match ours, no problem, just cut the exterior and lining pieces to your measurements instead.

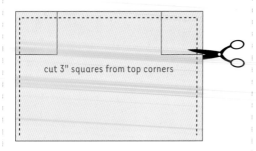

cut 3" squares from top corners

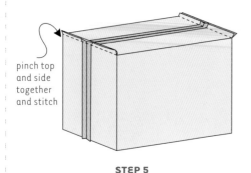

pinch top
and side
together
and stitch

STEP 5

④ Make the Exterior

Place the right sides of the two exterior pieces together, sandwiching the tab between them. Center the tab along the top of the cozy, and line up the raw edges of the tab with the raw edges of the cozy top. (The tab is essentially upside down between the two layers.) Stitch the sides and the top, catching the tab in the seam, and leaving the bottom edge open.

⑤ Customize the Corners

Measure and mark a 3" square in one top corner of the cozy. Cut the square out. Press the seams open. Pull the fabric layers apart at the cutout and pinch the side and top together. Line up the side and top seams and the raw edges of the cutout. Stitch the cutout edge shut to make the gusset (you will be making a seam that is perpendicular to the previous side/top seams). Repeat for the second top corner of the cozy and press the seams toward the top of the cozy. Repeat with the cozy lining pieces.

⑥ Join the Exterior and Lining

Place the lining piece inside the exterior piece, right sides together, aligning the side seams. Pin together and stitch around the edge, leaving a 3" opening for turning. Turn the lining to the inside through this opening — the wrong sides are now together. Neatly press the bottom edge of the tea cozy and topstitch along that edge, stitching closed the opening used for turning. Carefully pin the remaining length of ribbon along the outer bottom edge. Where the ends of the ribbon overlap, fold under one of the unfinished edges and pin it in place on top of the other raw edge. Stitch the ribbon to the cozy along the top and bottom edges of the ribbon.

wine-LOVers' special

Wine-Bottle Holders Designed by Sarah Hunter

Coasters Designed by Patricia Hoskins

Since the wine shop was having such a great wine sale, you decided to buy an extra bottle as a gift for your good friend. Thank goodness this project allows you to make two bags and two sets of four ingenious coasters that can slide right onto the base of the wineglass: you get to keep one set and give the other set away. Now your impulse purchase has become a gift of style and substance.

MATERIALS

* ✳ 1 yard of 44/45" fabric (any weight will do)
* ✳ 1 spool of coordinating thread
* ✳ 2 yards of ½" or 1" coordinating ribbon

Finished dimensions – wine-bottle holder is 7" × 14"; coaster size is determined by the size of your wine glass base

Seam allowance – ½" unless otherwise specified

Wine-Bottle Holder *(set of 2)*

① Measure, Mark, and Cut

Measure and mark the following pattern pieces directly on the wrong side of your fabric, leaving room for the coaster pieces coming up. Cut out the pieces, and also cut the ribbon into four 18" pieces.

* ✳ **Exterior and lining** 7" wide × 14" tall
  (cut 8 to make 2 bags)

NOTE: *Place "tall" dimensions along the grainline of your fabric.*

NOTE: *Measurements are based on a wine bottle with a 10" circumference and an 11" height.*

② Make the Linings

With right sides facing, pin two fabric pieces together. Stitch the sides and bottom, leaving the top edge open. Press seams open. Repeat with second set of lining pieces.

③ Make the Exteriors

Place two pieces of ribbon on the right side edge of one exterior piece, 2" down from the top edge, aligning the raw edges. Pin a second exterior piece (without ribbon) on top with right sides together, and stitch the sides and bottom, leaving the top edge open. The ribbon will be sandwiched between the layers. Press the seams open and turn the exterior right side out. Make a second exterior in the same manner.

④ Join the Exterior and Lining

With right sides together, fit the exterior inside the lining, aligning the side seams. Pin together and stitch around the top edge, leaving a 3" opening for turning. Through this opening, turn the lining to the inside (wrong sides will be together). Neatly press the top edge of the wine-bottle holder and topstitch along the top edge, turning under and closing the opening used for turning. With a pair of pinking shears, snip the ribbon ends to prevent fraying. Place the wine bottles into their holders, tie the ribbons, and you're good to gift!

Wineglass Coasters

① Measure, Mark, and Cut

Measure and mark the following pattern pieces directly on the wrong side of your fabric, then cut them out. (And if you're making the coasters before the wine-bottle holder, remember to leave room for those pieces as well!)

* **Coaster** 4½" diameter circle (cut 32; that's 4 per coaster to make 8)

NOTE: *Measurements are based on a standard-size wineglass. If you have a specific glass in mind, measure the diameter of the base and cut four circles that are 1" larger than the base.*

② Make the Coaster

* For the bottom, place two circles on top of each other, wrong sides together, aligning all raw edges.
* Fold the remaining two circles in half, wrong sides together, and press. Pin the half circles on top of the coaster base, with the folded edges meeting in the middle and raw edges aligned.
* Stitch completely around the circumference. Using pinking shears, trim the seam allowance close to the stitch line, being careful not to cut through the stitching.
* Turn the coaster right side out, hiding the pinked seam allowance. Press.

OBI-INSPIRED HOT-&-COLD PACK

Designed by Jessica Roberts

Inspired by the Japanese obi, this wrap holds a home-made, all-natural hot-and-cold pack, perfect for soothing a complaining back after too much time behind the vacuum cleaner. Heat or freeze the pack, then slip it inside the wrap and tie in place. Ahhhhh, relief!

MATERIALS

* ✳ 1 yard of 44/45" fabric (not suitable for one-way prints)
* ✳ 1 spool of coordinating thread
* ✳ 2 cups of whole flaxseeds or rice
* ✳ Funnel

Finished dimensions — The hot-and-cold pack measures 8" wide × 11" tall, and the entire obi measures 90" end to end.
Seam allowance — ½" unless otherwise specified

❶ Measure, Mark, and Cut

Place your fabric in a single layer with the wrong side facing up. Measure and mark the following pattern pieces directly on the wrong side of your fabric, then cut them out:

* ✳ **Ties** 42" wide × 11" tall (cut 2)
* ✳ **Pocket** 21" wide × 12" tall (cut 1)
* ✳ **Hot-and-cold pack** 19" wide × 11½" tall (cut 1)

NOTE: *Place "tall" dimensions along the grainline of your fabric.*

❷ Make the Ties

With right sides together, fold the ties in half lengthwise. Stitch along one short end and the long raw edge. Clip the corner, turn the right side out, and press.

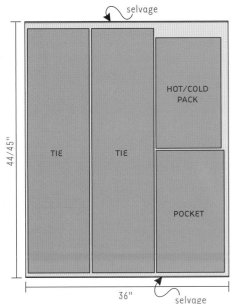

selvage

44/45"

TIE   TIE   HOT/COLD PACK

POCKET

36"

selvage

CUTTING LAYOUT

❸ Make and Attach the Pocket

* Press under both short ends of the pocket ¼". Press under another ¼" and topstitch close to the folded edge.
* Center the ties on each raw edge of the pocket, with right sides together, aligning raw edges. Baste in place using a scant ¼" seam allowance.
* With the pocket piece right side up, fold both finished edges of the pocket 5" toward the center of the pocket. The folded edges will overlap by 2", forming an envelope. Stitch through all layers along the raw edges, taking care not to catch the "tails" of the ties in the stitching lines. Clip corners, turn right side out, and press.

❹ Make the Hot-and-Cold Pack

With right sides together, fold the hot-and-cold-pack piece in half, aligning the short ends. Stitch along one long and one short end. Clip the corners, turn right side out, and press. On the open end, turn and press the fabric ½" to the inside of the pack.

❺ Fill the Hot-and-Cold Pack

Mark eight evenly spaced lines 1" apart, lengthwise, on the pack, creating nine channels to hold flaxseeds (or rice). Stitch along these lines to within ¼" of the open (short) end. Using a funnel, fill each channel with flaxseeds to within 2" of the top of each channel. Topstitch the open end closed to secure the seeds in the pack. Gently shake the heating pad to redistribute the flaxseeds.

❻ Use the Wrap and Pack

To heat the pack, place it in a microwave for 1 to 3 minutes on high. If necessary, heat further at 30-second intervals. To cool the pack, place it in the freezer for at least 1 hour. Once you've achieved the desired temperature, slip the pad into the pocket and tie the wrap around your waist — or wherever heating/cooling is needed. What a relief!

CHAPTER 4

CRAFT ORGANIZATION

A messy craft space is a well-used craft space, but wouldn't it be nice to be able to organize a bit? Here are a handful of projects to help you get there. Create some order out of crafting chaos, with a wall pocket, a compartmented box, a pincushion, or a smock — everything to keep yourself neat and tidy during those extra-messy do-it-yourself adventures.

ALL-YOU-NEED SEWING KIT

Designed by Erin Evans

At home or on the go, this roll-up sewing kit can handle all of your basic sewing supplies and notions, with snapped pockets for scissors and other sewing sundries, room for three or more spools of thread, and even a special needle holder. Roll it all up, tie it together, and you'll be the most stylish traveling crafter ever!

MATERIALS

* 1 yard of 44/45" fabric (quilting-weight cotton or cotton blend)
* 1 spool of coordinating thread
* 4 yards of trim such as rickrack or ribbon
* Decorative snaps (not sew-in) and a snap press, snap pliers, or other snap attacher
* ⅓ yard of ⅜" elastic

Finished dimensions – 16" tall × 11" wide
Seam allowance – ½" unless otherwise specified

① Measure, Mark, and Cut

Place your fabric in a single layer with the wrong side facing up. Measure and mark the following pattern pieces directly on the wrong side of your fabric, and cut them out:

* **Main body** 17" tall × 12" wide (cut 2)
* **Large pocket** 10½" tall × 8½" wide (cut 1)
* **Small pocket** 10½" tall × 4½" wide (cut 2)
* **Casing** 2" tall × 14" wide (cut 1)
* **Needle holder** 3½" tall × 2" wide (cut 2)
* **Ties** 20" tall × 2" wide (cut 2)

NOTE: *Place "tall" dimensions along the grainline of your fabric.*

② Make and Attach Pockets

On each of the three pockets (one large, two small), press under all edges with a narrow ¼" double-fold hem (*see page* 19). Stitch the top and bottom (short edge) hems, leaving the side edges pressed but unstitched.

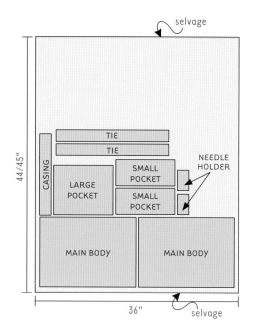

CUTTING LAYOUT

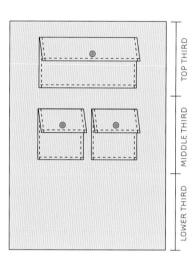

STEP 2

With the wrong side of the large pocket facing toward you, fold up the bottom edge 4", and fold the top edge down 1¾" to form a flap. Press the folds. Open the upper flap and stitch the side hems of the flap only. Repeat pocket finishing steps for the smaller pockets.

Position the pockets on the right side of one main body piece, with the large pocket centered in the top third of the body. Center the small pockets side by side in the middle third.

With flaps left open to avoid accidental stitching, edgestitch the sides and bottom of each pocket to the main body. Add snaps to the pocket and flaps, following the manufacturer's instructions.

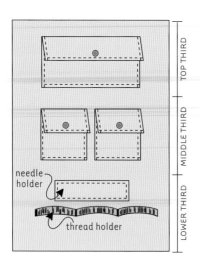

STEPS 3 & 4

❸ Make the Thread Holder

With right sides together, fold the casing strip lengthwise. Stitch along the long raw edge with a ¼" seam allowance, leaving the short ends open. Turn the casing right side out, fold under the raw ends ½", and press. Cut the elastic to 10" length and thread it through the casing. Stitch each end to secure.

Center the thread holder in the lower third of the main body. Turn the ends under and stitch it in place with a zigzag stitch. Divide the thread holder into three equal sections (or more sections if working with smaller spools) and stitch at the dividing lines.

❹ Make the Needle Holder

Pin the right sides of the needle-holder pieces together, and stitch around three sides, leaving one long side open. Turn right side out, and press under the raw edges at the opening ½".

Center the holder on the main body just above the thread holder. Edgestitch along the top (long) edge to secure it in place.

❺ Make the Ties and Trim

With right sides together, fold one tie in half lengthwise and stitch along one long edge, leaving the short ends open. Turn right side out. Position the seam in the center back of the tie and press. Tuck the raw edges inside ½" and slipstitch the opening closed. Center and topstitch the trim onto the front of the tie. Repeat with the second tie.

Pin the trim on all four sides of the pocketed main body, at least ½" from the raw edge. Stitch in place, taking care to turn under the raw edges of the trim.

❻ Finish the Sewing Kit

Stack both main body pieces, right sides together. Sandwich the ties between the layers, aligning their raw edges with the top center raw edge. Stitch all four sides, leaving a 5" opening on the bottom for turning. Clip the corners, turn the kit right side out, and edgestitch all four sides, stitching the opening closed as you go.

Hanging Wall Pocket

Designed by Kevin Kosbab

Sort your paper goods, whether it be sewing or craft patterns, files, bills, coupons – you name it, there is a place for it. If you're really feeling ambitious, you can even label the pockets for that next level of ultraorganization!

MATERIALS

* 1 yard of 44/45" or 54/60" fabric (home-decor or heavyweight preferred, but quilting weight will do)
* 2 yards of fusible interfacing (only if using quilting-weight fabric)
* 1 spool of coordinating thread
* ⅝ yard of ⅜" twill tape
* Alphabet rubber stamps and ink (preferably ink made for fabric)
* Fabric or basting glue (optional)
* 2 large grommets
* Grommet-setting tool (included in many grommet kits) and hammer

Finished dimensions – 30" tall × 13" wide
Seam allowance – ½" unless otherwise specified

1 Measure, Mark, and Cut

Place your fabric in a single layer with wrong side facing up. Measure and mark the following pattern pieces directly on the wrong side of your fabric. Mark three lines across one main body piece every 6", as indicated. Cut out the pieces.

* **Main body** 32" tall × 14" wide (cut 2)
* **Pockets** 8" tall × 14" wide (cut 4)

If using quilting-weight fabric, also cut from interfacing:

* **Main body** 31" tall × 13" wide (cut 2)
* **Pockets** 7" tall × 12" wide (cut 4)

Also, cut the twill tape into four 5½" lengths.

NOTE: *Place "tall" dimensions along the grainline of your fabric.*

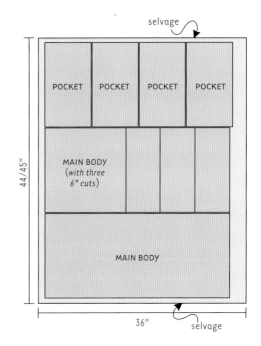

CUTTING LAYOUT

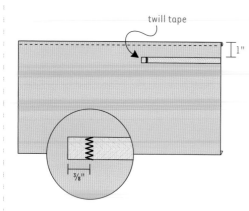

STEP 3
Attaching twill tape for labels

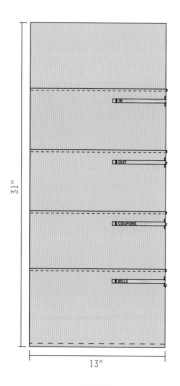

STEP 4
Pocket placement

② Apply Interfacing

If you're using quilting-weight fabric, center and fuse the interfacing onto the wrong side of each matching fabric piece.

③ Hem and Label the Pockets

Press under and stitch a ¼" double-fold hem along the top (long) edge of all pockets (*see page* 19). On three pockets, press under a ¼" double-fold hem along the bottom long edge, but do not stitch. (The fourth pocket is the bottom pocket.)

Pin twill tape on the right side of each pocket, 1" below and parallel to the top fold, with right raw edges aligned. Use a narrow zigzag stitch to topstitch the tape about ⅜" in from the left raw edge of the tape with a vertical stitch line. See illustration for twill tape and topstitch placement.

Baste the right edge of each piece of twill tape to a pocket.

The twill-tape pieces can be used as labels. Stamp the labels however you'd like; for instance, "skirts" or "tops" if you're organizing sewing patterns or "coupons," "bills," and so forth. Heat-set the ink if necessary. If you'd like, further secure the labels to each pocket with fabric glue.

④ Attach the Pockets

Place the bottom pocket (the one without a pressed bottom edge), right side facing up, on right side of one main body, aligning the bottom and side raw edges. Baste an edgestitch along the bottom and press open, leaving the pocket to one side and out of the way.

Select another pocket and open the unstitched fold at the bottom. With right sides together, place this pocket on the main body, aligning the opened fold with the first marked line 6" from the bottom. (The wrong side of pocket will be facing up, and the top hemmed edge will be hanging toward the bottom of the main body.) Stitch the pocket to the main body just above the opened fold line.

Attach the next two pockets to the main body in the same fashion, placing the opened fold at the 12" and 18" marked lines. When all pockets are stitched, fold them all up toward the top edge so that right sides are facing toward you. (The sides will get stitched closed in the next step.)

⑤ Stitch the Main Body

With right sides together, lay the remaining main body piece on top of the pocketed main body. Stitch around the perimeter, leaving a 5" opening on the bottom for turning. Clip the corners, turn right side out, and press. Press under the raw edges at the opening ½". Edgestitch around all four sides.

⑥ Make the Grommets

On the front main body, mark 1" in from the top and side of both top corners. Center a grommet barrel on each mark and trace the barrel onto the fabric. Cut out the circles through all layers of the main body. Insert and set the grommets, following the manufacturer's instructions. Hang and fill!

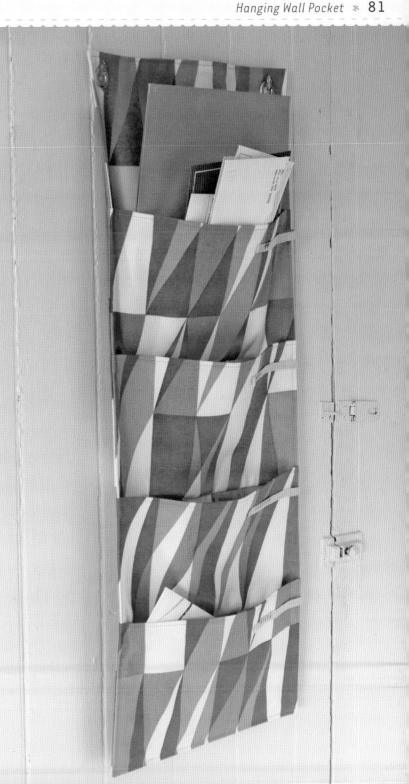

sewing tools trio

Sewing-Machine Cover Designed by Sarah Hunter

Pincushion and Needlebook Holder Designed by June Gilbank

Outfit your craft room with a snazzy sewing machine cozy and a matching wrist pincushion and needlebook holder — all from one yard of fabric!

MATERIALS

* 1 yard of 44/45" fabric (light- or medium-weight cotton)
* 1 spool of coordinating thread

Seam allowance – ½" unless otherwise specified

Sewing-Machine Cover

Finished dimensions – approximately 12" high × 16" wide × 6" deep

1 Measure, Mark, and Cut

With right sides together, fold your fabric in half lengthwise, aligning the selvages. Measure and mark the following pattern pieces directly on the wrong side of your fabric. If you're making all of the projects at once, you might want to lay them out and cut them together. Otherwise, cut carefully now to preserve enough fabric for the other projects later.

* **Cover** 15" tall × 23" wide (cut 2)
* **Pocket** 10" tall × 15" wide (cut 2)

NOTE: *Place "tall" dimensions along the grainline of your fabric. Measurements are based on a standard sewing machine size of 13" high × 16" wide × 6" deep. If your sewing machine is substantially bigger or smaller, measure its width, depth, and height and adjust the pattern accordingly.*

2 Make and Attach Pocket

With right sides facing, pin the pocket pieces together and stitch on all sides, leaving a 4" opening along the bottom (long) edge for turning. Clip the corners and turn right side out. Press under the raw edges of the opening ½" and press all around. Edgestitch the top pocket edge.

Center the pocket on the right side of one cover piece, with the bottom edge of the pocket aligned 1½" up from the bottom edge of the cover. Edgestitch the pocket to the cover along the sides and bottom, closing the pocket opening as you go.

③ Make the Cover

With right sides facing, pin the cover pieces together. Stitch the sides and top edges, leaving the bottom open. Press seams open.

Measuring from the raw edges of the top and right side of the cover, mark a 2½" square in both top corners of the cover. Cut out the squares. Pull the fabric layers apart at the cutout and pinch the side and top together and stitch. (See the illustrations for stitching the Tea Cozy, *page* 70.)

Make a narrow ¼" double-fold hem along the bottom edge and topstitch in place (*see page* 19).

Offset–Square Wrist Pincushion

ADDITIONAL MATERIALS

* ⅓ yard of ¾" ribbon or twill tape for wrist
* 1½" of ¾" Velcro
* 1 small bead or button
* Small quantity of fiberfill

Finished dimensions – 2½" square by 1" high

Seam allowance – ⅜" (unless otherwise indicated)

① Measure, Mark, and Cut

Measure and cut from fabric left over from sewing-machine cover:

* **Pincushion** 3½" square (cut 2)

On the wrong side of square A, mark a ⅜" seam allowance around all four sides and the center of each side, as shown. Make two placement marks on the right side of the square B, ⅜" down from the top raw edge on each side.

STEP 1

② Make the Wrist Strap

Measure the circumference of your wrist and add 3½". Cut the ribbon to this measurement.

Lay the ribbon down on a flat surface, and fold up 1" at one end. Position the Velcro hook side at this end, over the folded raw edge.

Stitch around all four sides of the Velcro, hiding the ribbon's raw edge.

Turn the ribbon over so the Velcro is face down. Fold up 1" at the other end of the ribbon and position and stitch the Velcro loop side as you did on the other side of the ribbon.

Place square A right side up on your work surface and lay the ribbon along the diagonal, with the Velcro loop side facing up. Make certain that equal amounts of ribbon extend on each side of the square, and stitch the ribbon to square A in a 1" square, right at the center of the square, as shown. Close the wrist strap and pin it out of the way for the following steps.

③ Make the Pincushion

Place square B right side up on the work surface, with the placement marks at the top edge. Place square A, right side down, on top of B. Offset square A by moving it upward until square A's center marks are aligned with square B's placement marks. Pin the squares together along the right-hand side.

To sew squares together, you will be stitching 7 lines, each half the length of one side of the square, then rotating either the upper or lower square before stitching the next line. It sounds trickier than it is: you will end up with a zigzag seam along the sides of your pincushion, formed by the half-seams you make as you go.

Starting at the center of the right edge of square A (point a) and the corner of square B (point b), stitch squares together from a/b to the corner of square A (and the middle of square B). With the sewing-machine needle in down position, lift the presser foot and rotate square A so that the next side of square A is aligned with the remainder of the first side of square B, and point c is directly over point d. Lower presser foot and stitch from the corner of square A to point c/d.

Again with sewing-machine needle in the down position, lift the presser foot and rotate square B so the next side is aligned with

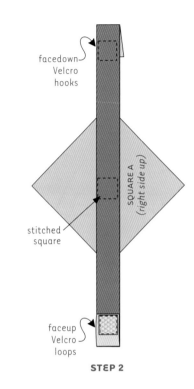

facedown Velcro hooks

SQUARE A (right side up)

stitched square

faceup Velcro loops

STEP 2

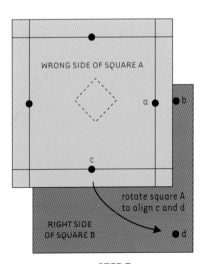

WRONG SIDE OF SQUARE A

a b

c

rotate square A to align c and d

RIGHT SIDE OF SQUARE B

d

STEP 3

the remainder of the side of A. Lower the presser foot and stitch from point c/d to the marked corner at end of this side of square A.

Continue rotating and stitching in this fashion until you reach the final side (top right corner of square A to point a). Leave this side open for turning.

Clip all corners and turn right side out, carefully. Push out the corners with a finger or turning tool. Turn the raw edges of the opening ⅜" to the wrong side and press.

Stuff the pincushion with fiberfill until firm. Slipstitch the opening closed.

❹ Finish Pincushion

Double a length of strong sewing thread, and thread both thread ends through a hand-sewing needle. Leave the thread loop longer than the two ends, and do not tie any knots. Push the needle through the center of the pincushion from top to bottom; you should come through in the middle of the stitched square on the wristband. Do not pull the thread all the way through; leave the loop extending from the top. Insert the needle back into the pincushion, close to where it came out, and come back up through the pincushion top and through the loop. Pull tight to dimple the center of the cushion.

Add a small button or bead to cover your stitch at the top, and go back through the pincushion to the back. Make one more small stitch on the back and come back through to the top. Unthread one of the two ends from the needle and go through the button or bead once more with the other end. Knot the two ends together under the button and then bury the ends inside the pincushion by rethreading the needle, coming back through the pincushion to the back and clipping the threads.

Attach the pincushion to your wrist, add some pins, and you're ready to go!

Needlebook Holder

ADDITIONAL MATERIALS

* ⅛ yard of fusible interfacing
* Felt scrap at least 5½" square
* 3"-long elastic cording or narrow ⅛" ribbon
* 1 button

Finished dimensions – approximately 3½" high × 3" wide

① Measure, Mark, and Cut

Measure and cut from fabric left over from the sewing-machine cover and/or the pincushion:

* **Cover** 4½" high × 7" wide (cut 2)

Cut from interfacing:

* **Cover** 3½" high × 6" wide (cut 1)

Cut from felt:

* **Needlebook piece** 3" high × 5¼" wide, with pinked or straight edges

② Apply Interfacing

Center and fuse the interfacing onto the wrong side of one fabric cover piece.

③ Make the Needlebook Cover

Stack the cover pieces, right sides together, with the interfaced piece on top. Stitch both long and one short side at the interfacing edge, leaving one short side open for turning. Clip corners, trim seam allowances, and turn right side out. Fold the raw edges of the opening in ½" toward the wrong side and press.

Fold elastic cording or ribbon in half and insert the raw ends ½" into the opening to form a loop, centering on the open edge. Edgestitch around all four sides of the cover, stitching the opening closed and securing the loop as you go.

Fold the needlebook in half and press the crease.

④ Assemble the Needlebook Holder

Fold the felt in half and place it inside the needlebook. Center on the crease. Pin and stitch two parallel lines along both sides of the center crease ⅛" apart.

Fold the ribbon loop around to the front to determine button placement, and mark. Handstitch a button in place, being careful not to let the stitches show on the inside of the needlebook cover.

ORiGaMi ORGaNiZeR

Designed by Katherine Donaldson

A twist on origami: use fabric instead of paper to make a tidy little notions box for your craft-room drawer! This can also come in handy as a dresser-top jewelry organizer or a kitchen-drawer catchall. It helps to have some experience with origami, as the construction techniques are a mixture of origami and traditional sewing, but don't be shy if you're new to this ancient Asian technique; we'll take you through the process step by step!

MATERIALS

* ✻ 1 yard of 44/45" fabric (quilting weight; small and/or geometric prints work best)
* ✻ 1 spool of coordinating thread
* ✻ 1¼ yard of 30"-wide medium- or heavyweight fusible interfacing
* ✻ 1 skein coordinating embroidery floss

Finished dimensions – about 12" square
Seam allowance – ½" unless otherwise specified

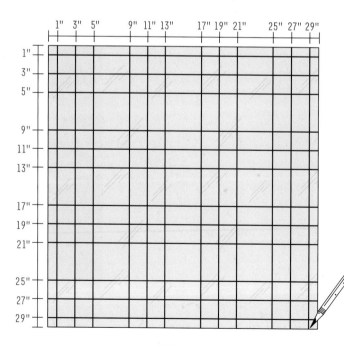

STEP 1

① Prepare the Interfacing

Cut the following pieces from interfacing. The large square must be trued up perfectly so the edges will line up when you fold the box, and there must be no wrinkles or creases in the interfacing.

* ✻ **Large square** 30" × 30" (cut 1)
* ✻ **Small square (not a true square, as one side is slightly wider)** 12" × 12¼" (cut 1)

  On the non-fusible side of the large square, mark guidelines for folding and pressing the box creases. From the left raw edge, draw vertical lines at 1", 3", 5", 9", 11", 13", 17", 19", 21", 25", 27", and 29", as shown. Repeat for horizontal lines, top to bottom.

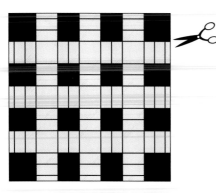

STEP 2

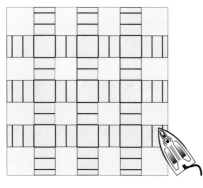

STEP 3

STEP 4

❷ Cut Out the Grid

Cut out the sections indicated in black from the interfacing with very sharp pointy scissors (smaller scissors may help).

❸ Attach Fabric and Interfacing

Line up the large grid of interfacing with the pattern on the fabric. Play with the interfacing and fabric pattern to determine best placement. To position the interfacing grid it is helpful to know that the 4" × 4" squares will become the bottoms of the box sections and the 2" × 4" rectangles will be most of the sides/dividers.

Fuse the 30" interfacing grid to the wrong side of your fabric, following manufacturer's instructions, making sure there is a 13" × 13¼" spot left in your yard for the box bottom. Trim the fabric to a 30" square flush with the outside edges of the interfacing.

Fuse the small interfacing square to the wrong side of your left-over fabric, following manufacturer's instructions, and trim the fabric to 13" × 13¼", leaving a ½" seam allowance on all four sides.

❹ Precrease the Grid Lines

Fold and press along each guideline, starting with the guidelines running top to bottom and then the guidelines running left to right. This is the origami prefold step, which creases the interfacing in the correct places to make folding up the box later go cleanly and easily. Guidelines running next to the cut-out sections should be folded right sides together, and all other guidelines should be folded wrong sides together. Follow the fold diagram for further instruction. Note that the top layer represents the right side, while the bottom layer is the wrong side.

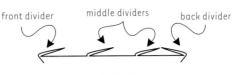

STEP 5

⑤ Fold the Box

Working from the right-hand row toward the left, fold up the sections for sides and press them away from you against the bottom sections of the boxes. Fold the back divider toward you against the bottom sections of the box. Fold the 1" strips under.

⑥ Stitch and Assemble the Box

Pin the folds down at the stitch lines. Stitch from front to back along the indicated creases/guidelines (at 1", 3", 11", 19", 27", and 29"). These stitch lines will become the top edge of the sides and dividers running top to bottom. Leave your thread tails long enough (1"–2") to tuck into the dividers or under the bottom. Pull up all the divider sections. Push the side edges in and everything should square up nicely.

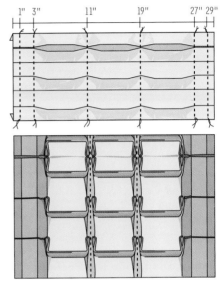

STEP 6

⑦ Square the Corners

For each of the 16 corners of box compartments, pull up the neighboring folded-down dividers and stitch in place with 3 strands of embroidery floss. To stitch the corners, bring a needle up from the bottom of the box through the sewn seam where the corners meet, take a few stitches through the corners, pulling them tight, then run the thread back down to the bottom of the box and tie off with a square knot. Leave several inches of tail for the knots at the edge corners so that you can easily tuck them out of sight in the underside of the dividers.

STEP 7

⑧ Finish the Bottom

Fold the loose side edges under the box and baste down wih slipstitch. Fold the ½" fabric border of the 13 × 13¼" fused fabric piece to the wrong side all around and press. Center this piece on the bottom of the box, wrong side toward the box, and baste in place with slipstitch. A 12" measurement should run front to back, and a 12¼" measurement should run left to right.

NOTE: *This bottom piece is slightly smaller than the box, so keep it centered on all sides. Tuck in any stray threads, make sure the top is square, and slipstitch the bottom piece to the box around all four sides. Sort and organize your notions or trinkets into various compartments.*

ARTIST BRUSHES CASE

Designed by Susan W. Schurz

Neatly store your paintbrushes in this handy carrying case! Not a painter? It's also perfect for knitting needles, or resize the pockets to make a cool tool roll.

MATERIALS

* 1 yard of 44/45" fabric (medium- or heavyweight cotton or cotton blend)
* 1 spool of coordinating thread
* 1 yard of 1½" ribbon

Finished dimensions – 16" wide × 21" tall, unfolded
Seam allowance – ½" unless otherwise specified

❶ Measure, Mark, and Cut

Place your fabric in a single layer with the wrong side facing up. Measure and mark the following pattern pieces directly on the wrong side of your fabric, and cut them out:

* **Front and back** 22" tall × 17" wide (cut 2)
* **Pocket** 9½" tall × 17" wide (cut 1)

NOTE: *Place "tall" dimensions along the grainline of your fabric.*

❷ Make and Divide the Pocket

Hem the top edge of the pocket piece with a 1" double-fold hem (*see page* 19). Topstitch in place. With the right side facing up, pin the hemmed pocket on the right side of the front piece, aligning the side and bottom edges.

Using a washable fabric pen or tailor's chalk, start 2½" in from each side and draw vertical lines on the pocket every 2". Topstitch along the lines through both layers of fabric, being sure to backstitch securely at the top edge. This will form eight 2"-wide pockets. Alternatively, you can make customized pockets: measure the tools or supplies you want to store, add in a little wiggle room, and stitch pockets in the widths that will meet your needs.

❸ Attach the Ribbon

On the right side of the back piece, mark a dot 3½" from the left (long) edge and 6¾" from the bottom (short) edge. Affix ribbon to the back with a box stitch.

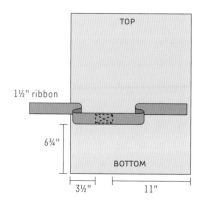

TOP

1½" ribbon

6¾"

BOTTOM

3½"   11"

STEP 3

④ Complete the Case

Stack the front and back pieces, right sides together, with the ribbon and stitched pocket facing each other at the same end. Stitch around all four sides, leaving a 6" opening at the top for turning. Clip the corners and turn right side out. Turn the raw edges of the opening in ½" to the wrong side and press all around. Edgestitch all around, stitching the opening closed as you go. You're done! Fill up the slots with brushes, knitting needles, or tools, flip the top edge over like a flap to protect precious contents, roll up, tie the ribbon, and off you go!

CRAFT OR GARDEN APRON

Designed by Rebecca Yaker

Whatever your craft — sewing, gardening, woodworking — this is the perfect handy half-apron for all your needs. Make it a tool belt for your domestic-repair needs, a gardening apron when it's time to plant your bulbs, or a sewing apron for your next One-Yard Wonder project!

MATERIALS

* ✳ 1 yard of 44/45" fabric (medium- to heavyweight)
* ✳ 3 yards of ½" double-fold bias tape
* ✳ 1 spool of coordinating thread

Finished dimensions – 23" wide × 10" tall

Seam allowance – ½" unless otherwise specified

① Measure, Mark, and Cut

Place your fabric in a single layer with the wrong side facing up. Measure and mark the following pieces directly on the wrong side of your fabric, and cut them out:

* ✳ **Tool loop** 5½" wide × 3" tall (cut 4)
* ✳ **Upper pocket** 21" wide × 4½" tall (cut 1)
* ✳ **Lower pocket** 25" wide × 7½" tall (cut 1)
* ✳ **Main apron** 21" wide × 10" tall (cut 2)

NOTE: *Place "tall" dimensions along the grainline of your fabric.*

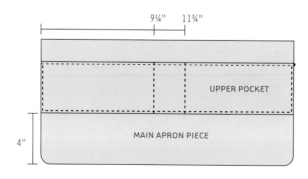

STEP 4

② Make Rounded Corners

On both pockets and main apron pieces, place a standard drinking glass upside down on one bottom corner of each piece and trace the portion of the glass that falls within the seam allowance using a fabric pen. Trim away the excess fabric. Repeat this step in the opposite bottom corner. (Another approach is to round both corners of one of the pieces and use it as a template to cut the corners on the other pieces.)

③ Assemble the Main Apron

With wrong sides together, place the main apron front and back sections together, matching all raw edges. Baste along all four sides with a ¼" seam allowance.

④ Make and Attach the Upper Pocket

Make a narrow ¼" double-fold hem and topstitch in place along the top edge of the upper pocket piece (*see page* 19). With right sides facing up, place the upper pocket on top of the main apron piece, placing the bottom edge of the upper pocket 4" up from the bottom of the main apron section, aligning the side raw edges. Stitch the upper pocket in place along the sides and bottom edge, with ¼" seam allowance.

Starting from the left side, measure and mark across the top edge of the upper pocket at 9¼" and 11¾". Mark the same measurements across the bottom edge of

the upper pocket. Draw a connecting line between the corresponding marks. Starting at the bottom edge, topstitch along both guidelines.

⑤ Make Pleats in the Lower Pocket

Make a narrow ¼" double-fold hem along the top edge of the lower pocket piece and topstitch in place (*see page* 19). Mark the placement of the two pleats along the bottom edge of the lower pocket at four points: two should each be 7" from each side (A) and two points should each be 9" from each side (B), as shown. Fold both B points toward the A points to create two pleats facing the outer edges of the lower pocket. Press. Baste across lower edge with a ¼" seam allowance to hold the pleats in place.

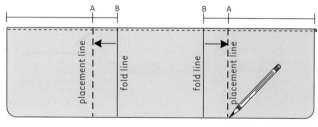

STEP 5

⑥ Attach the Lower Pocket

With right sides facing up, place the lower pocket on top of the main apron piece, aligning bottom edges and rounded corners. Stitch the lower pocket in place along the sides and bottom edge with ¼" seam allowances.

Starting from the left side, measure and mark across the top edge of the upper pocket at 8" and 13". Mark the same measurements across the bottom edge of the lower pocket. Draw a connecting line between the corresponding marks. Starting at the bottom edge, topstitch along both guidelines, through all layers.

⑦ Make and Attach the Tool Loops

Place two tool loop pieces with right sides together and stitch around three sides, leaving one short end open and unfinished. Clip

corners diagonally, turn right side out, and press. Edgestitch around three finished sides. Repeat with the second tool loop.

Position tool loops on opposite sides of the apron, aligning raw edges 4" down from the top edge of the apron. Stitch in place with ¼" seam allowance.

Place the finished end of the tool loops 3" away from the edge and topstitch in place through all layers. Note that the actual tool loop is longer than 3", but by placing it here, you are creating extra room for your tools.

⑧ Bind the Apron Edges

Cut a piece of bias tape 45" long to bind the sides and lower edge of the apron. Pin bias tape around the side and bottom of the apron and edgestitch in place, fully encasing the raw edges. (Remember to place the narrower edge on top so that you will catch the back of the bias tape in your stitching.)

⑨ Make Apron Ties

Use the remainder of the bias tape to bind the top edge of the apron and create the ties. Find the center of the bias tape and position it in the center of the top edge of the apron. Pin the bias tape in place, encasing the entire top edge. Starting at one end of the bias tape, edgestitch the entire length, across the top of the apron and to the end of the tie. Tie on your apron and fill it up!

Smock of All Ages

Designed by Beth Walker

This one-size smock can be made for many uses. Whip one up for a crafty kid or sew yourself a customized cover-up. What could be better than looking great while keeping your "real" clothes clean?

MATERIALS

* ✳ Locate the pattern in the front pocket (sheet #4)
* ✳ 1 yard of 44/45" (quilting-weight cotton)
* ✳ 1 spool of coordinating thread
* ✳ 1 package ½" double-fold bias tape

Finished dimensions – one size fits many
Seam allowance – ½" unless otherwise specified

1 Measure, Mark, and Cut

With right sides together, fold your fabric in half lengthwise, aligning the selvages. Position the pattern pieces, and measure and mark the additional pieces as shown. Cut out the pieces, and transfer the markings from the pattern pieces to the wrong side of the fabric.

* ✳ **Body** (cut 1 on fold)
* ✳ **Neck ruffle** (cut 1 on fold)
* ✳ **Pocket** 5" wide × 6½" tall (cut 1 on fold)

* ✳ **Ties** 2" × 20" (cut 2)

NOTE: *Place "tall" dimensions along the grainline of your fabric.*

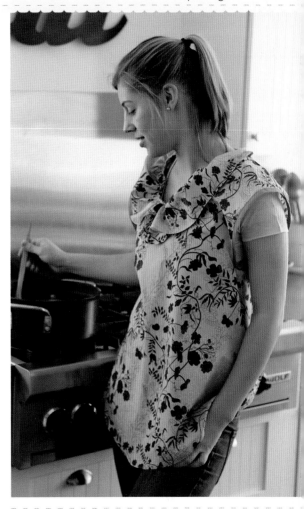

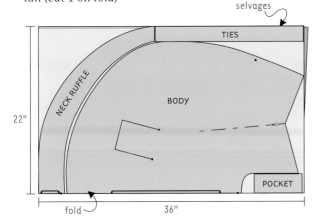

CUTTING LAYOUT

❷ Make the Pocket

Press under the top edge of the pocket ¼", and then press under another ½". Topstitch in place. Press under the remaining three edges ½". Position the pocket along the pocket placement lines (on the right or left side of the smock as you wish), and edge-stitch in place along three sides, leaving the top edge open.

❸ Prepare the Neck Ruffle

Finish the outer edge of the ruffle with a ¼" double-fold hem (*see page* 19). Use a basting stitch to gather the inner raw edge of the ruffle (*see page* 20).

❹ Attach the Neck Ruffle

Pin the right side of the gathered edge to the wrong side of the smock's neckline, aligning raw edges and center dots. It helps to start by pinning the outermost corners of the ruffle at the shoulder seam, then adjusting the gathers to fit, pinning it in place as you go.

Stitch the ruffle in place and trim the seam allowance to ¼". Clip to, but not through, the stitching line at the curved edge of the neckline.

Press the ruffle to the right side of the smock and neatly topstitch around this edge. Baste short, raw edges of the ruffle in place at the shoulder seams.

❺ Hem the Smock

From shoulder to shoulder, finish the outer rounded edge of the smock with a ¼" double-fold hem.

❻ Bind the Armholes

Pin bias tape along the armhole slits, fully encasing the raw edge — down one side of the slash and up the other. Stitch in place.

❼ Stitch the Shoulders

With right sides together, stitch the shoulder seams. Press the seam allowances toward the back of the smock.

❽ Make the Ties

Press under the short edges of each tie ½". Fold and press the ties as you would to make double-fold bias tape (*see page* 18). Neatly edgestitch around all four edges of each tie. Pin each tie on the back of the smock at the placement dots, and stitch in place on the wrong side of the smock close to the finished edge.

on THE GO

There are times when even the best all-purpose bag just won't do. When you're out and about and on the town, try these projects specially designed for that one oh-so-important task. In the car, at the beach, on the road, or at the market, these projects will help simplify your life.

Laptop sleeve

Designed by Becka Rahn

Show your laptop some love by appliquéing a sweet dog (as pictured) or other colorful critter on the flap. The sleeve can be custom-sized to fit your particular laptop's dimensions. Our version was made with a fabric that mimics patchwork.

MATERIALS

* Enlarge the appliqué pattern piece on page 279
* 1 yard of 44/45" fabric (home-decor weight)
* 1 spool of coordinating thread
* ½ yard of cotton batting
* Scraps of fabrics or felt for dog appliqué: 7" × 4" for body, 2" × 2" for ear, and 1" × 2" for collar
* 10" × 10" piece of paper-backed double-sided fusible web

* 1 package of ½" double-fold bias tape
* 6½" piece of sew-on Velcro
* 1 small button (optional)
* Black embroidery floss
* Sewing-machine walking foot (optional)

Finished dimensions – vary according to the size of your laptop

Seam allowance – ½" unless otherwise specified

① Measure Laptop Dimensions

Measure your laptop in two directions as shown:

* **Measurement A** = the circumference of the closed laptop, from the front latch to the hinges and back around to the latch, plus 2½".
* **Measurement B** = the width of the laptop, plus 1½".

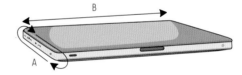

STEP 1
How to measure your laptop

② Measure, Mark, and Cut

Fold your fabric in half lengthwise, with right sides together, aligning the selvages. Measure and mark the following pattern pieces directly on the wrong side of your fabric, then cut them out:

* **Laptop sleeve** A wide × B tall (cut 2)
* **Binding, to finish inside seams** 2" wide × (A + 2") (cut 1)
* **Flap** 7" wide × 8" tall (cut 2)

Cut from batting:

* **Sleeve padding** A wide × B tall (cut 1)

NOTE: *Place "tall" dimensions along the grainline of your fabric.*

③ Appliqué the Flap

Trace the dog pattern pieces onto the paper backing of fusible web. Fuse the web to the wrong side of the dog body fabric scrap, following manufacturer's instructions.

Cut out the dog, peel off the backing paper, and fuse to one flap piece. Zigzag stitch around the raw edges of the dog appliqué. Appliqué the collar and ear pieces in the same fashion.

Use embroidery floss to embroider the eye (French knot) and nose (satin stitch) and attach the button as a dog tag on the collar if you like.

④ Assemble the Flap

Center and stitch the hook side of the Velcro onto the right side of the nonappliquéd flap piece, 1" from bottom edge. With right sides together, pin the flap pieces with raw edges aligned, and stitch around three sides, leaving the top edge open. Trim the corners, turn the flap right side out, and press. Set the flap aside.

⑤ Quilt the Laptop Sleeve

Lay two fabric rectangles with wrong sides together, and place a layer of batting between them. Pin through all three layers and use a disappearing fabric marker or tailor's chalk to mark the fabric with your choice of quilting lines (you could try diagonal lines at a 45-degree angle, 2" apart, but any pattern will do). Machine-quilt the layers together following the lines. You may want to use a walking foot, if you have one.

⑥ Attach the Loop Velcro

Decide which side will be the outside of your bag. Place the quilted rectangle with the right side (outside) facing up and the top (long) edge at the top. Fold the sleeve in half, wrong sides together, matching side raw edges and keeping the right side facing toward you. Measure 4" from the top edge, center the loop Velcro on the folded half, and pin in place. Unfold and stitch the Velcro in place.

⑦ Stitch the Sides

With right sides (the outside of the sleeve) facing, fold the quilted rectangle in half, matching short edges. Pin and stitch the side and bottom of bag, leaving the top open. Trim the seam allowances and bind them with the purchased bias tape, fully encasing the seam. Turn the sleeve right side out.

⑧ Attach the Flap

With right sides together and raw edges aligned, pin the flap to the center of the sleeve back. (Check to be sure the dog will show and the Velcro will align when you flip the flap over the top of the opening.) Baste in place with an edgestitch.

⑨ Bind the Top Edge of Bag

* Fold and press a binding strip as you would to make double-fold bias tape (*see page* 18). Open it up briefly and press under one short end ¼".
* Open up one long side of the binding and pin along the outside top edge of the sleeve, aligning raw edges, starting at the center of the flap with the pressed short end. Stitch in place, overlapping ends by at least ½" (trim if needed).
* Fold binding toward the inside of the sleeve and slipstitch in place, completely enclosing raw edges.
* Insert the laptop into the sleeve and you're ready to go!

CD POCKET

Designed by Irene Rodegerdts

This simple project holds a dozen of your favorite CDs, six on each side. Of course, you can make yours smaller or larger simply by adjusting the number of pockets. It's great for attaching to your car's sun visor, or you can keep it handy near your computer!

MATERIALS

* 1 yard of 44/45" fabric (quilting-weight cotton)
* 1 spool of coordinating thread
* 1⁄3 yard of double-sided fusible heavyweight interfacing such as Peltex or Timtex
* Chopstick or other turning tool
* 1⁄3 yard of 1⁄2" wide elastic (optional, if attaching to car visor)

Finished dimensions – approximately 5¼" × 10½"
Seam allowance – ½" unless otherwise specified

● Measure, Mark, and Cut

Place your fabric in a single layer with wrong side facing up. Measure and mark the following pattern pieces directly on the wrong side of your fabric, then cut them out:

* **Back piece A** 11½" tall × 12½" wide (cut 1)
* **Pocket piece B** 11" tall × 12½" wide (cut 1)
* **Pocket piece C** 10" tall × 12½" wide (cut 1)
* **Pocket piece D** 9" tall × 12½" wide (cut 1)
* **Pocket piece E** 8" tall × 12½" wide (cut 1)
* **Pocket piece F** 7" tall × 12½" wide (cut 1)
* **Front piece G** 6" tall × 12½" wide (cut 1)

Cut from interfacing:

* **Back piece A** 10½" tall × 5¾" wide (cut 2)

NOTE: *Place "tall" dimensions along the grainline of your fabric.*

● Hem the Pieces

Hem pieces B, C, D, E, F, and G along one long 12½" side by pressing under the raw edge ¼", then pressing under another 1". Topstitch at the top folded edge and the bottom edge of the hem.

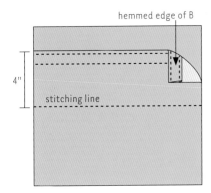
hemmed edge of B
4"
stitching line

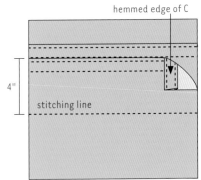
hemmed edge of C
4"
stitching line

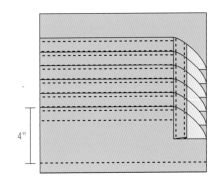
4"

STEP 3

③ Layer the Pockets

Throughout this step, the right side of all fabric pieces will be facing up.

* Place piece B on piece A, with the hemmed edge of B at the top, aligning side and bottom raw edges.
* Mark a line 4" down from the top hemmed edge of piece B across the entire width. Topstitch on this line to form the pocket.
* Repeat for pieces C, D, E, and F, layering pieces as you go.
* Place piece G on top of piece F, hemmed edge at top, matching side and bottom raw edges.

④ Assemble the Pockets

* Pin and baste all layers together with edgestitch along side and bottom edges.
* Fold in half lengthwise, right sides together, lining up all stitch lines and hemmed edges.
* If attaching to a car visor, insert a length of elastic between layers, centering one raw edge on the pocket's bottom raw edge. Pin the elastic in place.
* Stitch around the bottom and sides, taking care to catch the elastic only along the bottom edge, leaving the top of the edge open for turning. Clip corners, turn right side out, flatten so that side seams are truly along the side, and press. (When the project is complete, you should be able to insert CDs into both the front and back of the CD pocket, so you want to be sure that your side seam doesn't stray toward the back of the pocket and make those slots unusable.)
* At the opening, fold the top raw edges in ½" toward the wrong side and press.
* Insert both interfacing pieces into the pocket and press to fuse.
* If using elastic, insert the remaining raw edge into the center of the top opening. Pin the opening and edgestitch to close.
* Now your favorite tunes are right at your fingertips!

SCHOOL BINDER COVER

Designed by Charlene Caruso

Rock the halls at school with this totally awesome binder cover! Not only can you show off your individuality through the fabric and trim you select, you can also make lots of extra pockets for all those necessities.

MATERIALS
- ✳ 1 yard of 44/45" fabric (quilting-weight cotton)
- ✳ 1 spool of coordinating thread
- ✳ 2 yards of fusible interfacing
- ✳ Embellishments such as ribbons, beads, or other trims (optional)

Finished dimensions – vary according to binder size
Seam allowance – ½" unless otherwise specified

❶ Trace and Cut

Choose the binder you wish to cover and open it up. Trace the open binder onto tracing paper or other suitable pattern-making paper. Add an additional ½" to the width for ease, plus ½" to all four sides for seam allowance. Cut out and use this pattern piece to cut two pieces of fabric and two pieces of interfacing.

Fuse the interfacing to the wrong side of both fabric pieces. On the inside of the binder, measure the distance from the side edge to the binder rings. Add 1" for seam allowance, and cut one fused fabric piece into two pieces with this width. These pieces will become the inside cover.

❷ Make Slanted Pockets

Determine the size of the slanted pockets, using an inside cover piece as a guide. Add ½" to the side and bottom edges for seam allowance. Out of your left-over fabric and interfacing, you will cut two slanted pockets that are mirror images of each other. With this in mind, cut two fabric pieces and one inter-facing piece for each slanted pocket (4 of fabric, 2 of interfacing). Fuse the interfacing to the wrong side of two fabric pieces.

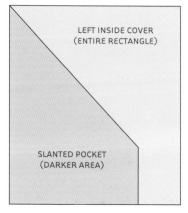

LEFT INSIDE COVER
(ENTIRE RECTANGLE)

SLANTED POCKET
(DARKER AREA)

STEP 2

With right sides together, pin each interfaced pocket to a matching fabric piece, aligning side and bottom raw edges. Stitch across the slanted edge, pivot at corner, and continue along short straight edge. Clip corner. Turn right side out, press, and edgestitch along the finished sides. Bottom and side edges will be left unfinished until a later step.

❸ Make the Small Pocket

From your leftover fabric, cut two small pocket pieces that are 6½" wide × 5" tall; also cut one from interfacing. Fuse the interfacing to the wrong side of one fabric piece. With right sides facing, pin the small pocket pieces together and stitch around all sides, leaving a 3" opening on the bottom edge for turning. Clip the corners, turn right side out, and press. Edgestitch along the top edge.

With the interfaced side on top, pin the finished small pocket on the right side of the slanted pocket piece. Stitch the sides and bottom edges in place. Stitch channels into the pocket as desired, using pen and pencil widths as guidelines.

❹ Complete the Inside Cover

Press under the inner edge of each inside cover piece ½" and edgestitch. Keeping in mind that these two inside covers will be the mirror image of one another, pin each slanted pocket piece (interfaced side on top) on the right side of an inside cover piece, aligning side and bottom raw edges. Baste together along the outside and bottom edges with a ¼" seam allowance.

❺ Finish the Binder Cover

With right sides together, pin both inside cover pieces to the outside cover piece, aligning raw edges. (There will be a gap in the middle between inside covers to accommodate the binder rings.) Stitch all around the outside edge. Clip the corners, turn right side out, and press. Edgestitch on all four sides. Slide the binder into the fabric cover. Finish by decorating with ribbons, beads, and other embellishments, as desired.

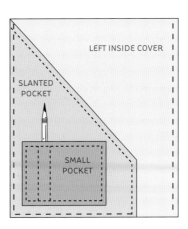

STEP 4

QUILTED LUNCH BAG

Designed by Mary Richmond

Goodbye brown-bag lunches, there's a new bag in town! There's nothing like noshing on a lunch you've lugged in a trendy tote — that keeps food as hot (or cool) as it looks!

MATERIALS

* 1 yard of 44/45" fabric (nondirectional, any weight)
* ¾ yard of insulated batting, cut to 22" × 36"
* 1 spool of coordinating thread
* 1 package (about 3 yards) of ¾" double-fold bias tape
* 3" of sew-on Velcro
* 1 decorative button
* Quilter's safety pins
* Sewing-machine walking foot (optional)

Finished dimensions — 9" wide × 10½" tall × 4" deep
Seam allowance — ½" unless otherwise specified

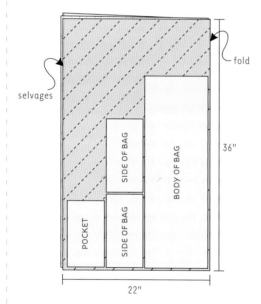

CUTTING LAYOUT

① **Quilt the Fabric**

With wrong sides together, fold your fabric in half lengthwise, matching up the selvages. Sandwich the 22" × 36" piece of insulated batting between the layers. Pin through all three layers and mark your choice of quilting lines using a disappearing marker, washable fabric pen, or tailor's chalk (you could try diagonal lines at a 45-degree angle, 2" apart). Machine-quilt the layers together, following your lines. You may want to use a walking foot, if you have one.

② **Measure, Mark, and Cut**

Measure and mark the following pattern pieces directly on the quilted fabric, then cut them out:

Body of bag 9½" wide × 27½" tall (cut 1)

Sides of bag 5½" wide × 10½" tall (cut 2)

Pocket 5½" wide × 9½" tall (cut 1)

NOTE: *Place "tall" dimensions along the grainline of your fabric.*

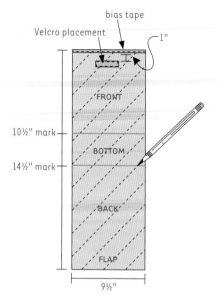

STEP 3

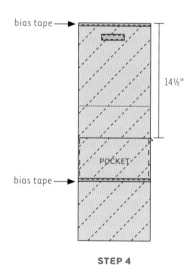

STEP 4

❸ Prep the Pieces

Encase one wide (top) edge of the pocket with bias tape and stitch. Do the same at one short end of the body piece and one short end of each side piece. Stitch the loop side of the Velcro to the center of the body piece 1" below the bias tape. From the top, mark the body piece as shown along both long sides at 10½" and again at 14½". These marks will be your pivot points for attaching the side pieces.

❹ Attach the Pocket

With right sides together, pin the raw edge of the pocket to the body piece at the 14½" mark with the bound pocket edge pointing toward the Velcro. Stitch along the raw edge. Flip pocket over and press so the right side is facing out and the seam is covered. Baste in place along the side edges.

❺ Stitch the Sides

With wrong sides together, align bound edge of body piece and one side piece. Pin in place and stitch to the 10½" mark. Pivot to turn the corner, and stitch the pieces together to the 14½" mark. Pivot again and stitch the pieces together to the top edge of the side piece (the remaining body section will become the flap). Do the same with the second side piece.

❻ Bind the Edges

Press under one end of the remaining bias tape ½". Starting at the top front of one of the side seams, encase the raw edges with bias tape and stitch. Continue working your way around the entire raw edge of the bag, neatly folding the bias tape (mitering the corners) at the top of the bag. As you approach the opposite end of the bag, trim the bias tape and turn under ½" and overlap the beginning raw edge of the tape for a neat finish. Stitch the hook side of the Velcro to the center of the flap underside, 1" below the bias tape. Add a decorative button on the outside if desired.

PLANNER SLEEVE

Designed by Helen Ringrose

Don't want your nice expensive organizer or date book to get bashed around in your overstuffed handbag? Sew up this little sleeve for a bit of protection. Don't have an organizer? Use it to hold a small notebook and pens, or use it as a cosmetics purse.

MATERIALS LIST

* ✳ 1 yard of 44/45" fabric (quilting-weight cotton)
* ✳ 1 spool of coordinating thread
* ✳ 8" × 18" piece of cotton batting
* ✳ 1 yard of ½" double-fold bias tape
* ✳ Closure of choice: Velcro, 1 button, or 48" length of ribbon
* ✳ Sewing-machine walking foot (optional)

Finished dimensions – designed to fit a 4¼" × 5½" pocket organizer
Seam allowance – ½" unless otherwise specified

① Measure, Mark, and Cut

Fold your fabric in half lengthwise, with right sides together, aligning the selvages. Using the cutting diagram as a guide, measure, mark, and cut two pieces from the fabric and cut one from the batting.

NOTE: *If using unidirectional fabric, place the cutting layout vertically along the design, with the square end at the top.*

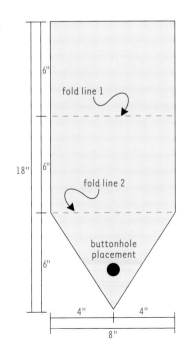

6"

fold line 1

18"   6"

fold line 2

6"   buttonhole placement

4"   4"

8"

CUTTING DIAGRAM

② Assemble the Pieces

Use disappearing marker, washable fabric pen, or tailor's chalk to mark the fold lines on the right side of one fabric piece (see cutting diagram). With wrong sides facing, place the fabric pieces together, sandwich batting in between, and align all raw edges. Pin through all layers to keep them from shifting. Using a zigzag stitch (and a walking foot, if you have one), stitch about ¼" from the edge.

③ Bind One End

Trim the short, straight raw edge, encase it with bias tape, and stitch (*see page* 18).

④ Make an Envelope

Fold the fabric along fold line 1, so that the edge meets fold line 2, making an envelope shape. If you wish a specific side to be the sleeve exterior, that side should be facing toward you on the folded section. Stitch the side seams. Trim the raw edges close to the stitching line, and enclose raw edges all the way around the sleeve with bias tape.

⑤ Make the Closure

Stitch on Velcro, or use a buttonhole and button, or hand-sew a length of ribbon to the envelope flap for a pretty tie. See the illustration for suggested ribbon placement.

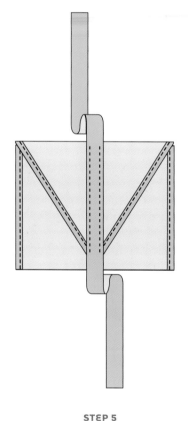

STEP 5

NOT-UGLY CaR TRASH BaG

Designed by Jessica Vaughan

It's time to rid your vehicle of random rubbish! Hook this trash bag around the headrest and hang it on the back of your car's seat to make decluttering a delight. A front pocket allows for extra storage.

MATERIALS

* 1 yard of 44/45" fabric
  (quilting- or home-decor weight cotton)
* ¼ yard of 44/45" contrasting fabric
  (quilting- or home-decor weight cotton) (optional)
* 1 spool of coordinating thread
* One 1" parachute buckle (sometimes called
  a quick-release clip) such as Dritz #470

Finished dimensions – 15½" × 8¾"
Seam allowance – ¼" unless otherwise specified.

① Measure, Mark, and Cut

Place your fabric in a single layer with wrong side facing up. Measure and mark the following pattern pieces directly on the wrong side of your fabric, then cut them out:

* **Long strap** 18" tall × 4¼" wide (cut 1)
* **Short strap** 8" tall × 4¼" wide (cut 1)
* **Front pocket** 10¼" tall × 9¼" wide (cut 1)
* **Main pocket** 16" tall × 9¼" wide (cut 2)

Cut from contrasting or main fabric:

* **Binding (no need to cut on the bias)**
  2½" tall × 13½" wide (cut 3)

NOTE: *Place "tall" dimensions along the grainline of your fabric.*

② **Make Straps**

Fold and press the straps as if making double-fold bias tape (*see page* 18). Open up briefly, and press under both short ends ¼". Edgestitch on all sides.

③ **Attach the Buckle**

Thread the short strap through the female half of the buckle and fold, matching short edges. To strengthen the strap, stitch a box stitch close to the buckle (*see page* 14). Thread the long strap through the male half of the buckle. This end is meant to be adjustable, so don't stitch it in place.

④ **Make and Attach Binding**

Using the binding piece, fold and press to make double-fold bias tape (*see page* 18). Stitch bias tape along the top edge of the front pocket, fully encasing raw edge. Repeat for the two main pocket pieces. Do not trim binding ends yet.

⑤ **Assemble the Bag**

With right sides facing, align both main pocket pieces. Sandwich the shorter front pocket piece between the layers (checking to be sure it will be facing the right way), matching side and bottom raw edges. Stitch along both sides and the bottom, leaving the top edge open. Clip the bottom corners and excess binding. Zigzag along the seam allowance to reinforce the seam, and turn the bag right side out.

⑥ **Attach the Straps**

Center the short strap on one side seam and stitch into place with a box stitch placed just under the binding. Do the same with the long strap on the opposite side seam. Prepare for a clean car!

MATT'S MAP BAG

Designed by Matt DeVries

Cyclists of both the pedaling and motoring variety will appreciate this small messenger-style bag with a transparent map pocket on the flap. Never get lost again!

MATERIALS

* 1 yard of 44/45" fabric (heavyweight)
* 2 yards of 1½" or 2" webbing
* ¼ yard of double-sided fusible web interfacing
* 1 metal or plastic slide, 1½" or 2" wide, depending on webbing width
* 1 metal or plastic rectangle ring, 1½" or 2" wide, depending on webbing width
* 1 sew-on magnetic snap
* ¼ yard of thin clear sew-on vinyl

Finished dimensions – 11" tall × 8" wide × 2" deep
Seam allowance – ½" unless otherwise specified

1 Measure, Mark, and Cut

With right sides together, fold your fabric in half lengthwise, aligning the selvages. Following the cutting layout, measure and mark the pattern pieces directly on the wrong side of your fabric, then cut them out:

* **Flaps** 12" tall × 9" wide (cut 2)
* **Main panels** 12" tall × 9" wide (cut 4)
* **Side panels** 12" tall × 3" wide (cut 4)
* **Bottom panels** 3" tall × 9" wide (cut 2)

Cut from interfacing:

* **Flap** 10" tall × 7" wide (cut 1)

Cut from vinyl:

* **Map pocket** 8" tall × 8" wide (cut 1)

NOTE: *Place "tall" dimensions along the grainline of your fabric.*

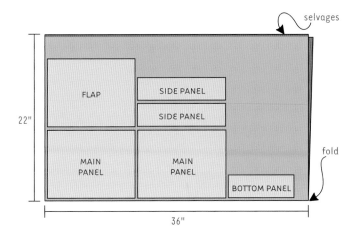

selvages

fold

22"

FLAP

SIDE PANEL

SIDE PANEL

MAIN PANEL

MAIN PANEL

BOTTOM PANEL

36"

CUTTING LAYOUT

② Make the Exterior

With right sides together, pin one flap piece and one main-panel piece together. Stitch across top 9" raw edge. Open up and press seam allowances toward the main panel. This panel is now the back of the bag.

With right sides together, pin the side-panel pieces to the back main-panel piece, aligning side and bottom raw edges (top of side panels will extend ½" above flap seam). Stitch side seams, stopping ½" from the bottom raw edge. Pin the side panels to the second main-panel piece in the same fashion, aligning side and bottom raw edges. Stitch together, again stopping ½" from the bottom raw edge.

With right sides together, pin the bottom panel to each main panel, lining up the corners and raw edges. Stitch together, leaving ½" free at each end. Attach the bottom panel to the side panels in the same fashion, again leaving ½" free at each end. All bottom panel seams should meet each other ½" from the corner raw edges. Press the seams open. Mark this as the exterior of your bag and leave wrong side out.

③ Make the Lining

Apply interfacing to wrong side of the remaining flap piece, 1" from each raw edge, and fuse following manufacturer's instructions. Leave the paper backing on for now.

Repeat step 2 with the lining pieces using the interfaced flap piece and the remaining main, side, and bottom-panel pieces. Turn lining right side out and remove the paper backing from the double-sided interfacing.

④ Attach the Strap

Cut a 4" piece of webbing. Thread through the rectangle ring and fold in half, edgestitching to secure. Center on the right side of one lining side panel, aligning raw edges. Edgestitch to attach.

Center and pin the remaining webbing piece on the right side of the opposite lining side panel with raw edges aligned. Edgestitch to attach.

⑤ Attach the Lining

Insert the lining inside the exterior piece, right sides together. Tuck the handle

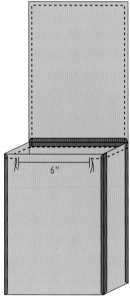

STEP 5

pieces between the layers so that they are completely hidden from view. Align all raw edges, corners, and vertical seams and pin securely in place. Mark a 6" opening in the center of the front main panel and stitch around, starting on one edge of the opening, across the side panel, then up, across, and back down the flap, across the second side panel, and across the front to the other side of the opening.

6 Finish the Bag

Turn bag right side out through the opening. Hand-sew magnetic snap halves to the inner flap and the front main panel.

Turn the raw edges at the opening in ½" to the wrong side and press. Continue pressing all seams. Press front and back of flap to fuse the second side of the interfacing.

Edgestitch all around, starting at the front main panel to close the opening. When you reach the flap, place the vinyl piece on top of the outer flap, aligning side and bottom edges, and stitch into place with edgestitch.

7 Finish the Strap

Thread the slide onto the long strap. Thread the long strap end through the rectangle ring on the opposite side panel from outside to inside, taking care not to twist the strap. Thread the strap back through the slide, fold the raw edge under, and stitch to secure close to the slide.

Beach-Time Towel Tote

Designed by Michele Chisholm

This is truly a beach or poolside must-have! This towel bag will hold all your sunning necessities like books, suntan lotion, and a hat, plus there's a small zippered pouch for keys, wallet, and other easy-to-lose items. Once large items are removed, you can slip it over your lawn chair for a soft, cozy place to relax. Speaking of comfort, slip it over the car seat on the way home to protect your upholstery (or protect your legs from sun-baked car seats).

MATERIALS

* Beach towel
* 1 yard of 44/45" fabric (quilting- or home-decor-weight cotton)
* 1 spool of coordinating thread
* 30" of 1½" webbing
* One 14" zipper
* Sewing-machine zipper foot

Finished dimensions – 15" tall × 20½" wide
Seam allowance – ½" unless otherwise specified

① Measure, Mark, and Cut

Place your fabric in a single layer with the wrong side facing up. Measure and mark the following piece directly on the wrong side of your fabric, then cut it out:

* **Pouch** 32" tall × 21½" wide (cut 1)

NOTE: *Place "tall" dimensions along the grainline of your fabric. This width will fit a standard folding beach chair. If you have a special chair in mind, measure its width and add 1" to determine the bag's width.*

② Prepare the Zipper Seam

Fold fabric in half across the width, right sides together, to form a rectangle that is 16" tall × 21½" wide. Place this piece with the fold at the bottom. Mark a stitching line ½" down from the top raw edge all the way across. Along the top edge, make two marks, each 4½" in from side raw edges.

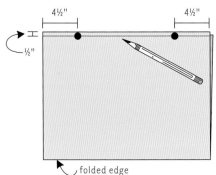

STEP 2

Lay the zipper along the stitching line to check length: with zipper centered, the marks should be just inside the ends of the zipper tape. (Note: If you adjusted the cut fabric width in step 1, you may also need to adjust the marks for zipper placement. Zipper tape should slightly extend past both marks.) Put zipper aside.

Using a normal stitch length, stitch along the ½" marked line from one side to the first zipper placement mark. Backstitch and cut the threads. Stitch from the second zipper placement mark to the other side in the same fashion. Between the zipper placement marks, stitch a longer basting stitch along the marked line. Press the seam open.

③ Install the Zipper

On the wrong side of the fabric, center closed zipper, right-side down, along the basted seam, keeping the ends of zipper tape extending beyond the ends of the basting line. The zipper head should be flush with the left side of the basting stitch. Pin in place.

Turn fabric right side out. Make sure zipper teeth are still centered on the basted seam. Pin along both sides of the seam and zipper to secure. Using a machine zipper foot and starting on the right side of the zipper head, stitch down one side of zipper, across the bottom just above the metal stop, and up the other side.

Remove the basting threads and press, using a low heat setting so as not to melt zipper teeth.

④ Complete the Pouch

Turn the fabric wrong side out. Fold so that zipper is 2" below top fold. (If your fabric has a directional print, position the zipper and top fold so that the fabric below the zipper is upside down.)

Unzip zipper halfway for turning and stitch the side seams. Zigzag just inside the seam allowance to reinforce. Turn the zippered pouch right side out, press, and zip the pouch closed.

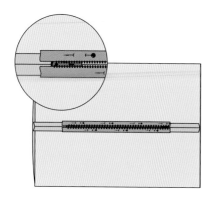

STEP 3

NOTE: *You may want to unzip the zipper a few inches to get started; after stitching an inch or two, stop, leaving the needle down in the fabric, and zip closed to keep the zipper head out of the way. When coming up the other side, you may want to again unzip zipper when you are a couple of inches from the top.*

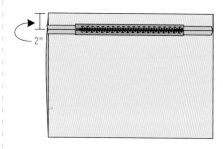

2"

STEP 4

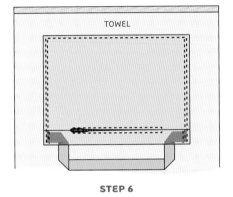

4"

TOWEL

STEP 5

TOWEL

STEP 6

⑤ Attach the Pouch to the Towel

Lay towel right side down, with one short end at the top. Place the zippered pouch 4" below this top short edge, centered from the sides. The zippered side should be facing up, with zipper oriented at the bottom. Edgestitch around three sides, leaving zipper (bottom) side open.

⑥ Attach the Strap

Tuck a 30" length of webbing between the pouch and the towel, near the bottom open edge of the pouch, centered between the zipper and the folded edge. The raw ends of the webbing should butt up to the edgestitching from the previous step. Pin securely in place and stitch ½" inside the edgestitching seam along both side seams of the pouch. Backstitch again over the strap to reinforce and secure in place.

⑦ Enjoy Your Bag

Flip the bag so that the zippered side is on the interior. Fold the towel and tuck the far end into the bag to meet the bag's bottom seam. Fold again to tuck the rest of the towel into the bag. Load it up, sling the strap over your shoulder, and hit the beach! At the beach, unfold the towel and slip the pouch end over a lawn chair for a comfy slipcover.

Jewelry Roll

Designed by Valerie Williams

Here's the perfect at-home accessory for neatly organizing your earrings, necklaces, baubles, and bangles. And if you've got travel plans, use this fashionable gem to keep your jewels tidy, protected, and easy to find.

MATERIALS

* Locate the pattern in the front pocket (sheet #4)
* 1 yard of 44/45" fabric (quilting-weight cotton)
* 1 spool of coordinating thread
* ½ yard of lightweight woven fusible interfacing
* Two 7" zippers
* 1½ yard of ⅜"-wide grosgrain ribbon
* Sewing-machine zipper foot

Finished dimensions – 7" wide × 13" tall
Seam allowances – ½" unless otherwise specified

① Measure, Mark, and Cut

Place your fabric in a single layer with the wrong side facing up. Cut out all pattern pieces from both the fabric and the interfacing as indicated below. Apply the interfacing to the wrong side of each fabric piece, following manufacturer's directions.

* **Body** (cut 2)   * **Flap** (cut 1)   * **Pocket** (cut 4)   * **Ring placket** (cut 1)

② Hem the Pieces

Turn the following raw edges in ½" toward the wrong side and press:

* The top edge of four pockets
* The bottom edge of the flap
* The top and bottom edges of the ring placket

③ Install the Zippers

With wrong sides facing, pin two pocket pieces together, aligning all edges, particularly the pressed top folds. Sandwich the left side of the zipper tape between the top folds, leaving the zipper teeth outside the fabric; center the zipper ½" in from both sides and pin. Topstitch the zipper in place, using a zipper foot. Do the same for the other zipper and the remaining pocket pieces.

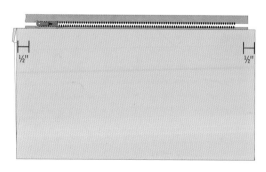

STEP 3

④ Make the Pockets

With right sides facing up, place one pocket on one body piece, aligning bottom and side raw edges. This is now the bottom pocket.

With right sides facing up, place the ring-placket piece right side up just above the bottom pocket, so the folded bottom edge of the placket covers the top half of the zipper tape. Topstitch the ring placket to the zipper and body using a zipper foot.

With right sides facing up, pin the flap piece on the body piece, aligning the top curved edge and side raw edges.

Position and pin the remaining pocket between the flap and the ring placket so that the folded bottom edge of the flap covers the top half of the zipper tape and the folded top edge of the placket covers the bottom raw edge of the pocket.

Topstitch the flap to the zipper and body, using the zipper foot, and topstitch the placket to the pocket and body.

⑤ Attach the Ribbons

Cut two 7" lengths of ribbon. Pin the end of one ribbon to the left side of the ring placket, aligning raw edges, as marked by a large dot on the pattern. Baste with a zigzag stitch within a ¼" seam allowance. Repeat on the right-hand side.

Cut two 20" lengths of ribbon. Pin one end of each at center top, as marked by a large dot on the pattern, aligning raw edges. Baste with a zigzag stitch within a ¼" seam allowance.

⑥ Finish the Roll

With right sides facing, pin both body pieces together, making sure all ribbons are tucked between layers and out of the way of the stitching line. Stitch around the outside edge of the roll, leaving a 5" opening on the bottom edge for turning. Stitch again at a scant ⅜" seam allowance to reinforce this seam.

Clip corners and clip to, but not through, the seam along the top curve to ease fullness.

Turn the roll right side out, and press the raw edges into the opening. Slipstitch the opening closed and press all edges.

Thread the rings onto the ribbon, and tie the ends together loosely so the rings lie on the placket. Fill the pouch with jewelry and fold the roll in three parts, with the curved edge and top ribbons on top. Wrap these ribbons around and tie into a pretty bow.

COLLAPSIBLE SHOPPING TOTE

Designed by Shelley Crouch

Collapsible, reusable shopping bags that fit in your purse are all the rage, but why buy an expensive tony tote when you can make your own? A Velcro or snap strip holds it together so it can stay purse- or pocket-size, but it's always ready to whip out at the farmer's market or your local co-op. So let's go sew — to save some money and the environment!

MATERIALS

* Locate the pattern in the front pocket (sheet #4)
* 1 yard of 44/45" fabric (quilting-weight cotton)
* 1 spool of coordinating thread
* 1 package of ½" double-fold bias tape
* 1 snap fastener or Velcro square/circle

Finished dimensions – approximately 14" wide × 15" tall (not including strap)

Seam allowance – varies, so adjust as indicated

① Measure, Mark, and Cut

With right sides together, fold your fabric in half lengthwise, aligning the selvages. Cut the pieces below, and transfer all markings from the pattern to the wrong side of the fabric:

* <u>Tote pattern</u> (cut 2 on the fold)
* <u>Strap</u> 2" wide × 14" tall (cut 1)

NOTE: *Place "tall" dimensions along the grainline of your fabric.*

② Make the Strap

Press under both short ends of the strap ½", then fold and press as if making double-fold bias tape (*see page* 18). Edgestitch all four sides. Fold in half across the width and press a crease at the center. Once folded, the strap will be about 6½" long.

❸ Stitch the Handles

With wrong sides facing, fold one bag piece in half lengthwise and stitch the short handle ends together with scant ¼" seam. Trim to ⅛" and press open.

Reposition the bag pieces so that the right sides are facing. Fold the same bag piece in half lengthwise, and stitch again with ¼" seam to encase the raw edges from the first seam; this is a French seam. (For more about French seams, *see page* 16.) Press seam allowance to one side. Stitch the handle on the other bag piece in the same way.

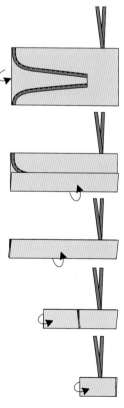

COLLAPSE YOUR TOTE

❹ Stitch the Bag

Place both bag pieces, wrong sides together, and stitch the sides and bottom of bag with a scant ¼" seam allowance.

On one side of the bag, measure 2½" up from the bottom of the bag. Align the center fold of the strap with the raw edge at this location (the finished ends of the strap will be toward the center of the bag). Stitch the folded edge of strap in place with a ¼" seam allowance.

Trim the seam allowance of the bag (including folded end of strap) to ⅛" and clip corners. Pin the loose ends of the strap to one side to keep it out of your way in the following steps.

To complete the French seam, turn the bag wrong side out and press. Stitch around the sides and bottom of the bag with a ¼" seam, press, and turn right side out again. Press the seam allowance to one side at the top of each seam.

❺ Bind Handles

Stitch bias tape around the raw edge of one handle, fully encasing the raw edges and carefully easing bias tape around curves. When back at the beginning of the binding, trim the bias tape, fold it under ½", and stitch to secure, hiding the beginning raw edge of bias tape under the folded edge. Repeat for the second handle and top of bag.

✳ How to Collapse Your Tote

With handles on the left and the strap at the bottom right, fold the bag as follows:

* Fold bag in half lengthwise, aligning the handles, then fold the handles down toward the body of the bag.
* Fold bag in thirds lengthwise, starting with edge closest to you and folding toward closing strap.
* Fold in thirds from handles at left and move toward the right.
* Wrap ends of strap around folded bag to meet at top. Determine placement of closure and mark. Attach snap or Velcro closure as desired.

YOGa MaT BaG

Designed by Gene Pittman

Have you ever been able to find the perfect yoga bag that was utilitarian, attractive, and had a pocket for your wallet and keys? Well, look no further! Not only does this bag fulfill all of the above requirements, it also allows quick access, yet keeps the mat in place while biking or walking from yoga class. How Zen.

MATERIALS

* ✳ 1 yard of fabric (any weight will do)
* ✳ 1 spool of coordinating thread
* ✳ 1 yard of coordinating 1" webbing
* ✳ 1 pair of 1" D-rings
* ✳ 22" of ½" elastic

Finished dimensions – 9" wide × 25" tall
Seam allowance – ½" unless otherwise specified

➊ Measure, Mark, and Cut

With right sides together, fold your fabric in half lengthwise, aligning selvages. Measure and mark the following pieces directly on the wrong side of your fabric, then cut them out:

* ✳ **Exterior and Lining** 17½" wide × 29" tall (cut 2)
* ✳ **Pocket** 6" wide × 8" tall (cut 2)
* ✳ **Bottoms** 16½" diameter circle (cut 2)
* ✳ **Strap Loop** 3" wide × 2" tall (cut 1)
* ✳ **D-ring tab** 3" wide × 6" tall (cut 1)

NOTE: *Place "tall" dimensions along the grainline of your fabric.*

➋ Make the Pocket

With right sides together, pin pocket pieces together. Stitch around all four edges, leaving a 2" opening along the center bottom edge for turning. Clip corners, turn pocket right side out, and press raw edges of opening in ½" toward wrong side.

Press and topstitch along the top edge of the pocket. Center the pocket on the bag exterior 8½" down from the top edge. Stitch in place close to the edge along three sides, leaving the top edge open.

❸ Stitch the Exterior

With right sides together, fold the bag exterior in half lengthwise. Stitch the long back seam and press open. Fold and press one end of the webbing under ½" for the bottom edge of the strap. Center this folded edge on the back seam of the right side of the exterior, 1" up from the bottom raw edge, with the fold facing toward bottom. The unattached end of the strap will thread through the fabric tube toward the top raw edge. Securely stitch in place. With right sides together, pin the bottom (circle) to the bottom edge of the bag, easing the straight edge of the bag to fit around the curved edge of the circle. Stitch the circle to the bag and trim seam to ¼". Turn right side out.

❹ Line the Bag

With right sides together, fold the bag interior in half lengthwise. Stitch the long back seam and press open. With right sides together, pin the other bottom (circle) to the bottom edge of the bag, easing the straight edge of the bag to fit around the curved edge of the circle. Stitch the circle

to the bag and trim the seam allowance to ¼". Place the lining inside the exterior with wrong sides together, aligning center back seams. Baste along the top edge to hold pieces together. Press under the top edge ½", then press under ¾" and stitch in place, leaving a 2" opening at the seam. Thread elastic through the casing, overlap the ends ½", and stitch together securely. Stitch the casing opening closed (see page 19).

❺ Make the Strap Loop

Press under both short ends of the strap loop ¼". Fold and press the strap loop as you would to make bias tape (see page 18). Edgestitch along both long edges. Center this loop over the center back seam, 1½" below (and parallel to) the top edge. Securely stitch both short ends, and slide the webbing through this loop to hold in place.

❻ Finish the Bag

Fold and press the D-ring tab as you would to make bias tape. Edgestitch along both long edges. Slide D-rings onto the tab and stitch short raw edges together. Press under raw edges ½". Center the folded pressed edges on the front of the bag, 2" above the top of the pocket. Stitch in place securely. Slide your yoga mat into the bag, thread the strap up and over the top of the bag and through the D-rings, and off to the gym you go!

CHAPTER 6

FROM HEAD TO TOE

Your clothes reflect your personality, and it can sometimes be so hard to find exactly the right top or skirt in a print and color you like. Create perfect, great-fitting pieces to incorporate into your wardrobe for morning, noon, and night! Who ever dreamed it would only take one yard to make a skirt or dress? Get ready to revamp your wardrobe with some one-yard magic.

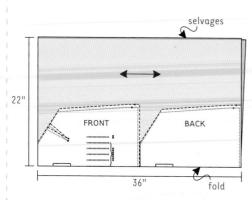

CUTTING LAYOUT FOR SIZES XS, S

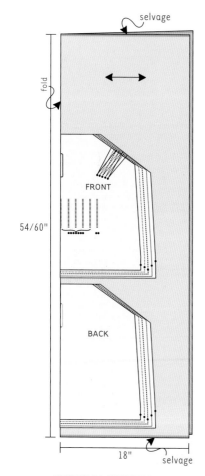

**CUTTING LAYOUT FOR SIZES
M, L, XL, 1X, 2X**

PINTUCKED TOP

Designed by Robin Dodge

*What a great way to showcase your favorite fabric —
make it wearable! Simple tops always come in
handy during those hot summer months. This little
summery top, with bias-tape shoulder ties and
pintucks, is the perfect addition to your wardrobe.*

MATERIALS

* ✳ Locate the pattern in the front pocket (sheet #4)
* ✳ 1 yard of fabric (XS-S: 44/45", directional fabric may be used; M-2X: 54/60", nondirectional fabric must be used) (quilting-weight cotton)
* ✳ 1 spool of coordinating thread
* ✳ 4 yards of ½" double-fold bias tape

Sizes – XS, S, M, L, XL, 1X, 2X
Seam allowance – ½" unless otherwise specified

① Determine Your Size

Select your size based on your full bust measurement.

	XS	S	M	L	XL	1X	2X
Bust measurement	32"	34"	36"	38"	40"	42"	44"
Finished top measurement	35"	38"	40"	42"	44"	46"	48"

② Measure, Mark, and Cut

Place the pattern pieces on the fabric as shown in the appropriate cutting layout and cut out two front/back pieces on the fold. Transfer all markings to the wrong side of the front fabric piece, noting that the center pintuck will straddle the fold line. The back is the same size and shape as the front but has no dart or pintucks.

③ Create the Pintucks

Pintucks appear on the right side of the fabric. Therefore, on the front only, with wrong sides together, stitch a ⅛" pintuck along each of the pintuck marks by stitching each set of double lines together (*see page* 19). Sizes XS–XL will have 9 pintucks, while 1X and 2X will have 11.

④ Make the Darts

With right sides together, fold each front armhole down the middle of the dart; pin and stitch dart along lines. Press the darts toward the side seams.

⑤ Join the Front and Back

With right sides together, stitch front and back together at both side seams. Create a 1" double-fold hem at the bottom edge (*see page* 19).

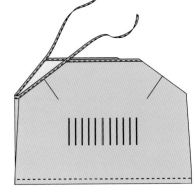

STEP 5
Binding the armholes and making the ties

⑥ Finish the Top

Stitch bias tape along the top straight edges of the front and back, fully encasing the raw edges (*see page 18*).

Measure 60" of bias tape and mark the halfway point. Pin the halfway point at the bottom of the armhole side seam and pin the tape along the armholes, fully encasing the raw edges. The ends will extend off the garment in both the front and the back. Stitch the entire length of the bias tape. Repeat this step with the other armhole.

Try on the top and tie the bias-tape straps in bows over shoulders. Trim to the desired length and knot the ends to eliminate fraying.

STRAPLESS BELTED TUNIC

Designed by Sharon Madsen

Get ready to make the perfect date-night tunic. What better way to showcase your favorite yard of fabric? It's versatile enough to be worn all four seasons: by itself, belted, unbelted, or layered underneath a shirt or jacket.

MATERIALS

* 1 yard of 44/45" (sizes XS–L) or 54/60" (size XL) fabric (quilting-weight cotton)
* 1 spool of coordinating thread
* 1 yard of ⅜" elastic
* French curve (*See* Glossary *on page* 280.)

Sizes – XS, S, M, L, XL

Seam allowance – ½" unless otherwise specified

1 Determine Your Size

Choose your size based on your full bust measurement. Each size is designed with approximately 5" of wearing ease. For example, if your bust measures 34", the finished width of the tunic would be 39". The tunic is a straight rectangle that gets its shaping from the slight curve and elastic at the upper chest. The finished width will be the same for both the bust and hip area.

	XS	S	M	L	XL
Bust measurement	32"	34"	36"	38"	40"
Finished tunic measurement	37"	39"	41"	43"	45"

2 Measure, Mark, and Cut

With right sides together, fold your fabric in half lengthwise, aligning the selvages. Measure and mark the following pieces directly on the wrong side of your fabric, then cut them out:

	XS	S	M	L	XL
Piece dimensions	wide × tall	wide × tall	wide × tall	wide × tall	wide × tall
Tunic front (cut 1)	19" × 28"	20" × 28½"	21" × 29"	22" × 29½"	23" × 30"
Tunic back (cut 1)	19" × 27"	20" × 27½"	21" × 28"	22" × 28½"	23" × 29"
Belt (cut 2)	36" × 3"	36" × 3"	36" × 3"	36" × 3"	36" × 3"

NOTE: *Place "tall" dimensions along the grainline of your fabric.*

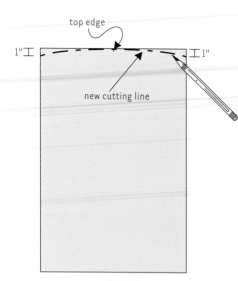

STEP 3

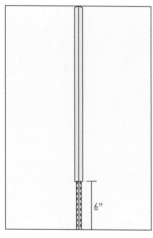

STEP 4
Making a slit

③ **Shape the Front Piece**

On the right and left sides of the front piece, measure 1" down from the top edge and draw a mark. Place a third mark at the center top edge of the front piece. Use a French curve to draw a gently curved line from each side seam to the mark at the center front. This slight curve along the upper front edge will allow for a better-fitting tunic. Trim the fabric above the curve.

④ **Stitch the Sides**

With right sides together, stitch the side seams to within 6" of the bottom edge. Clip the seam at the end of your stitching within the seam allowance to (but not through) your stitching line. Press seams open. To create the side slits or vents, turn the seam allowance of the remaining 6" to the inside of the tunic. Make a narrow ¼" double-fold hem and topstitch in place (*see page* 19).

Turn the tunic right side out and hem the bottom edge with a ⅝" double-fold hem.

⑤ **Make the Top Casing**

Place the elastic around your upper chest (under your arms and above your full bust) stretching it slightly until it feels comfortable. Add ¾" to that measurement and cut. Press under the top edge of the tunic ¼", and press under another ¾". Topstitch close to the folded edge of the casing, leaving a 1" opening at one side seam. Insert elastic through casing with safety pins, and try on for fit. Overlap the ends of the elastic by ½" and stitch together securely. Stitch the casing opening closed (*see page* 19).

⑥ **Make the Belt**

With right sides together, stitch the belt pieces together at one short end to make one long belt strip. Press the seam open and press under the short raw ends ½". Topstitch around all edges. This long belt will fit all waist sizes, and it can be worn in a variety of ways. You'll look stunning!

Bias Skirt

Designed by Isabelle Brasme

This bias-cut skirt hangs perfectly from all your curves in just the right way. As an added bonus, the slight A-line shape is flattering to all!

MATERIALS

* Locate the pattern in the front pocket (sheet #1)
* 1 yard of 54/60" fabric (quilting-weight cotton in a nondirectional print)
* 1 spool of coordinating thread
* 1 yard of ¼" elastic
* Optional: lace or other decorative trim for the bottom edge of the skirt

Sizes – 6-16
Seam allowance – ½" unless otherwise specified

① Determine Your Size

Choose your size based on your waist and hip measurements. Keep in mind that this skirt is cut on the bias. Although the finished skirt may appear form-fitting, it will use the natural, bias stretch of the fabric and will move with you very nicely. The skirt length for all sizes is 20½".

	Size 6	Size 8	Size 10	Size 12	Size 14	Size 16
Waist measurement	24½"	25½"	27"	28½"	30½"	32½"
Hip measurement	34"	35½"	36¾"	38½"	40"	41½"

② Measure, Mark, and Cut

Place your fabric in a single layer with wrong side facing up (see diagram on next page). Trace a copy of the skirt pattern, noting the different grainline arrows for front and back. Place the pattern piece as shown in the cutting layout and cut out one front piece and one back piece on the bias.

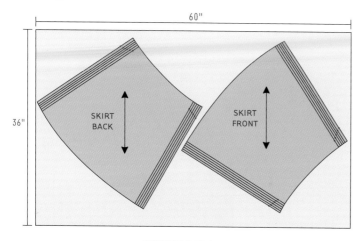

60"

36"

SKIRT BACK

SKIRT FRONT

CUTTING LAYOUT

IMPORTANT NOTE ON BIAS LAYOUT: *Take extra care to lay out the pattern piece precisely on the bias of the fabric. The skirt front and back are cut from the same pattern piece.*

③ Stitch the Sides

With right sides together, stitch the skirt front to the skirt back along both side seams. Press seams open.

④ Make the Waistline Casing

Press under the top edge of the skirt ¼", and then press under another ½". Topstitch close to the folded edge of the casing, leaving a 1" opening at one side seam. Insert the elastic into the casing, safety-pin in place, put on the skirt, and adjust the length of the elastic to fit comfortably. Once you have established a good fit, cut the elastic, overlap the ends by ½" and stitch together securely. Stitch the casing opening closed (*see page* 19).

⑤ Hem the Skirt

Hem the skirt with a narrow double-fold hem (*see page* 19). Depending on the style you're after, you may want to add a decorative trim to the bottom of your skirt. Pin it along the hemline, and stitch in place to achieve your desired look.

summer nightie

Designed by Rae Hoekstra

Perfect for those hot summer nights, this easy, breezy summer top is so comfy for sleeping — and even looks great with your favorite pair of jeans. Everyone loves a little versatility!

MATERIALS

* Locate the pattern in the front pocket (sheet #2)
* 1 yard of 44/45" fabric (quilting-weight cotton or lighter)
* 1 spool of coordinating thread
* 3½ yards of contrasting 2" bias trim, or 1 package of ½" double-fold bias tape
* 1 yard of ¼" natural elastic
* 12" of ⅛" ribbon for bow

Sizes – S, M, L
Seam allowance – ½" unless otherwise specified

❶ Determine Your Size

Choose your top size based on your measurements and bra cup size. The skirt piece will be the same for all sizes.

	Small	Medium	Large
Cup size	A/B	B/C	C/D
Finished bust measurement	41"	45"	49"

❷ Measure, Mark, and Cut

Place your fabric in a single layer with the wrong side facing up. Place the pattern pieces for the top as shown in the cutting layout. Measure and mark the skirt front and back directly on the wrong side of the fabric. Cut out the pieces and transfer the dots from the bodice pattern to the wrong side of the fabric. Also, mark the center of the skirt front and skirt back on the top edge.

* **Bodice triangles** (cut 2)
* **Skirt front/back** 21" top length × 26" bottom length × 17" height (cut 2 trapezoid shapes)

NOTE: *Place bodice pattern pieces as marked. Place height dimensions of the skirt along the grainline of your fabric.*

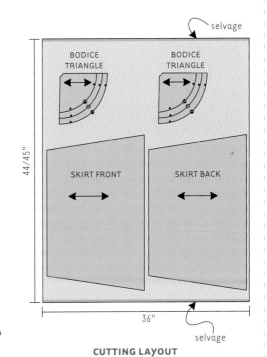

CUTTING LAYOUT

❸ Stitch the Sides

With right sides together, stitch the side seams of the skirt and press seams open. Turn right side out.

❹ Bind the Bodice Triangles

Use packaged ½" double-fold bias tape, or make your own by cutting 3½ yards of bias strips from the contrasting fabric. Press and fold into bias tape (*see page* 18).

Lay the bodice triangles side by side, just as they will be on the nightie. Enclose the outside straight edge of both triangles with bias tape, cutting the trim at the point of the triangle. Attach using a zigzag stitch.

To bind the inner edges, start at the bottom of the straight edge (the curved edge gets attached to the top of the skirt) and allow at least 16" of extra trim to extend at the top of the triangle for the shoulder straps. Attach using a zigzag stitch, enclosing the raw edge and reinforcing where the trims overlap at the top of the triangle. Continue stitching up the sides of the bias tape to finish the straps.

❺ Bind the Hemline

Encase the raw edge at the bottom of the nightie with bias tape using a zigzag stitch.

❻ Gather the Triangles

Use a basting stitch to gather the raw edge of the bodice triangles by stitching between the dots (*see page* 13). With right sides and raw edges together, place the inside corner of each triangle at the center mark of the skirt front, with the other corner at the side seam. Adjust gathers to fit. Stitch both triangles in place with a ¾" seam allowance. Press seams open, and trim *only* the triangle seam allowance to ¼".

⑦ Make the Underbust Casing

Fold the bodice triangles out of the way and press ¼" of the skirt's seam allowance toward the wrong side around the entire top edge of the skirt. Press this allowance under another ½" to form the casing for the elastic (*see page* 19). Topstitch close to the folded edge of the casing, leaving a 2" opening at one side seam for inserting the elastic. Insert the elastic into the casing, safety-pin in place, and try on the nightie to adjust for fit. Once you've determined an ideal length, cut and overlap the ends of the elastic ½" and stitch. Stitch the casing opening closed.

⑧ Add Decoration

Tie the ribbon into a bow and machine-stitch or hand-sew to the center front of the nightie.

⑨ Position the Shoulder Straps

Try on the nightie and, with the assistance of a loved one, pin the ends of the straps to the back of the nightie wherever they are the most comfortable (you may need to shorten them). Make sure that the straps are not twisted. Remove the nightie and stitch the straps to the wrong side of the skirt, just underneath the elastic casing. You have just created the perfect saucy nightie top!

PERFECT-FIT SLEEP SHORTS

Designed by Jessica Roberts

These shorts will fit women of all sizes with a fit based upon your own measurements. They are truly customizable, as you will control the ease as well as the length to create a perfect-fitting pattern. Get ready for a slumber party!

MATERIALS
* 1 yard of 44/45" fabric (quilting-weight cotton)
* 1 spool of coordinating thread
* ½" elastic, long enough to comfortably fit your waist
* Tracing paper to create the paper pattern

Size – custom fit
Seam allowance – ½" unless otherwise specified

① Determine Your Measurements

You make the pattern for this project by taking a few key personal measurements and plugging them into the formulas provided. Use the results to graph out your dream sleep shorts, ones that will fit you and only you – perfectly!

② Draft Your Pattern Pieces

* **To make the front pattern piece (see diagram).** At the top of your tracing paper, start at one edge and draw a line the length of measurement A. Mark this point as A. From the end of that line, measure out another 1½" and then down the length of measurement B. Mark this point as B. Connect the end of the measurement A line to point B using a shallow curve, as illustrated. From point B, draw a line down the length of measurement D. Mark this point as D. From here, draw a perpendicular line from point D back to the edge of the paper. Note that the edge of the paper represents the grainline.

REQUIRED MEASUREMENTS:

Hip measurement: __

Total rise, front to back: __

Desired length from waist: __

Once you've got these three measurements determined, plug them in to the following equations:

A = Hip measurement __ + 7" (for seam allowance and ease) ÷ 4

B = Total Rise measurement __ ÷ 2

C = Waist to bottom of shorts __ + 2½" (for seam allowance)

D = C − B

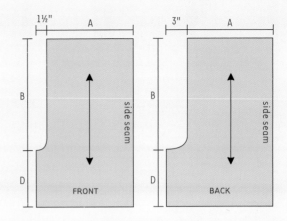

* **To make the back pattern piece (see diagram).** At the top of your tracing paper, start at one edge and draw a line the length of measurement A. Mark this point as A. From the end of that line, measure out another 3" (this is different from the front piece) and then down the length of measurement B. Mark this point as B. Continue making the back pattern piece as you did for the front.

❸ **Lay Out and Cut**

With right sides together, fold your fabric in half lengthwise, aligning the selvages. Pin your pattern pieces in place, along the grainline of your fabric. Cut two front pieces and two back pieces.

❹ **Stitch the Seams**

With right sides together, stitch a front to a back along the side seam, then stitch the inside leg seam. Repeat for the remaining front and back pieces.

Turn one front/back piece right side out and slip it inside the other with right sides together, matching inner leg seams. Stitch the entire crotch seam from front to back. Stitch again, this time using a ¼" seam allowance, to reinforce this seam. Trim the seam close to the second stitch line.

❺ **Hem the Shorts**

To hem each leg opening, press under ¼", then press under 1". Topstitch close to the folded edge (*see page* 13).

❻ **Make the Waistband Casing**

Press under the top edge ¼", then press under ¾". Topstitch close to the folded edge of the casing, leaving a 1" opening at one side seam. Insert the elastic into the casing, safety-pin the elastic in place, try on the shorts, and cut the elastic to fit. Overlap the ends of the elastic ½" and stitch together securely. Stitch the casing opening closed.

MOTHER-DAUGHTER HALTER TOPS

Designed by Lisa Powers

A throwback to the 1970s, this lightweight halter top is just right for summer sun and fun. Which is better – making a mother-daughter duo or creating coordinating tops for friends? You be the judge! But whichever way you go, you'll have two very cute and comfortable tops in short order.

MATERIALS

* ✳ 1 yard of 44/45" fabric (quilting-weight cotton)
* ✳ 1 spool of coordinating thread
* ✳ 1-2 yards of coordinating ½" ribbon

Size – custom fit

Seam allowance – ½" unless otherwise specified

❶ Determine Your Size

Choose your size based on the chart.

Toddler	Child/Teen	Adult
Fits sizes 2T-6T	Fits sizes 7-14	Fits sizes S-2X

❷ Measure, Mark, and Cut

Measure and mark the halter top directly on the wrong side of your fabric and cut it out:

Toddler	Child/Teen	Adult
15" wide × 15" tall	20" wide × 20" tall	25" wide × 25" tall

NOTE: *Place "tall" dimensions along the grainline of your fabric.*

❸ Stitch the Top

Finish all four edges of the fabric square to your liking. The most common method would be to neatly hem all four edges, but you can also experiment with some different options. Pinking all four edges creates a whimsical look, or you could go a little more rustic by stitching a straight line ½" from all raw edges, allowing the fabric a controlled fray. This effect will increase with washing but will never go beyond that stitching line.

④ **Make the Casing and Neck Tie**

Place your fabric square with the wrong side up and fold over one of the corners 5" to the wrong side. Topstitch 1" from the fold. Thread ribbon through casing. Try the top on by tying the ribbon around your neck to see if the length needs to be adjusted. Be sure to cut the ribbon long enough so you can tie it comfortably around your neck. You may want to knot the ends of the ribbon to deter fraying.

⑤ **Finish the Ties**

Try the halter back on by tying it around your neck. The halter top will form a V at the bottom (waist) edge, and the two points to the right and left at your midsection can be tied behind you for a snug look or you can add ribbon to them for a roomier fit. If you decide to use ties, cut a length of ribbon long enough to go around your midriff and be tied in a bow. Cut that length in half and stitch one length on each side corner on the wrong side.

simply Beautiful sundress

Designed by Madeline Elizabeth Steimle

You needn't look any further for your perfect summer wardrobe staple. This very feminine dress can also be shortened and worn as a tunic. Whip it up and go get some sun!

MATERIALS

* Locate the pattern in the front pocket (sheet #2)
* 1 yard of 44/45" fabric (quilting-weight cotton; not suitable for a unidirectional print)
* 1 spool of coordinating thread
* ¼" elastic, 2" shorter than your rib circumference just below your bust
* 1 package of ½" double-fold bias tape

Sizes – S, M, L

Seam allowance – ½" unless otherwise specified

① Determine Your Size

	S	M	L
Bust measurement	31"–34"	34"–36"	36"–39"
Waist measurement	24"–26"	26"–28"	29"–31"
Hip measurement	33"–36"	36"–38"	39"–41"

② Measure, Mark, and Cut

With right sides together, fold your fabric in half lengthwise, aligning the selvages. Place the bodice pattern pieces as shown in the cutting layout. Also measure out the skirt front/back, in your size, and mark it directly on the wrong side of the fabric. Cut out the pieces, and transfer all markings to the wrong side of the bodice fabric. Place a mark at the center front on the top edge of the skirt front piece.

* **Bodice front** (cut 2)   * **Bodice back** (cut 2)
* **Skirt front/back** (cut 2)

Small	Medium	Large
19" wide × 22" tall	21" wide × 22" tall	22" wide × 22" tall

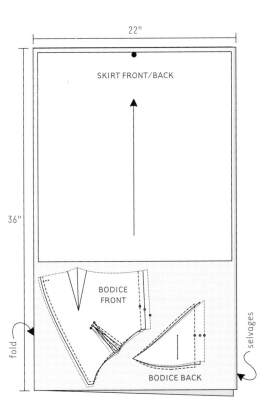

CUTTING LAYOUT

NOTE: *Place pattern pieces as shown, with "tall" dimensions along the grainline of your fabric.*

STEP 3

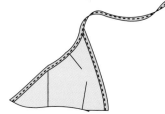
STEP 4
Inner edge

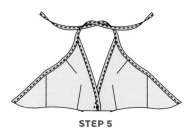
STEP 4
Outer (armhole) edge and strap

STEP 5

STEP 6

❸ Prepare the Bodice Pieces

Stitch the darts in both bodice front pieces. Press the armhole darts toward the side seam and the underbust darts toward the center. With right sides together, stitch bodice front to bodice back at side seams. Press seams open.

❹ Bind the Bodice Edges

Encase the inner edge of each bodice piece in bias tape and stitch in place. Encase the outer (armhole) edge of each bodice piece in bias tape, letting the ends extend 18" beyond the bodice (to allow enough length for it to tie behind your neck). Stitch in place.

❺ Join the Bodice Pieces

Overlap and pin the bodice pieces in the center, matching dots. Stitch.

❻ Stitch the Bodice to the Skirt

With right sides together, stitch front and back skirt pieces at both side seams. Press seams open. Use a basting stitch to gather the top raw edge of the skirt front (*see page* 13). With right sides and raw edges together, pin the bodice to the skirt, adjusting the skirt gathers to fit the bodice front, matching side seams. Stitch in place. Divide both the ¼" elastic and waist-edge seam allowance into quarters. Pin the elastic to the waist seam allowance, matching the quarter marks. Using a zigzag stitch, stitch the elastic in place within the ½" seam allowance of the waist seam by stretching the elastic to meet the fabric.

❼ Finish the Edges

At the center back of the dress, press the seam with elastic to the inside of the skirt. Topstitch from the outside to hide the elastic. Hem the bottom edge of the dress with a ⅝" double-fold hem (*see page* 19).

spats

Designed by Rebecca Yaker

Get ready, because spats are back! Add some flair to your footwear and turn any shoe into a boot. After all, leg warmers aren't just for knitters anymore.

MATERIALS

* Locate the pattern in the front pocket (sheet #2)
* 1 yard of fabric (any width, home-decor weight preferred)
* 1 spool of coordinating thread
* ½ yard of fleece or batting
* 4 yards of coordinating ⅝" grosgrain ribbon, cut into eight 18" pieces
* 4 yards of ¼" elastic
* ½ yard of ¾" elastic, cut into 2 pieces, each 9" in length
* 8 buttons, 1" or larger
* Sewing-machine walking foot, optional

Size – one size fits most

Seam allowance – ½" (unless otherwise specified)

1 Measure, Mark, and Cut

With right sides together, fold your fabric in half lengthwise, aligning the selvages. Use the pattern to cut out the following pieces. Use chalk or disappearing ink to transfer markings from all pattern pieces to the right side of the fabric.

* **Spat front** (cut 4)
* **Spat back** (cut 4)

Cut from fleece or batting:

* **Spat front** (cut 2)
* **Spat back** (cut 2)

NOTE: *Place pattern pieces as marked along the grainline of your fabric.*

2 Quilt the Pieces

For each fleece (or batting) piece, place a matching fabric piece on top with the wrong side facing the fleece. Pin through both layers and mark your choice of quilting lines with a fabric pen; for instance, you could try diagonal 3" squares. Machine-quilt the two layers together, following the lines. You may want to use a walking foot, if you have one. Quilt two fronts and two backs.

3 Join the Quilted Pieces

With right sides together, stitch a quilted front to a quilted back along the center front edge, aligning raw edges and notches. Press the seam open and topstitch ⅛" away from the seam on both sides. Repeat with the remaining quilted pieces.

④ Make the Lining

With right sides together, stitch the nonquilted front and back pieces together in the same manner as the quilted pieces, aligning raw edges and notches. Press seams open.

⑤ Assemble the Spats

Complete the following steps for both spats.

* Place ¾" elastic along the bottom edge on the back of a quilted spat at elastic placement mark (the one farther from center front seam). Align raw edges and pin in place. (This will be a kind of stirrup to keep your spats from riding up; the other end will be attached later.)

* Cut four pieces of ¼" elastic, each 3" in length. Make loops with the elastic by folding in half and aligning raw edges. Position loops at placement marks along raw edge of spat front, aligning raw edges.

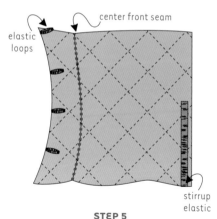

STEP 5
Right spat, right side

* With right sides together, align raw edges and notches of one quilted exterior and one spat lining, sandwiching the elastic in between the layers. Pin and stitch around all four sides, leaving a 4" opening along the bottom edge as indicated on pattern piece. Clip corners, turn right side out, and press. Turn edges of opening to wrong side ½" and press.

⑥ Create Ribbon Casings

On four pieces of the grosgrain ribbon, turn under one short end ½". Starting with this end, pin ribbon pieces in place on the right side of the spat exterior along placement lines. Trim other ribbon ends to necessary length, leaving ½" to turn under. Stitch ribbons in place along both long edges, starting seams ½" from ribbons' folded edge and leaving both short ends open. These openings will allow you to pull the elastic through the casing and secure before stitching the ribbon ends closed.

Insert an 11" length of elastic into the top casing. At each end, fold ribbon back and stitch elastic securely to spat. Topstitch end of the ribbon casing closed, fully concealing the elastic. Repeat with the second casing. Use a 10" length of elastic in the lower two casings. Repeat with second spat.

⑦ Add Buttons

Sew buttons securely in place at the end of the casing opposite the elastic loops on both spats.

⑧ Determine Bottom Stirrup Length

Try on the spats over your favorite shoes. Place the seam up the front of your leg and the buttons along the outside of your leg. Pull the bottom strap elastic until it fits snugly, and pin. Remove the spat, and trim the elastic to desired length. Tuck the raw edge between the spat exterior and lining at placement mark, taking care that the elastic is not twisted. Edgestitch across the bottom edge of the spat, closing the opening used for turning and securing the elastic strap in place.

FABRIC OPTIONS

Lightweight wool, heavy silk, heavy polyester blend, or other medium-weight fabrics are recommended for this project. You want the fabric to have a nice drape. If you like, make the binding from contrasting fabric or use packaged 2" bias tape (sometimes called quilt binding).

THE MOD CAPER

Designed by Christine Haynes

The cape never really goes out of style; it just takes a special kind of woman to pull it off. You're that kind of woman, aren't you? It's a bold choice but one that should not be forgotten. This classic, classy look is easier to pull off (and make!) than you might think, so grab some fabric and drape yourself in a bold new cape.

MATERIALS

* 1 yard of 60" fabric (medium weight, see left for options)
* 1 spool of coordinating thread
* 1-2 yards of coordinating ½" ribbon

Size – one size fits most
Seam allowance – ½" unless otherwise specified

1 Measure, Mark, and Cut

With right sides together, fold your fabric in half lengthwise, aligning the selvages. Measure and mark the following pattern pieces on the wrong side of your fabric, and cut them out:

* **Cape body.** Measure 29" up the right side, from fold to selvage. Do the same along the folded edge of the fabric, as shown. From the bottom right corner, pivot a measuring tape or string from edge to fold, measuring out a series of 29" marks and connecting the dots to create a smooth, circular curve.

    To create the neck opening, measure 8" up the right side from the fold and mark. Do the same along the folded edge of the fabric. From the bottom right corner, pivot a measuring tape, ruler, or string, measuring out a series of 8" marks and connecting the dots to create a smooth, circular curve. Cut 1 body piece.

* **Binding strips.** With the remainder of the fabric, use a straight edge to cut over 60" worth of 3"-wide strips on the bias to use as binding.

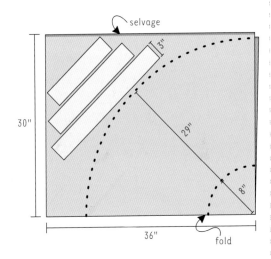

CUTTING LAYOUT

❷ Hem the Cape

Make a narrow ¼" double-fold hem along the bottom and front edges of the cape (*see page* 19).

❸ Make the Binding

Join enough of the bias strips together to form one long strip that is 3" wide and 54/60" long. Fold and press to make bias tape (*see page* 18).

❹ Finish the Neck

Find and mark the center point of the neck. Use a basting stitch to gather the neck opening of the cape (*see page* 13). Adjust the gathers so that the neck edge measures 21". Find the center point of the bias strip and mark. Lining up both center points, encase the entire neck edge with the bias strip. Pin in place. Before stitching, check the length of the ties. Trim any excess and fold under and press the short raw edges. Stitch the bias strip closed, working from one end to the other, making sure to catch both sides of the tape (and the cape fabric when you get to it) as you go. Press, wrap your cape around your shoulders, and enjoy!

"GOOD HAT DAY" HAT

Designed by Rebecca Jo Malmström

The pattern creates a fully reversible, neatly finished hat that showcases the back side of the printed fabric for a slightly more subdued look. Some of the pieces are reversed to take advantage of the muted look of the wrong side of the fabric — this option is up to you. The instructions are written so that all right sides are facing out for the hat's exterior, except for the top.

MATERIALS

* Locate the pattern in the front pocket (sheet #1)
* 1 yard of fabric (any width, weight, and content will do)
* 1 spool of coordinating thread
* ½ yard of heavyweight fusible interfacing

Size – custom fit

Seam allowance – ½" unless otherwise specified

① Measure, Mark, and Cut

Making a hat that fits perfectly depends on one crucial factor: the size of your head! Measure around your head just above your ears and add 1½" inches to this measurement. (Or, if you normally prefer to wear your hair up under your hat, add 3".) Use this key measurement to mark and cut out the following pieces from your fabric:

* **Hat strip A** 2" tall × your head circumference (cut 3)
* **Hat strip B** 3" tall × your head circumference (cut 2)
* **Hat strip C** 1½" tall × your head circumference (cut 1)
* **Top** a circle that matches your head circumference plus ½" (cut 2)
* **Brim** same for all sizes (cut 2)

Cut from interfacing:

* **Brim** (cut 2)

NOTE: *Place "tall" dimensions along the grainline of your fabric.*

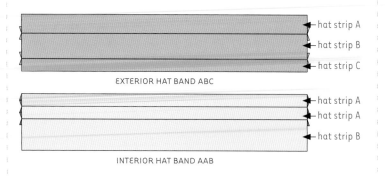

EXTERIOR HAT BAND ABC

— hat strip A
— hat strip B
— hat strip C

INTERIOR HAT BAND AAB

— hat strip A
— hat strip A
— hat strip B

STEP 2

② Stitch the Hat Strips

With right sides together, stitch hat strip A to hat strip B along one long edge. Stitch hat strip C to the other raw edge of B, creating exterior hat band ABC. Press seams open. With wrong sides together, stitch short ends of this band together and press seam open.

With wrong sides together, stitch the remaining hat strips in a different pattern: stitch one remaining hat strip A to the final hat strip A along one long edge. Stitch hat strip B to the other long raw edge of the final A strip, creating interior hat band AAB. Press the seams open. With right sides together, stitch short ends of this band together and press seam open. On interior hat band AAB, stitch a ½" hem on the long raw edge of strip A.

③ Make the Brim

Fuse interfacing to the wrong side of both brim pieces following manufacturer's instructions. With right sides facing, pin brim pieces together and stitch around the outside curved edge. Clip to, but not through, the stitching line to ease fullness. Turn right side out and press. Pin through brim layers and topstitch ¼" from finished edge of brim. Topstitch ½" away from the first stitching line and repeat three additional times, each at ½" intervals. This will help stiffen the brim.

④ Attach the Brim and Hat Bands

Find the center of the inner raw edge of the brim and mark. Fold the interior hat band AAB in half and mark the center of the B strip. Fold the exterior hat band ABC in half, and mark the center of the A strip. Align the center points of the raw edges, sandwiching the brim between the hat bands, and stitch in place.

Turn right side out, press, and topstitch ¼" from the finished edge, taking care not to catch the brim. (You are only stitching through the interior and exterior hat bands, not the brim.)

⑤ Attach the Top of the Hat

With right sides together, pin the circular top pieces together. Then pin both pieces to the raw edge of exterior hat band ABC, aligning markings. Ease extra fullness out of the hat by stretching the hat band as you pin. Turn the hat inside out, pin the hemmed edge of interior hat band AAB in place, taking care to cover the seams. Slip-stitch the interior hat band to the top.

CHAPTER 7

CaRRY IT ALL

Accessories are a girl's best friend, the best of the best being the perfect handbag. Bags for day, bags for night, bags for the grocery store, and even a couple of uniquely compact diaper bags for Mom. You'll be sure to find one, two, or more new favorites in this special collection of purses and totes.

FLOUNCY BAG

Designed by Nina Perkins

Appropriate for girls of all ages, this gathered purse is a delightful touch of femininity! If you like, further embellish it with a personalized label, buttons, additional ribbons, or other accessories.

MATERIALS

* 1 yard of 44/45" fabric (quilting-weight cotton or cotton blend; nondirectional print)
* 1 spool of coordinating thread
* 2 D-rings
* 2 yards of 3" ribbon cut into two 18" pieces and one 36" piece
* 1 package of ready-made piping with flange

Finished dimensions – approximately 15" wide × 12" tall (not including strap)

Seam allowance – ½" unless otherwise specified

① Measure, Mark, and Cut

Place your fabric in a single layer with the wrong side facing up.

Measure and mark the following pieces directly on the wrong side of your fabric, then cut them out:

* **Exterior** 30" tall × 12" wide (cut 2)
* **Lining** 10" tall × 12" wide (cut 2)
* **Top band** 3½" tall × 10" wide (cut 4)
* **Strap** 36" tall × 3½" wide (cut 2)
* **Bottom** 4" tall × 10" wide ovals (cut 2)

NOTE: *Place "tall" dimension along the grainline of your fabric.*

② Make the Strap and D-Ring Loops

* Center and pin the 36" length of 3" ribbon onto the right side of one strap piece. Topstitch in place. With right sides facing, pin both strap pieces together; stitch along both long sides. Turn the strap right side out and edgestitch all around.
* Cut two 4" tabs off one end of strap for D-ring loops. Thread one D-ring onto each tab. Fold each tab in half and edgestitch the short edges together to hold the D-rings in loops.

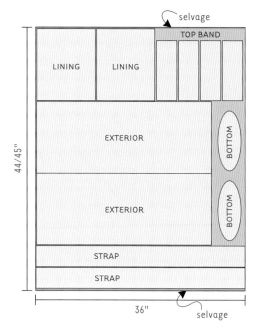

CUTTING LAYOUT

③ Add the Piping

With right sides facing, pin two top band pieces together, and stitch along one short side. Press the seam allowance open. Use your zipper foot to stitch the piping to the bottom raw edge of the top band. With right sides facing, pin together the short ends of the top band and stitch, forming a circle. Press the seam allowance open.

④ Assemble the Exterior

With right sides together, pin exterior pieces together and stitch along both short sides. Use a basting stitch to gather the top and bottom raw edges of the exterior (*see page* 13). With right sides together and raw edges even, pin the exterior top edge to the top band's piped edge. Matching side seams and adjusting gathers to fit, pin the exterior of the bag to the band, and stitch. With right sides together and raw edges even, pin one bottom oval to the bottom of the bag exterior, orienting the oval so that the smaller ends line up with the side seams. Adjust the gathers and stitch.

⑤ Make the Lining

* With right sides together and raw edges aligned, stitch one top band piece to one lining piece along the 10" edge. Repeat for the remaining top band and lining pieces.

* On right side of one lining piece, stitch one of the 18" ribbon pieces 4" up from bottom edge, keeping the ribbon parallel to the bottom edge. Stitch the ribbon every few inches, creating loops in the ribbon. These loops will keep the contents of your bag organized, so keep that in mind when determining loop size. Repeat with the other lining piece and other piece of ribbon.

* With right sides facing, pin the lining pieces together. Stitch them together along the sides. With right sides together and raw edges even, pin and stitch the remaining bottom oval to the bottom of lining as you did for the exterior.

⑥ Finish Bag

* Press under the top raw edge of both exterior and lining ½". Turn the exterior right side out and insert the lining into the exterior, wrong sides together, matching side seams and top folded edges.

* On each side of the bag, insert raw edges of D-ring loops in between the exterior and lining, centered over side seams. Edgestitch around the top edge, closing up the top band and reinforcing at the D-ring loops. Thread the long strap ends through the D-rings. Turn under both raw ends of the handle ½" and topstitch to close. Fold the handle ends over the D-rings and add a boxstitch to secure. Hand-sew any desired embellishments to the outside of the bag.

FOLKLORE BAG

Designed by Lauren Booth

A wonderful showcase for those whimsical Japanese prints you've been eyeing online. A yoke and pleats add to the awesome stylishness.

MATERIALS

* Locate the pattern in the front pocket (sheet #1)
* 1 yard of 44/45" fabric (home-decor weight)
* 1 spool of coordinating thread
* 1½ yards of medium-weight fusible interfacing
* 1 magnetic purse closure

Finished dimensions – 13½" wide × 10" tall (not including straps)

Seam allowance – ½" unless otherwise specified

① Measure, Mark, and Cut

With right sides together, fold your fabric in half lengthwise, aligning selvages. Use the pattern to cut out the following pieces. Also measure and cut the pocket and straps. Transfer all markings from the pattern pieces to the wrong side of the fabric.

* **Bag front/back** (cut 2)
* **Lining front/back** (cut 2)
* **Sides/bottom** (cut 2)
* **Top band** (cut 4)
* **Pocket** 4½" tall × 6" wide (cut 2)
* **Straps** 5" tall × 25" wide (cut 2)

Cut from interfacing:

* **Bag front/back** (cut 2)
* **Side** (cut 1)
* **Top band** (cut 4)

NOTE: *Place pattern pieces along the grainline of your fabric.*

② Apply the Interfacing

Fuse interfacing to the wrong side of both bag front/back pieces and one side/bottom piece, following manufacturer's instructions.

❸ Make Exterior Pleats

Make the pleats on both front/back pieces by folding the fabric, right sides together, and matching pleat lines. Press the pleats as indicated on the pattern. Tack them in place at the top raw edge with a basted edgestitch.

❹ Assemble the Exterior

With right sides together, pin the interfaced side/bottom to a front/back piece, aligning top corners and raw edges. Stitch together. Clip the curves within the seam allowance to ease fullness (*see page* 17). Attach the second front/back piece to the interfaced side/bottom in the same way. Press seam allowance toward the side/bottom. Turn right side out and topstitch each front/back ¼" from the seam line.

❺ Make the Lining

With right sides facing, pin the pocket pieces together and stitch on three sides, leaving one short side open for turning. Clip the corners and turn right side out. Press under raw edges ½" at the opening. Position the pocket on one lining piece as indicated on the pattern, and edgestitch on both sides and bottom. Stitch the remaining side/bottom to both lining pieces in the same fashion as the exterior (step 4), except for the topstitching.

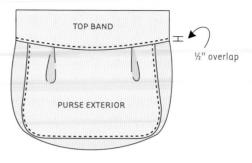

STEP 6

❻ Make and Attach Top Pieces

With right sides facing, pin two top band pieces together, and stitch both short sides to form a circular band. Repeat with the other two top band pieces.

Press under the bottom raw edge of each top band ½", taking care to preserve the bottom curve. Turn right side out and position the top band over the exterior with the pieces overlapping by ½", centering the top band side seams on each side of the side/bottom piece. Topstitch ¼" above the top band's folded bottom edge to attach the band to the purse body. Attach the remaining top band to the lining in the same way.

❼ Add the Closure

Attach the magnetic purse closure to the lining's top band, following manufacturer's instructions. Position one half of the closure on each side, taking care that the halves are centered vertically and horizontally, and align with each other.

❽ Make the Straps

With wrong sides facing, fold one strap piece in half lengthwise and press. Unfold and then press under both long raw edges ½" toward the crease. Refold the strap in half lengthwise, press, and edgestitch all around. The finished strap will be 2" wide. Make the second strap in the same way.

⑨ Attach the Straps

Pin one strap on the right side of the exterior, directly above the pleat. Align the strap's raw edges with the raw edge of exterior top band. Make sure the strap is not twisted and is bending toward the bottom of bag, as shown. Do the same with the second strap on the other side of the exterior. Stitch both straps in place with ¼" seam allowance.

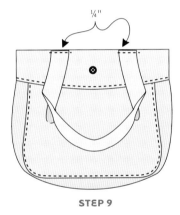

STEP 9

⑩ Finish the Bag

Turn the lining wrong side out. Place the exterior inside the lining so the right sides are facing. Pin the lining to the exterior, sandwiching the straps between the two layers. Align side seams and top raw edge. Stitch around the top of the bag, back-stitching at each strap for reinforcement. Leave an opening on one side between the straps for turning.

Turn the purse right side out and tuck the lining inside the exterior. Press under the raw edges of bag opening ½". Edge-stitch all around the top edge, stitching the opening closed as you go.

Bohemian Banana Bag

Designed by Ellen Baker

This versatile bag can be worn across your chest, leaving you unfettered to chase kids on the playground or head off to a picnic. The embroidered ribbon gives it an old-world feel, yet it's supersimple to make.

MATERIALS

* Locate the pattern in the front pocket (sheet #2)
* 1 yard of cotton canvas (any weight)
* 1 spool of coordinating thread
* 3½ yards of 1½" embroidered ribbon, cut into two 63" (1¾ yard) lengths
* One 16" zipper

* Sewing-machine zipper foot, unless attaching zipper by hand

Finished dimensions – approximately 17" wide × 10" tall

Seam allowance – ½" unless otherwise specified

❶ Measure, Mark, and Cut

With right sides together, find the center of the fabric by folding it in half lengthwise, aligning selvages. Open it back up and fold both sides to the center. Cut four pieces (two exteriors and two interiors) along the two folds.

❷ Make Bag Exterior and Lining

* With right sides facing, pin two exterior pieces together. Stitch sides and bottom curve, leaving the top open. Clip to (but not through) the seam along the rounded corners to ease fullness. Stitch again within the seam allowance to reinforce this seam using a zigzag or overcast stitch.
* Repeat with the other two fabric pieces for the lining. Turn the lining right side out, leaving the exterior wrong side out.

❸ Assemble the Bag

* With right sides facing, insert the lining into the exterior. Matching side seams and raw edges, stitch along the top seam, leaving a 5" opening on one side for turning.
* Turn the bag right side out and press under raw edges of opening ½". Press and slip-stitch opening closed.

④ Make and Attach the Strap

With right sides together, fold the ribbon in half across the width and stitch the short ends together to make a loop.

Repeat with the second piece of ribbon. Place ribbon loops wrong sides together, matching seams and side edges.

Find the center of the bag bottom and position the ribbon seam there. Starting at this point, pin the ribbon to the bag, keeping side seam centered underneath the ribbon. After you have reached the top corner of the bag, you will simply be pinning the sides of the ribbon together. Repeat with the other half of the ribbon, pinning from the bottom to the opposite top corner, then completing a continuous loop of ribbon that will form the strap. Hand-sew the ribbon to the bag with a slipstitch, and continue slipstitching the edges of ribbon strap together.

⑤ Attach the Zipper

Hand-sew the zipper to the bag's top edge with the zipper open, centering the zipper teeth at the opening.

QUILTED CIRCLES SHOULDER BAG

Designed by Heidi Massengill

Quilting and appliqué seem to go hand in hand, so what better way to show off your mad quilting skills than this small bundle of cuteness?

MATERIALS

* Locate the pattern in the front pocket (sheet #3)
* 1 yard of 44/45" fabric (quilting-weight cotton)
* 1 spool of coordinating thread
* Cotton batting
* Double-sided fusible web interfacing
* Up to 10 scraps of contrast fabric, approximately 4" × 4" for each appliqué
* 1 package of ½" double-fold bias tape (pre-packaged, or make your own with scrap fabric)
* Magnetic closure
* Sewing-machine walking foot (optional)

Finished dimensions – approximately 13½" wide × 8" tall (not including straps)

Seam allowance – ½" unless otherwise specified

1 Cut and Quilt the Fabric

Cut the pieces below from the main fabric, leaving 4" along the selvage for the strap. Also cut two of the same size rectangles from the batting.

* **Rectangles.** 20" wide × 18" tall (cut 4)

Lay two fabric rectangles with wrong sides together, and place a layer of batting between them. Pin through all three layers and use a disappearing fabric marker or tailor's chalk to mark the fabric with your choice of quilting lines (you could try diagonal lines at a 45-degree angle, 1" or 2" apart, but any pattern will do). Machine-quilt the layers together following the lines. You may want to use a walking foot, if you have one.

2 Measure, Mark, and Cut

Use the pattern and also measure and mark the following pieces from the remaining quilted fabric.

* **Closure tabs** 3" wide × 3" tall (cut 2)

Cut from nonquilted fabric:

* **Closure tabs** 3" wide × 3" tall (cut 2)
* **Strap** 4" wide × 22" tall (cut 1)

Cut from batting:

* **Strap** 4" wide × 22" tall (cut 1)

3 Make the Circle Appliqués

Fuse double-sided interfacing to the wrong side of each piece of scrap fabric, following manufacturer's instructions. Cut the circles, peel off the paper backing, and fuse the circles to the outside of the bag as desired.

With your sewing machine (and a walking foot, if available) free-motion-stitch a spiral on each circle, beginning at the center and working to the outside edge. The fusible web prevents the outer raw edges from fraying.

4 Assemble the Bag

Staystitch along the outer edge of each bag piece. Fold and pin along dart lines, right sides together, and stitch along dart line. With right sides facing, pin the bag pieces together and stitch along the outer edge.

Trim the seam allowance, if necessary, and pin bias tape around the outer-edge seam allowance, fully encasing raw edges. Stitch, taking care to catch the back side of the bias tape. Enclose the top curved raw edges with bias tape in the same fashion. Do not bind the short top straight edges, which will be turned under during handle placement.

⑤ Make the Closure

Center and attach male side of magnetic closure to right side of one quilted closure tab.

With right sides together, pin this tab to non-quilted tab piece, and stitch along three sides with ¼" seam allowance. Clip corners and turn right side out. Turn under raw edges and press all around.

Repeat to make the other closure tab, using the female side of the magnetic closure. Center the tabs on each side of the bag opening, pinning them to the lining just below binding, and topstitch in place.

⑥ Make and Attach Strap

Pin the batting strap piece to the wrong side of the fabric strap. Edgestitch along all four edges. Press under the raw edges ½". Fold the strap in half lengthwise, wrong sides together, and press. Edgestitch both long edges.

At marks for the strap placement, fold the top raw edges of the bag pieces to the wrong side ½" and press. Insert the short ends of the strap into each side of the bag by at least ½". Edgestitch openings closed, catching strap ends. Stitch again ¼" within seam allowance to reinforce, catching all bag and handle layers.

SCRUNCHIE BAG

Designed by Regina Lord

The scrunched elastic top helps keep all your goodies nice and secure inside this roomy bag. With a festive ribbon on the strap, you're ready with your girlie finest!

MATERIALS

* 1 yard of 44/45" fabric (quilting-weight cotton)
* 1 spool of coordinating thread
* 1¼ yard of ⅝" or ⅞" decorative ribbon
* 1¼ yard of 1" webbing (cotton)

* Three 1½"-diameter metal rings
* 30" of ½" elastic

Finished dimensions — approximately 18" wide × 14½" tall (not including strap)

Seam allowance — ½" unless otherwise specified

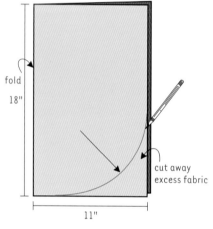

fold

18"

11"

cut away excess fabric

STEP 1
Shaping the bag

① Measure, Mark, and Cut

Cut the yard of fabric into quarters, making four 18" tall × 22" wide pieces. With right sides together, fold one piece in half lengthwise, and draw a curved line on the outside bottom fold as shown. Cut along the line. Unfold the piece and use it as a pattern to cut three more pieces from the remaining fabric.

From the remaining fabric scraps, cut:

* **Ring tabs** 4" × 3" (cut 2)

② Make the Strap and Closure

Cut both the ribbon and the webbing into a 38" piece and a 6" piece. Pin each ribbon piece to the corresponding webbing piece and edgestitch both long sides. Thread one metal ring onto the 6" strap. Fold the strap over about 1" and edgestitch along the short raw edge to secure.

STEP 2   1"

③ Make the Ring Tabs

With right sides together, fold one ring tab in half lengthwise and stitch along the long raw edge. Turn right side out and press. Do the same with the remaining ring tab. Thread one metal ring onto each tab. Fold the tabs in half and edgestitch along the short raw edge to secure.

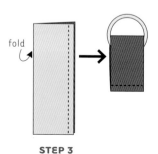

fold

STEP 3

④ Assemble the Bag

To make the exterior, pin two semicircles with right sides together and stitch along the rounded edge. Clip to (but not through) the seam along the curves to ease fullness. Do the same with the remaining pieces to make the lining, leaving 4" open at the bottom for turning.

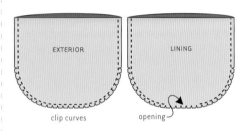

clip curves   opening

STEP 4

⑤ Attach the Ring Tabs

Turn the exterior right side out. On the right side, center the ring tabs at the side seams, aligning raw edges. Pin in place and edgestitch. Center the closure on one side, aligning raw edges. Pin in place and edgestitch.

STEP 5

⑥ Stitch the Lining to the Exterior

With right sides facing, insert the exterior into the lining. Pin around the top edge, with the tabs and closure sandwiched between the layers. Stitch the top raw edge and turn the bag right side out through the hole in the lining. Fold the edges of the opening to the wrong sides and press. Slipstitch the opening closed, and press all around.

⑦ Scrunch the Bottom of the Bag

Lay the bottom of the bag on a flat surface. Cut 6" of elastic and center it on the bottom seam of the bag lining. Pin the center of the elastic to the center of the bag, then stretch the elastic first in one direction and then the other, stitching each side in place, using a zigzag stitch, through all layers.

⑧ Make the Casing

Edgestitch around top edge of the bag. Topstitch 1" away from the first stitching line and once more another ¾" from the second stitching line. These last two stitching lines will form the casing. With a seam ripper, carefully open a lining side seam to insert the remaining elastic. Thread the elastic through the casing, adjust the length, overlap the ends, and stitch together (*see page 19*). Slipstitch the side seam closed.

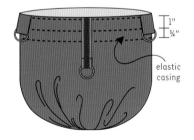

elastic casing

STEP 8

⑨ Attach the Straps

Thread each end of the long strap to each of the side-seam metal rings, fold under, and pin. Check that the length is right for you, make any adjustments, and topstitch to secure (*see page 13*).

Hands-Free Belt Bag

Designed by Rebecca Yaker

You don't have to be a tourist to sport an updated belt bag! It's amazing how many uses these bags have, especially when carrying a purse or other tote is just too much to handle. Perfect for bicycling, long walks, art fairs, and dance-floor nights, this bag will hold it all without the strain on your shoulder or back. As an added bonus, it's fully compatible with the many belts in your wardrobe.

MATERIALS

* 1 yard of 44/45" fabric (preferably home-decor weight)
* 1 spool of coordinating thread
* One 9" coordinating zipper (metal, coil, or molded plastic)
* 1½ yards of 2" webbing
* One pair of 2" D-rings
* 3½" of ¼" elastic
* One 1" swivel clasp
* Sewing-machine zipper foot (optional)

Finished dimensions – 9" wide × 5" tall × 2" deep
Seam allowance – ½" unless otherwise specified

1 Measure, Mark, and Cut

With right sides facing, fold your fabric in half lengthwise, aligning the selvages. Measure and mark the following pattern pieces directly on the wrong side of your fabric, then cut them out. Be efficient with your cutting layout, as you will be cutting several more pieces after you cut these.

* **Bag exterior/lining** 10" wide × 6" tall (cut 4)
* **Top gusset** 10" wide × 1¾" tall (cut 4)
* **Main gusset** 20" wide × 3" tall (cut 2)
* **Pocket flap** 4½" wide × 3" tall (cut 2)
* **Belt loops** 4" wide × 3½" tall (cut 2)

Place the remaining fabric in a single layer with the wrong side facing up.
Measure and mark the following pattern pieces on the wrong side:

* **Interior pocket** 8" wide × 8" tall (cut 1)
* **Pleated pocket** 5" wide × 5" tall (cut 1)
* **Flat pocket** 4½" wide × 4½" tall (cut 1)
* **Swivel-clasp tab** 7" wide × 2½" tall (cut 1)

NOTE: *Place "tall" dimension along the grainline of your fabric.*

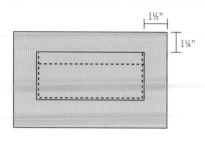

STEP 2
placing the interior pocket

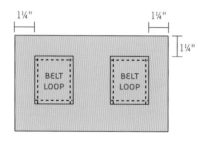

NOTE: *If you will be wearing the bag on a belt that is wider than 2¼" you may need to cut wider belt loops in step 1.*

STEP 4

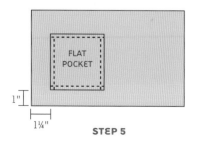

STEP 5

② Make the Interior Pocket

With right sides facing, fold the interior pocket piece in half, aligning the raw edges. Stitch around three sides, leaving a 2" opening along the bottom (8") edge for turning. Clip the corners, turn right side out, and press. Topstitch across the top folded edge at a ¾" allowance.

Center the pocket on one bag lining piece, 1½" in from each side and 1¼" down from the top edge. Edgestitch in place along the side and bottom, leaving the top edge open. This is now the back lining piece.

③ Make the Tab and Attach the Clasp

Fold and press the swivel-clasp tab as you would to make bias tape (*see page* 18). Edgestitch along the long open edge. Fold under one short end ½" and press. Slide the pressed end of the tab through the swivel clasp, turning in another 1" on end, enclosing the clasp. Stitch close to fold. Pin raw edge of tab to right side of back lining 1¼" from top on right edge, aligning raw edges. Baste in place. Set back lining piece aside.

④ Make the Belt Loops

Make a double-fold ¼" hem along the 4" side edges of both belt loops and topstitch close to the folded edges (*see page* 13). Press under the top and bottom edges ½". Position the belt loops on the right side of the back exterior 1¼" down from the top edge and 1¼" in from each edge. Stitch in place along the top and bottom edges of the loops. Set the back exterior aside.

⑤ Make the Flat Pocket

Create a double-fold ¼" hem (*see page* 19) along the top edge of the flat pocket and topstitch close to the folded edge. Press under the side and bottom edges ½" and position the pocket on the left side of the front exterior 1¼" from the left-side edge and 1" up from the bottom edge. Topstitch close to the folded edges.

⑥ Make the Flap

Press under the upper edge of one pocket flap ½". With right sides together, pin the flap pieces together, aligning side and bottom raw edges. Stitch around three sides, leaving the top edge open. Clip corners, turn right side out, and press. Edgestitch the flap at ⅛" along three finished edges. Position the flap over the flat pocket, abutting the raw edge of the flap with the top finished edge of the pocket. Stitch at ½" seam allowance from the raw edge, keeping the pressed edge of the flap facing free. Press the seam allowance of the flap up and tuck it under the pressed facing edge. Press the flap down and topstitch ¼" from the top edge through all layers.

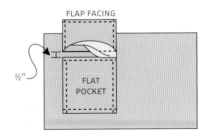

FLAP FACING

½"

FLAT POCKET

STEP 6

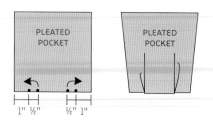

STEP 7

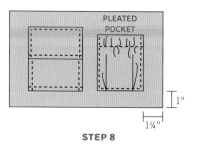

STEP 8

⑦ Make the Pleated Pocket

To form pleats along the bottom edge of the pleated pocket, measure in 1½" from the left edge, pinch fabric, and position pleat ½" to the left. Pin in place. Repeat pleat on the right side of the bottom edge. Baste across bottom edge to hold pleats in place.

⑧ Attach the Pleated Pocket

Press under the top edge of the pleated pocket ¼". Press under another ¾" and topstitch close to the folded edge. Insert elastic into the top edge of the pocket; pin the elastic at one end, and pull it through the opposite opening; baste the elastic in place on both ends. Press under the side and bottom edges ½" and position the pocket on the right side of the front exterior 1¼" from the right-side edge and 1" up from the bottom edge. Topstitch close to folded edges. Set front exterior aside.

⑨ Install the Zipper

Press under one long edge of all top gusset pieces ½". With the folded edge of one gusset piece parallel to the zipper, pin the folded edge to one side of the zipper, ⅛" from the zipper teeth. (Raw short edges of the gusset should extend ½" longer than the zipper at each end.) Topstitch, using a zipper foot. Repeat with the second top gusset piece on the opposite side of the zipper. Trim the zipper tape if necessary. Set the two remaining top gusset pieces aside for the lining.

⑩ Assemble the Gussets

Staystitch the long edges of both main gusset pieces. Place marks along both raw edges 5½" from each end and notch to the staystitch line at these points. These are the pivot points for the corners when attaching the gusset to the bag.

With right sides together, align the short ends of one main gusset piece and the zippered top gusset pieces. Stitch. Press seam allowances toward the main gusset and topstitch at ¼".

⑪ Make the Exterior

With right sides together, pin one front exterior piece to the gusset, aligning the raw edges. Match up gusset notches with bottom corners of the front. (Note that gusset seams will line up with top corners of front.) Stitch, pivoting at corners. Turn right side out, fold the bag and gusset along the seam, and edgestitch ⅛" from the seam around the front exterior. Unzip the zipper, turn the bag wrong side out again, and attach the bag exterior piece to the gusset raw edge in the same way but without the edgestitching.

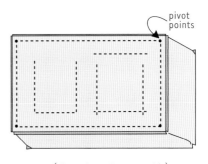

(shown from the wrong side)

STEP 11

⑫ Make the Lining

With right sides together, align the short ends of the other main gusset piece and the top gusset lining pieces. (Note that there will be a ½" gap between the top gusset lining pieces in order to accommodate the zipper.) Stitch and press seam allowances toward the main gusset and topstitch at ¼" on the side of the seam allowance. Using the remaining bag exterior/lining pieces, assemble the gusset lining and bag lining in the same manner as the exterior of the bag, disregarding edgestitching on the front edges. Turn the lining right side out.

⑬ Finish the Bag

With wrong sides together, place the exterior inside the lining. Slipstitch the folded edges of the top gusset to the zipper tape (for a clean edge and to clear the zipper teeth, you will need to turn in the lining seam allowance as you go). Turn the bag right side out. Measure your waist at the location you intend to wear the bag. Add 10" and cut the webbing to this measurement. Create a ½" double-fold hem on one end of the webbing (*see page* 19). On the opposite end, turn under ½" and press. Slide the pressed end of the webbing through the D-rings, turning the end under 1" to enclose the rings. Stitch close to the folded edge. Slide the belt through the loops on the back of the bag and hit the town!

GROCERY TOTE

Designed by Jessie Senese

Replicate that good old brown-paper grocery bag out of your favorite heavier vintage or modern fabric! This version even has nice, crisp, structured side and bottom edges to emphasize that classic boxy shape. You'll never go back to paper or plastic again!

MATERIALS

* 1 yard of 44/45" or 54" fabric (home-decor weight; not suitable for unidirectional prints)
* 1 spool of coordinating thread
* One 5" × 11" piece of heavyweight interfacing (such as Peltex or Timtex)

Finished dimensions – 13" tall × 12" wide × 5½" deep (not including handles)

Seam allowance – ½" unless otherwise specified

① Measure, Mark, and Cut

Place your fabric in a single layer with wrong side facing up. Measure and mark the following pattern pieces directly on the wrong side of your fabric, then cut them out:

* **Bag exterior** 36" tall × 19" wide (cut 1)
* **Bag lining** 36" tall × 19" wide (cut 1)
* **Handles** 18" tall × 4" wide (cut 2)

NOTE: *Place "tall" dimension along the grainline of your fabric.*

② Make the Bag

* With right sides facing, fold the exterior piece in half to make an 18" × 19" rectangle. The folded edge will become the bag bottom. Stitch both sides and the folded bottom, leaving the top open.
* Measuring from the raw edge, mark a 3" square in each bottom corner of the exterior piece. Cut out the square corners and press side seams and bottom seams open.
* Pull bag sides apart at cutout and pinch side and bottom seams together, lining up seams and raw edges. Stitch across corner of bag to create gusset, and zigzag stitch within seam allowance to reinforce gusset. Leave exterior wrong side out.
* Repeat with lining piece to make lining. Turn lining right side out.

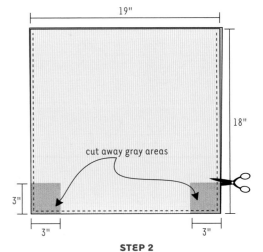

19"

18"

cut away gray areas

3"

3"

3"

STEP 2

❸ Make the Handles

With wrong sides together, fold one strap piece in half lengthwise and press. Open the strap and fold the long raw edges halfway (½") toward the crease on the wrong side and press. Refold the strap in half lengthwise, press, and edgestitch all around. Repeat for the second strap.

❹ Position the Handles

Pin one handle to the right side of the lining, positioning each end of the strap 6" from each side seam, aligning the raw edges of the strap ends with the raw edge of the exterior. Be sure the handle is not twisted and is bending toward the bottom of the bag. Repeat with the second handle on the other side of the lining. Stitch the handles in place with a ¼" seam allowance.

❺ Add the Lining

Place the lining inside exterior with right sides together, sandwiching the handles in between the two layers. Align the side seams and top raw edge. Stitch around the top of the bag, backstitching on each handle for reinforcement, leaving an opening at least 4" wide on one side between the handles for turning.

❻ Finish the Seams

Turn the bag right side out and tuck the lining inside the exterior. Insert the heavyweight interfacing piece through the opening in the liner and position it at the bottom of the bag. Fold under the raw edges of the bag opening ½" and press the top edge. Edgestitch around the top edge, stitching the opening closed as you go.

⑦ Structure the Side Seams

* Using disappearing marker, washable fabric pen, or tailor's chalk, measure and mark a vertical line 3" from each side of both side seams. The bottom of these marks should end at the bottom corners. Pinch and fold all layers of fabric along these marks to create four long vertical creases. Pin in place, being sure to pin through both exterior and lining on both sides of the mark.

* Repeat for the bottom side edges. When pinning the bottom side edges, keep the interfacing (which is about 1" smaller all the way around) out of the pinned seam.

* Edgestitch beginning at the top of one pinned side, topstitch down, stopping ½" from the bottom corner. Keeping the needle in the fabric, pivot to begin stitching along the long bottom pinned edge. Pivot at the next corner in the same fashion to continue stitching up the opposite side. Repeat for the other pinned edges.

* Now grab and go to the grocery store!

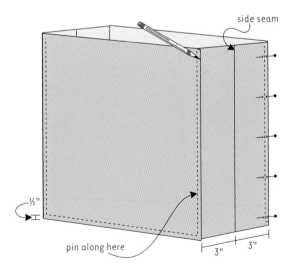

side seam

½"

pin along here

3"   3"

STEP 7

petite Diaper Tote

Designed by Jana Nielson

This diaper purse was created for those times when you are running to the store or zipping out on some other short errand and you don't want to take your giant diaper bag with you. It is also great when your baby is a little older, but you still have daily changing duties.

MATERIALS

* 1 yard of 44/45" fabric (home-decor weight will wear better)
* 1 yard of fusible interfacing
* 1 yard of fusible fleece
* 1 spool of coordinating thread
* 1 magnetic snap
* 7" piece of Velcro
* Sewing-machine walking foot (optional)

Finished dimensions – 7½" wide × 7" tall × 3½" deep
Seam allowance – ½" unless otherwise specified

① Measure, Mark, and Cut

Fold your fabric in half lengthwise with wrong sides together, matching selvages. Measure and mark the following pieces directly on the wrong side of your fabric, then cut them out:

* **Bag exterior** 12" wide × 10" tall (cut 2)
* **Bag lining** 12" wide × 10" tall (cut 2 on fold)
* **Strap** 36" wide × 4" tall (cut 1 on fold)
* **Tab** 8" wide × 6" tall (cut 1 on fold)
* **Changing pad** 16" wide × 22" tall (cut 2)

Cut from fusible interfacing:

* **Bag exterior** 12" wide × 10" tall (cut 2)
* **Strap** 36" wide × 4" tall (cut 1)
* **Tab** 8" wide × 6" tall (cut 1)

Cut from fusible fleece:

* **Changing pad** 16" wide × 22" tall (cut 2)

NOTE: *Place "tall" dimension along the grainline of your fabric.*

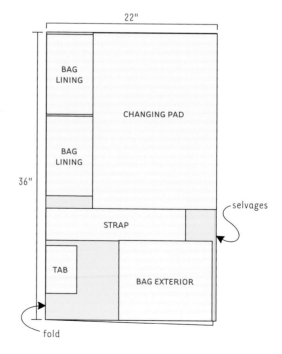

CUTTING LAYOUT

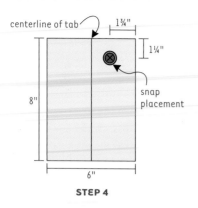

centerline of tab

1¾"

1¼"

8"

snap
placement

6"

STEP 4

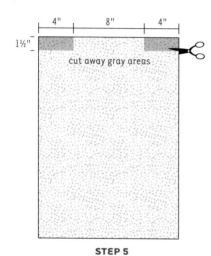

4" 8" 4"

1½"

cut away gray areas

STEP 5

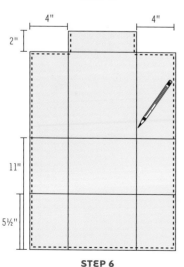

4" 4"

2"

11"

5½"

STEP 6

② Apply Fusible Interfacing

Following manufacturer's instructions, fuse strap interfacing to the wrong side of the strap and tab interfacing to wrong side of tab. Fuse bag exterior interfacings to wrong side of bag exteriors.

③ Make the Strap

Press and stitch the strap as you would to make double-fold bias tape (*see page* 18). Topstitch along both long edges.

④ Make the Tab

On the right side of the tab piece, position the male side of the magnetic snap 1¼" down from top raw edge and 1¾" from right raw edge. Attach snap to tab piece according to manufacturer's instructions.

 With right sides together, fold tab in half lengthwise, aligning raw edges. Stitch across the top and down the open edge, leaving bottom edge open. Clip the corners, turn right side out, and press.

⑤ Make the Changing Pad

* Following manufacturer's instructions, iron fusible fleece to the wrong sides of changing pad pieces. On the wrong side of one of the changing pad pieces, measure down 1½" from the top short end and draw a line. Measure 4" in from each side edge and draw a line perpendicular to the first line. Cut away the two 1½" × 4" rectangles from the top corners. Repeat with second changing pad piece.
* With right sides facing, pin the changing pad pieces together. Stitch around all sides, pivoting at corners. Leave the 8" edge along the top open for turning. Clip all corners, turn right side out and press. Topstitch around all finished edges at ¼".

⑥ Quilt the Changing Pad

Using a disappearing marker, washable fabric pen, or tailor's chalk, mark quilting lines on the changing pad as shown.

Machine-quilt the layers together following your lines. (You may want to use a walking foot.) Fold and press the changing pad along the vertical quilting lines. Repeat, folding and pressing along the horizontal quilting lines.

⑦ Make the Bag Lining

With right sides facing, pin the bag lining pieces together, aligning raw edges. Stitch together along the side and bottom edges, leaving the top open. Using a disappearing marker, washable fabric pen, or tailor's chalk, mark a 2" square in each bottom corner, measuring from the raw edges. Cut out square corners as shown.

Press the seams open. Match side seam with bottom seam, and stitch across the corner of the bag. Press the seam open. Repeat with the second corner. Press under the top edge ½".

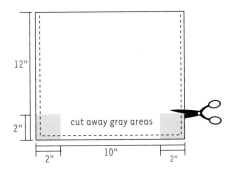

STEP 7

⑧ Assemble the Exterior

With right sides facing, pin the bag exterior pieces together. Stitch side seams, leaving bottom seam open. Slide the changing pad in between the bag exterior pieces and center the changing pad's 8" raw edge along the bottom raw edge of the exterior pieces. Pin together and stitch across the bottom edge of the bag, through all layers. Assemble the bottom corners of the bag exterior, as you did with the lining in step 7. Turn the exterior right side out (note that the changing pad will be folded into the back of the bag). Attach the female side of the snap on the center front of the bag's exterior, 1½" down from the top edge. Center 7" of Velcro's loop side on the side of the changing pad facing away from the bag back, below and parallel to the 11" quilting line from step 6. Stitch in place. Fold up the changing pad and mark the position of the loop Velcro on the back of the bag. Stitch the hook Velcro in this location. This will secure the folded changing pad when it is not in use.

⑨ Finish the Bag

Center raw edge of tab (snap side up) on the back of the bag exterior. Stitch in place at ½" seam allowance. Center each strap end on a side seam on the right side of bag exterior, matching raw edges (making sure strap is not twisted). Stitch across the edges at ½" seam allowance. Press under the top open edge of bag exterior ½". Place lining inside exterior, matching side seams. Stitch around the top of the bag at ¼". Your diaper purse is done: fill it with wipes, diapers, a bottle, your wallet . . . and run!!

Latte Changing Pad

Designed by Anne Lindholt Ottosen

This compact changing pad and sleeve can hold a small package of wet wipes and two or three toddler diapers. It is intended for the toddler mom who no longer needs a big diaper bag, as it can be rolled up and tucked right inside your purse. Perfect for a trip to the coffee shop!

MATERIALS

* 1 yard of 44/45" fabric (home-decor weight will wear better)
* ⅓ yard of fleece
* 1 spool of coordinating thread
* 1" piece of Velcro
* 1 yard of coordinating ribbon, up to ½"

Finished dimensions – Pad and sleeve are 7" wide × 11" long
Seam allowance – ½" unless otherwise specified

① **Measure, Mark, and Cut**

Place your fabric in a single layer with the wrong side facing up. Measure and mark the following pieces directly on the wrong side of your fabric, then cut them out:

* <u>Sleeve exterior</u> 7" wide × 22" tall (cut 1)
* <u>Sleeve lining</u> 7" wide × 22" tall (cut 1)
* <u>Flap</u> 7" wide × 4" tall (cut 2)
* <u>Changing pad</u> 11" wide × 24" tall (cut 2)

Cut from fleece:

* <u>Changing pad</u> 11" wide × 24" tall (cut 1)

NOTE: *Place "tall" dimension along the grainline of your fabric.*

② **Make the Sleeve Exterior and Lining**

With right sides together, fold the sleeve lining in half crosswise, aligning short raw edges. Stitch along the sides, leaving top short edge open. Clip corners. Repeat with the exterior pieces. Turn the exterior piece right side out, and press.

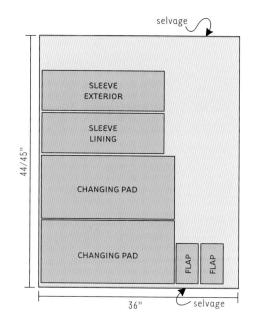

CUTTING LAYOUT

❸ Make the Flap

Create two rounded corners on one long edge of the flap: With right sides together, align flap pieces and place a standard drinking glass upside down on one bottom corner. Using a fabric pen, trace the portion of glass that falls within the seam allowance. Trim away the excess fabric. Repeat this step for the opposite corner. With right sides together, pin the flap pieces together along the sides and curved edge, leaving the straight edge open. Stitch. Notch the seam around curve, turn the right side out, and press. Topstitch along the finished edge. Stitch the hook side of the Velcro piece in the center of the flap, ½" from the edge. (Note that the side of the flap with Velcro is the wrong side.)

❹ Assemble the Sleeve

With right sides together, center the flap (with the Velcro facing away from the bag) between the side seams on the top edge of the sleeve exterior, aligning raw edges. Stitch in place with a scant ¼" seam allowance. Place the sleeve exterior inside the lining, right sides facing, sandwiching the flap in the center, aligning side seams and raw edges. Stitch around the top edge, leaving a 4" opening for turning on the side opposite the flap. Turn right side out and press. Press under the edges of the opening ½" and edgestitch around the top of the sleeve. Position the loop side of the Velcro piece on the front center of the sleeve, 1½" from the finished edge. Stitch in place.

❺ Make the Changing Pad

Place the changing pad pieces with right sides together, aligning raw edges. Position both changing pad pieces on top of the fleece and pin together through all layers. Stitch around all four sides, leaving a 4" opening along the bottom short end. Clip corners, turn right side out so that the fleece is the center layer, and press. Topstitch ¼" from the edge around all four sides of the pad, closing the opening used for turning. Mark the center of the ribbon. Position the center point of the ribbon 7" down from the top edge of the changing pad, with the length of the ribbon parallel to the long edge. Stitch in place at the center mark. Hem or knot the ribbon ends to keep them from fraying. Your sleeve will store compactly inside the changing pad.

CHAPTER 8

OUTFIT YOUR SMALL WONDER

Every child deserves to look fantastic, and it's up to you to make this happen! One-yard clothing options are almost limitless for children. We've got irresistible, adorable outfits for wee ones from newborn on up to school age! A baby jacket will make a quick, easy gift for all those showers, and you can also keep that little one well dressed in a smart selection of skirts, jumpers, tops, and dresses.

NEWBORN FLYAWAY JACKET

Designed by Anna Buchholz

This is the perfect cozy little jacket for the newborn in your life. The size range is 0 to 3 months, but could easily go up to 6-month size by adding a little extra to the sleeve length. Make several for your baby or to give as gifts.

MATERIALS

* Locate the pattern in the front pocket (sheet #1)
* 1 yard of 44/45" fabric (flannel recommended; not suitable for unidirectional prints)
* 1 spool of coordinating thread
* 1 package of ½" double-fold bias tape
* 1 sew-in snap

Size – 0-3 months
Seam allowance – ½" unless otherwise specified

① Measure, Mark, and Cut

With right sides together, fold your fabric in half lengthwise, aligning the selvages. Place the pattern on the fabric as shown. Transfer markings from all pattern pieces to wrong side of fabric. Cut out the jacket, leaving the back center fold intact and cutting through the front center fold to make the front opening of the jacket.

NOTE: *Place pattern piece along the grainline of your fabric.*

② Stitch the Sides

With right sides together, stitch sleeve and side seams, matching notches and pivoting at underarm. Carefully clip seam to stitching at underarm pivot point. Press seams open and turn jacket right side out.

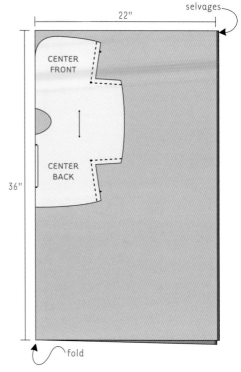

CUTTING LAYOUT

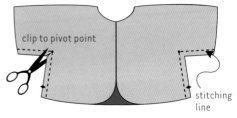

STEP 2

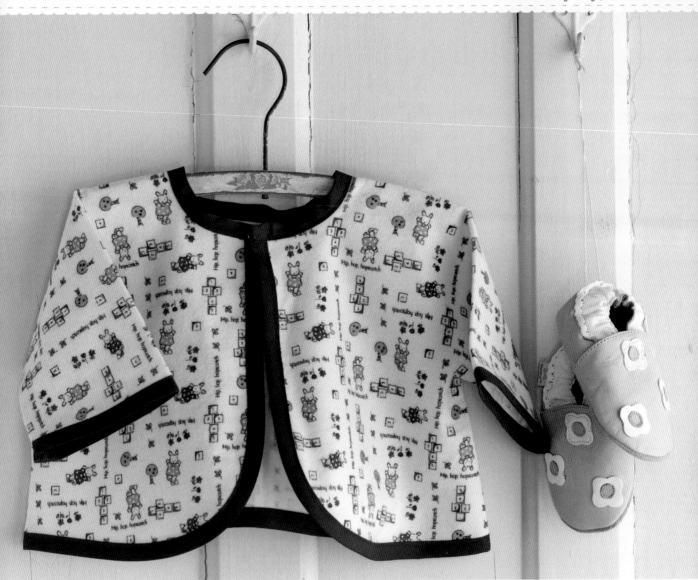

③ Bind the Edges

Pin double-fold bias tape along bottom edge and around jacket front openings and neck, enclosing all fabric raw edges in bias tape. Repeat with sleeve ends. Stitch bias tape in place, making sure to catch the back side of the bias tape in stitching (*see page* 18).

④ Add the Neck Closure

At neckline, overlap top jacket fronts slightly to determine the placement of the snap. Mark. Hand-sew one side of the snap to each side of the jacket.

TODDLER PINAFORE SMOCK TOP

Designed by Donna Pedaci

The pinafore smock top is open in back and ties with a ribbon bow. It has a square neckline and empire waist. It's the perfect feminine year-round look for your little girl. Wear with pants and shirt in cold weather, over shorts or a skirt in warm weather.

MATERIALS

* Locate the pattern in the front pocket (sheet #1)
* 1 yard of 44/45" fabric (quilting-weight cotton, not suitable for unidirectional fabric)
* 1 spool of coordinating thread
* 1½ yards of ⅝" coordinating ribbon, cut into two 27" pieces
* 2 buttons (for embellishment)

Sizes – 2T-4T

Seam allowance – ½" unless otherwise specified

1 Determine Your Child's Size

Determine which smock size you are going to make based on the child's chest size.

Toddler size	2T	3T	4T
Chest size	21"	22"	23"

2 Measure, Mark, and Cut

Place your fabric in a single layer with wrong side facing up, then fold one selvage end over about 7" or 8", enough to accommodate the bodice pattern pieces in the correct size. Place the pieces as shown, and measure and mark the pieces listed. Cut everything out and transfer ribbon placement markings to the wrong side of the fabric.

* **Bodice front** (cut 2 on fold)
* **Bodice back** (cut 4)
* **Skirt front** 28" wide × 18" tall (cut 1)
* **Skirt back** 14" wide × 18" tall (cut 2)

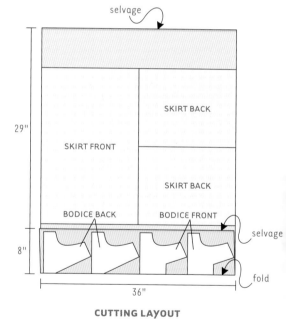

CUTTING LAYOUT

NOTE: *Place "tall" dimensions and pattern pieces along the grainline of your fabric.*

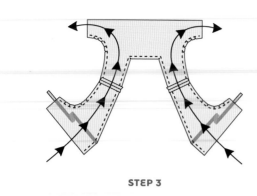

STEP 3

❸ Assemble the Bodice

With right sides together, stitch one bodice front to one bodice back at the shoulders. Press seams open. Repeat with the second bodice pieces — these will form a lining. With right sides together, pin the bodice lining to the bodice exterior, matching side seams. Stitch around armholes. Clip curved seam allowance around armhole to, but not through, the stitching line.

Pin each piece of ribbon on the right side of bodice backs, centering the ends over the placement dots. Sandwich ribbons between the lining and exterior with all raw edges even. Stitch around entire neckline and back opening. Clip corners on front neckline to, but not through, the seam allowance. Turn right side out. Press.

Open out lining at sides to work top and lining separately. Pin top front piece to back pieces at side seams, right sides together, aligning raw edges. Stitch, and press seams open. In a similar manner, pin lining sections together, stitch, and press seams open.

❹ Make the Skirt

With right sides together, stitch skirt back pieces to skirt front at side seams. Press seams open. Stitch a narrow double-fold hem along skirt-back raw edges (*see page* 19).

❺ Attach the Skirt and Bodice

Use a basting stitch to gather the top raw edge of the skirt (*see page* 13). With right sides together and raw edges even, pin the bodice front to the skirt, matching side seams, and adjusting the skirt gathers to fit. Stitch in place, taking care not to catch the bodice lining in your seam. Press seam toward the bodice. Press under the bottom raw edge of lining ½", and slipstitch in place over gathered seam of skirt, covering seam.

❻ Add the Finishing Touches

Press under a 2" double-fold hem on lower edge of skirt and stitch in place (*see page* 19). Sew buttons to the bodice front for a little extra embellishment. Either hem the ends of the ribbon ties or use a pair of pinking shears to snip the ends to prevent fraying.

ALL-AGES CLASSIC JUMPER

Designed by Amanda Sasikirana

This simple jumper has a wide band and straps with elastic in the back to ensure a perfect fit. You can adjust the length to make it a jumper, tunic, or top.

MATERIALS

* ✳ 1 yard of 44/45" fabric (any weight/content, not suitable for unidirectional prints)
* ✳ 1 spool of coordinating thread
* ✳ ½ yard of 1" elastic
* ✳ ¼ yard lightweight fusible interfacing
* ✳ Two 1" buttons

Sizes — 6, 12, 18, and 24 months; 2T–5T
Seam allowance — ½" unless otherwise specified

❶ Determine Your Child's Size

Determine which jumper size you are going to make based on the child's chest size.

Infant sizes	6 months	12 months	18 months	24 months
Chest size	17"	18"	19"	20"

Toddler sizes	2T	3T	4T	5T
Chest size	21"	22"	23"	24"

❷ Mark, Measure, and Cut

Place your fabric in a single layer with wrong side facing up. Select the appropriate size and, following the layout, measure and mark the following pattern pieces directly on the wrong side of your fabric, then cut them out:

Infant sizes	6 months	12 months	18 months	24 months
Piece dimensions	wide × tall	wide × tall	wide × tall	wide × tall
Skirt front/back (cut 2)	15½" × 12"	16½" × 13"	17½" × 14"	18½" × 15"
Top band, front (Fabric: cut 1) (Interfacing: cut 1)	10" × 5"	10½" × 5"	11" × 5"	11½" × 5"
Top band, back (cut 1)	15½" × 5"	16½" × 5"	17½" × 5"	18½" × 5"
Straps (cut 2)	11½" × 5"	12" × 5"	12½" × 5"	13" × 5"
Elastic (cut 1)	10" long	10½" long	11" long	11½" long

Toddler Sizes	2T	3T	4T	5T
Piece dimensions	wide × tall	wide × tall	wide × tall	wide × tall
Skirt front/back (cut 2)	19½" × 16"	20½" × 17"	21½" × 18"	22" × 19"
Top band, front (Fabric: cut 1) (Interfacing: cut 1)	12" × 5"	12½" × 5"	13" × 5"	13½" × 5"
Top band, back (cut 1)	19½" × 5"	20½" × 5"	21½" × 5"	22" × 5"
Straps (cut 2)	13½" × 5"	14" × 5"	14½" × 5"	15" × 5"
Elastic (cut 1)	12" long	12½" long	13" long	13½" long

NOTE: *Place "tall" dimensions along the grainline of your fabric.*

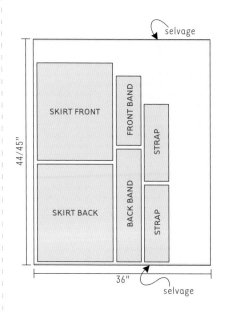

CUTTING LAYOUT

❸ Make the Straps

Press under the short ends of the straps ½". Press under both long edges ½". Press and fold the straps in half lengthwise with wrong sides together, aligning folded edges. Topstitch ⅛" from the edge around all four sides of both straps.

❹ Make the Top Band

Iron the interfacing to the wrong side of the band front according to manufacturer's instructions. With right sides together, pin the short ends of the front and back bands together and stitch. Press seams open. Press under the top raw edge of the bands ½". (Note that the back band is longer than the front.)

⑤ Stitch the Skirt

Use a basting stitch to gather the top edge of the skirt front (*see page* 13). With right sides and raw edges together, stitch the skirt front and back pieces together along the side seams, keeping basting threads free. Press seams open.

⑥ Join the Skirt and Bands

With right sides together, pin the raw, unfolded edge of the band with the top of the skirt, matching side seams. Adjust the skirt front gathers to fit the front band, pinning in place as you work the gathers. Stitch around the top edge. Press the seam allowance toward the band.

⑦ Place and Attach the Straps

Place the straps on the back band 3" from the side seams (for sizes 6 months to 24 months) or 4" (for sizes 2T to 5T). Box stitch a 1¾" square to secure the straps to the band (*see page* 14).

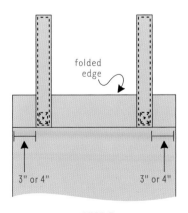

folded edge

3" or 4"   3" or 4"

STEP 7
strap placement

⑧ Finish the Band

Fold the band in half with wrong sides together so that the folded edge covers the gathered skirt seam. Pin the band in place from the outside. On the right side of the jumper, topstitch the band ⅛" from the seam, making sure that you catch the inside edge of the band and enclose the gathered edge of the skirt. Leave a 2" opening at both side seams.

⑨ Insert the Elastic

Insert the elastic into the back band, pinning each end to the side seams to secure. Stitch the elastic in place along the side seams through all layers. Topstitch both openings closed.

⑩ Finish the Jumper

Make vertical buttonholes 1" from the end of each strap to accommodate your buttons. For sizes 6 months to 24 months, center the buttons on the front band 2½" from the side seams. For sizes 2T to 5T, center the buttons on the front band 3" from the side seams. Stitch a narrow ½" double-fold hem along the bottom edge of the skirt (*see page* 19).

STRAPLESS BANDEAU SHORTY JUMPER

Designed by Stephanie Sterling

Inspired by an adult-sized halter-top jumper, but nowhere near as saucy as the 1980s version, this rendition takes on a life of its own when your little one puts it into action. You may want to consider adding straps (either shoulder or halter) for some extra playground fun!

MATERIALS

* Locate the pattern in the front pocket (sheet #3)
* 1 yard of fabric (for 2T-4T: 44/45"; for 5T: 54"/60")
* 1 spool of coordinating thread
* 2 decorative buttons
* Two 1" D-rings
* ½ yard of ¼" elastic

Sizes – 2T-5T

Seam allowance – ½" unless otherwise specified

① Determine Your Child's Size

Sizing is determined according to the chest and waist measurement.

Toddler size	2T	3T	4T	5T
Chest size	21"	22"	23"	24"
Waist size	20"	20½"	21"	21½"

② Measure, Mark, and Cut

Fold your fabric in half lengthwise, with right sides together, aligning the selvages. Place the pattern pieces, and mark and measure the piece below. Cut out the pieces and transfer markings from all pattern pieces to wrong side of the fabric.

* **Front and back** cut 4
* **Belt** 26" wide × 2¾" tall (cut 1)

NOTE: *Place "tall" dimensions and pattern pieces along the grainline of your fabric.*

③ Stitch the Jumper

With right sides together, pin one front piece and back piece together, and stitch along the inside leg seam. Press seam open. Repeat with the second set of front and back pieces. With right sides together, stitch the center seam from front to back along the curve, matching inner leg seams. Stitch again at a ¼" seam allowance to reinforce this seam. Trim the seam allowance close to the second stitching line to eliminate bulk. With right sides together, pin and stitch the front and back along the side seams. Press seams open.

④ Make the Casing

Place the elastic around the child's upper chest under her arms, stretching it slightly until it feels comfortable. Add ¾" to that measurement and cut. To make the casing, press under the upper edge of jumper ¼", then press under another ½". Stitch in place close to the fold, leaving a 1" opening at the side seam. Thread elastic through casing, overlapping the ends ½", and stitch them together securely. Stitch the casing opening closed (*see page* 19).

⑤ Make the Belt

Press under both short ends of the belt ½". Fold and press the belt as you would to make bias tape (*see page* 18). Topstitch around all four edges. Insert one end of the belt through both D-rings, fold end over ¾", and stitch close to the rings to secure.

⑥ Add the Finishing Touches

Finish the leg openings with a ½" narrow hem (*see page* 19). Sew two decorative buttons at center front underneath the elastic casing.

summer fun play top

Designed by Maggie Bunch

This lined play top is roomy enough to wear a T-shirt or turtleneck underneath, extending the lifetime of the garment through all four seasons. It's so cute, your little one is going to want it in her wardrobe all year long.

MATERIALS

* Locate the pattern in the front pocket (sheet #2)
* 1 yard of 44/45" fabric (quilting-weight cotton)
* 1 spool of coordinating thread
* Three ½" buttons

Sizes – 2T-6T

Seam allowance – ½" unless otherwise specified

❶ Determine Your Child's Size

Determine which play-top size you are going to make based on your child's chest size.

Toddler size	2T	3T	4T	5T	6T
Chest size	21"	22"	23"	24"	25"

❷ Measure, Mark, and Cut

Place your fabric in a single layer with wrong side facing up. Measure and mark the following pattern piece directly on the wrong side of your fabric along one edge, then cut it out:

* **Peplum** 43" wide × 5" tall (cut 1)

After cutting out the peplum piece, fold your remaining fabric in half lengthwise, right sides together, aligning the selvages. Select the appropriate-size pattern pieces, place them on the fabric, and cut them out. Transfer markings to the wrong side of the fabric.

* **Front** (cut 2 on fold)
* **Back** (cut 4)

③ Stitch the Sides

With right sides together, stitch one front to one back at the shoulders. Press seams open. Repeat with the other two pieces – these will form the lining. With right sides together, pin the exterior to the lining, matching side seams. Stitch around armholes, neckline, and back opening. Clip seam allowance around armhole and neckline curves to, but not through, the stitching line. Turn right side out, as shown by the arrows, and press.

Open out the lining at the sides to work the top and lining separately. Pin the top front piece to the back pieces at the side seams, right sides together, aligning raw edges. Stitch, and press seams open. In a similar manner, pin the lining sections together, stitch, and press seams open.

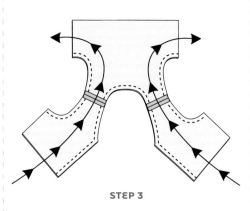

STEP 3

④ Make the Peplum

Fold the peplum in half lengthwise with right sides together and stitch the short ends, in a curve if desired. Clip corners or curved edge, turn right side out, and press. Along the raw edge, place a mark at 4½", 16½", 25½", and 37½". Use a basting stitch to gather the seam allowance between these marks (*see* diagram).

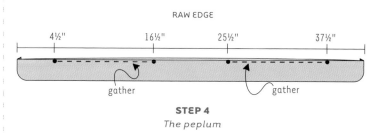

RAW EDGE

4½" 16½" 25½" 37½"

gather   gather

STEP 4
The peplum

⑤ Attach the Peplum to the Top

With right sides together, pin the peplum to the bottom edge of the top exterior, leaving the lining free, matching center front, both ends, and all four dots. Adjust the peplum gathers to fit the top, centering gathers over the side seams. Pin in place as you work the gathers. Stitch together, taking care not to catch the lining in your stitching. Press seam toward the top. Press under the raw edge of the lining ½", and slipstitch in place, covering the seam.

⑥ Make the Buttonholes

Make horizontal buttonholes on the right back, as indicated on the pattern, taking care to make buttonholes the right size for your chosen buttons. The second buttonhole should be centered between the top and bottom button placement lines. Sew on the buttons.

"TWIST & SHOUT" TWIRL SKIRT

Designed by Maggie Bunch

Come on and work it on out! This is the perfect comfortable and stylish skirt for your preschool-age girl to pull on for rocking out.

MATERIALS

* ✳ 1 yard of 44/45" fabric (quilting-weight cotton; not suitable for unidirectional prints)
* ✳ 1 spool of coordinating thread
* ✳ 1 yard of ½" elastic
* ✳ 1 yard of ⅛" piping (prepackaged or make your own)
* ✳ Sewing-machine zipper foot

Sizes — Adjustable, fits up to a 27" waist
Seam allowance — ½" unless otherwise specified

① Determine Your Child's Size

This skirt pattern is appropriate for preschool-age girls, fitting ages 2 to 5. (You will adjust the waist elastic according to your child's size.) The main difference between the sizes is often as simple as adjusting the skirt length. These instructions make a skirt with a finished length of 14½", but if you need to make it longer or shorter, simply increase or decrease the tall measurement of the skirt piece by the appropriate amount.

② Measure, Mark, and Cut

Place your fabric in a single layer with wrong side facing up. Following the layout, measure and mark the following pattern pieces directly on the wrong side of your fabric, then cut them out:

* ✳ <u>**Yoke and waistband**</u> 6" wide × 30" tall (cut 1)
* ✳ <u>**Skirt front/back**</u> 30" wide × 9" tall (cut 2)
* ✳ <u>**Bias strip (for binding)**</u> 2" × 32" (cut 4)
* ✳ <u>**Bias strip (for piping)**</u> 1" × 32" (cut 4)

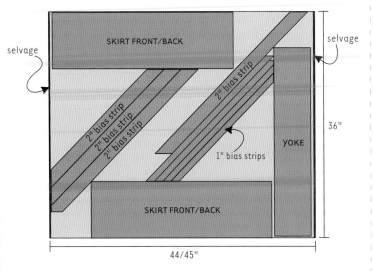

CUTTING LAYOUT

NOTE: *Place "tall" dimensions along the grainline of your fabric.*

❸ Make the Binding and Piping

* Stitch short ends of all 2" bias strips together to make one long strip. Press seams open. Fold and press this strip to make bias tape (*see page* 18).

* To make the custom piping, stitch short ends of all 1" bias strips together to make one long strip. Press seams open. Make the piping (*see page* 20), using a long stitch and a zipper foot to stitch binding close to the piping.

❹ Stitch the Yoke and Waistband

Align raw edges of piping to bottom raw edge of yoke on the right side. Stitch together using zipper foot. With right sides facing, fold the yoke piece in half crosswise, and stitch the short ends together. Press seam open. Turn and press ¼" of upper yoke edge to the wrong side. Then turn and press another 1". Stitch in place, close to the fold, leaving a 2" opening at the side seam. Measure elastic around your child's waist for a comfortable fit, and cut. Thread the elastic through the casing, overlapping the ends ½" and stitching them together securely. Stitch the casing opening closed (*see page* 19).

❺ Stitch the Skirt

With right sides together, pin and stitch the skirt side seams (the short edges). Press seams open. Use a basting stitch to gather the top edge of the skirt (*see page* 13).

❻ Attach the Yoke and the Skirt

With right sides together, align the raw edges of the yoke and attached piping with the top of the skirt, matching side seams. Adjust the skirt gathers to fit the yoke, pinning in place as you work the gathers. Stitch in place and press the seam allowance toward the skirt. (The piping will show on the front of the skirt.)

❼ Hem the Skirt with Bias Tape

Open up bias tape. Pin long raw edge of right side of the tape to the wrong side of skirt hem. Press bias strip up and over the raw edge of the skirt to the right side of the skirt. Pin in place and topstitch the bias strip close to the folded edge, making sure to catch the back edge of the bias tape as you go.

BaLLeT-NeCK TODDLeR DReSS

Designed by Rachael Theis

This is the modern-day variation on the classic pillowcase dress. The one-size-fits-many styling is very forgiving, as the elastic waist will help you adjust the size as needed. The dress is intended to be worn long, but if you've got a particularly tall girl, she can throw on a pair of leggings and be good to go.

MATERIALS

* Locate the pattern in the front pocket (sheet #2)
* 1 yard of 44/45" fabric (quilting-weight cotton)
* 1 spool of coordinating thread
* 1 package of ½" single-fold bias tape
* 2 yards of ¼" elastic
* 1½ yards of trim for the bottom edge (optional)

Sizes – 2T-6T
Seam allowance – ½" unless otherwise specified

➊ Measure, Mark, and Cut

Fold fabric in half lengthwise along the grainline with right sides together, aligning selvages. Measure and mark the following pattern pieces directly on the wrong side of your fabric, then cut them out:

* **Front and back** 22" wide × 36" tall (cut 2)

NOTE: *Place "tall" dimensions along the grainline of your fabric.*

➋ Assemble the Pieces

With right sides together, stitch front and back at both long edges, which are the side seams. When sewing the left side seam, stitch 5" down from the top edge, leave a ¾" opening, then continue stitching the seam. (The gap later serves as the opening for the neck casing.) Press seams open. Make a narrow ¼" hem at top edge (*see page* 19). Fold and press another 5½" to the wrong side along the top edge to create an armhole facing for step 3. Topstitch ⅝" from the folded top edge.

➌ Cut the Armholes

Place the dress right side out with the front piece on top. Position sleeve template on the top right-hand corner of the dress, aligning the top edge and side seam. Trace the armhole cutting line onto the dress and cut through all layers of fabric. Repeat on the left side of the dress. (You may need to reinforce the side seams where the armhole has been cut.)

4 Finish the Armholes

On the dress piece, staystitch around the armhole opening ¼" from the cutting line. Repeat staystitching on the armhole facing. (*Note:* Do not stitch through both layers at once.) Make angular cuts from the end of the armhole opening toward the corners of the staystitching, being careful to clip to (but not through) your stitching line.

Notch the seam around the curved edge, taking care to not clip through staystitching. Neatly turn the armhole raw edge ¼" to the wrong side at the newly formed armhole opening on both the dress and the facing. Invisibly slipstitch the two folded edges together to finish the armhole, on both the bottom (concave) edge and the top (convex) edge of the armhole.

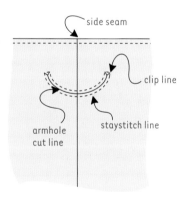

STEP 4

5 Make the Belt Casing

Determine belt placement based on child's size:

Toddler size	2T	3T	4T	5T	6T
Placement below armhole	3¼"	4"	4¾"	5½"	6¼"

Press one end of the single-fold bias tape ½" to the wrong side. Pin folded edge of bias tape onto the right side of the dress at the desired position beginning at one side seam. Pin the bias tape around the waist, abutting the ends of the bias tape but leaving them open. Neatly edgestitch in place along both long sides of tape, leaving ends open at side seam. Measure the elastic around your child's waist, add an extra 1", and cut. Thread the elastic through the casing, overlapping the ends ½", and stitching together securely. Hand-sew the casing opening closed (*see page* 19).

6 Finish the Neck Edge

Thread a 20" piece of elastic into the neck casing, overlapping the ends ½" and stitching them together securely. Hand-sew the casing opening closed (*see page* 19).

7 Hem the Dress

Try the dress on your child to determine finished length and make a double-fold hem accordingly (*see page* 19). You may also choose to add a row or two of trim around the bottom edge and sleeves.

PLEATED GIRLY SKIRT

Designed by Rebecca Yaker

A plethora of pleats makes this skirt pleasing for toddler girls who love to twirl! (And what toddler girl doesn't?) When you're done, crank up some up-tempo tunes and watch your dervish work the pleats of this cute little number!

MATERIALS

* 1 yard of 44/45" fabric (any weight/content will do)
* 1 spool of coordinating thread
* ¾ yard of ¾" elastic
* 1¼ yard grosgrain ribbon, rickrack trim, or embellishment (optional)

Sizes – 2T, 4T, 6T

Seam allowance – ½" unless otherwise specified

① Determine Your Child's Size

Sizing is determined according to the waist measurement.

Toddler size	2T	4T	6T
Waist size	22"	24"	26"

② Measure, Mark, and Cut

Fold your fabric in half lengthwise, with right sides together, aligning the selvages. Measure and mark the following pattern pieces directly on the wrong side of your fabric, then cut them out:

Toddler size	2T	4T	6T
Piece dimensions	wide × tall	wide × tall	wide × tall
Skirt front and back (cut 2)	18" × 10"	19¼" × 11½"	20½" × 12½"
Waistband (cut 1)	23" × 3"	25½" × 3"	27½" × 3"

NOTE: *Place "tall" dimensions along the grainline of your fabric.*

③ Make the Pleats

Fold the skirt front in half, with right sides together, aligning the side raw edges. Press a light crease on this folded edge to mark the center. Along the top raw edge, measure and

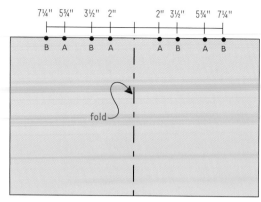

7¼" 5¾" 3½" 2"   2" 3½" 5¾" 7¼"

B A B A   A B A B

fold

NOTE: *Pleat placement is the same for all three skirt sizes.*

STEP 3

mark a point 2" on each side of the center crease. Both of these marks are called A. Measure and mark two more points called A, each 5¾" on each side of the center crease.

Also along the top edge, measure and mark four points called B: the first two should be placed 3½" away from the center crease; and the second set placed should be 7¼" away from the center crease. (The B marks are 1½" away from the A marks.)

Fold and press points A toward points B toward the outside edges of the skirt front to create two pleats on each side of center. Press pleats in place and machine-baste along upper edge to secure the pleats. Repeat pleat placement for the skirt back.

4 Stitch the Sides

With right sides together and raw edges aligned, pin and stitch the side seams of the front and back skirt sections. Press seams open.

5 Add the Waistband

With right sides together, stitch the short ends of the waistband together, forming a loop. Press seam open. Press under the top raw edge of the waistband ½". With right sides facing, pin raw edges of the skirt and waistband together, matching up the side seams. Stitch and press the seam allowance toward the waistband.

6 Make the Casing

Fold the waistband in half, toward the inside of the skirt, so that the folded edge overlaps and covers the seam. On the inside of the skirt, slipstitch the waistband in place, leaving a 2" opening at one side seam for inserting the elastic. Cut elastic the appropriate length to snugly but comfortably fit around your little one's belly, adding an extra 1". Thread the elastic through the waistband casing, overlap the ends ½" and stitch together securely. Stitch the casing opening closed (*see page* 19).

7 Hem the Skirt

Press under the bottom edge of the skirt ¼", then press under another ¾" and stitch close to the pressed edge.

8 Add Embellishing Touches

In this optional step, you may choose to add a row of grosgrain ribbon or rickrack (with a little bow, of course) around the bottom of the skirt, or put ball fringe at the hem — you name it! If you decide to add trim, always measure and use pins: you don't want your end result to look crooked!

CHAPTER 9

ACCESSORIZE YOUR LITTLE ONE

As children get growing and start exploring, equip them with the right accessories and tools for work and play. Make your budding carpenter a tool belt or your precocious artist a smock. Chart their progress with a personalized growth chart, or give them a dinner-table boost with a beanbag booster seat.

mini CRAFT & TOOL BELT

Designed by Mellissa Abreu

Help your creative little one make the most of his or her time at the easel or the workbench. Tie on this little apron and fill with a generous helping of crayons or mini tools. Now step back and watch the imagination take flight!

MATERIALS

* 1 yard of 44/45" fabric (any weight will do)
* 1 spool of coordinating thread
* ¼ yard lightweight fusible interfacing

Size – Small (toddler, up to 3T) and Large (child, up to 6)

Seam allowance – ½" unless otherwise specified

① Measure, Mark, and Cut

Fold your fabric in half lengthwise, with right sides together, aligning the selvages. Measure and mark the following pattern pieces directly onto the wrong side of your fabric, then cut them out:

Piece dimensions	Small (toddler size) wide × tall	Large (child size) wide × tall
Apron (cut 2)	13½" × 9"	15½" × 10½"
Waistband (cut 1)	13½" × 5"	15½" × 6"
Ties (cut 2)	23½" × 5"	23½" × 6"
Pocket (cut 2 from fabric) (cut 1 from interfacing)	10½" × 4"	12½" × 4"

NOTE: *Place "tall" dimensions along the grainline of your fabric.*

② Prepare the Pocket

Iron interfacing to the wrong side of one pocket piece according to the manufacturer's instructions. With right sides facing, pin pocket pieces together, stitching around all four sides, leaving a 2" opening along the bottom edge for turning. Clip corners, turn right side out, and press. Topstitch around all four edges at a ¼" allowance.

③ Assemble the Apron

With right sides facing, pin apron pieces together. Stitch around both sides and bottom edges, leaving top edge open. Clip corners, turn right side out, and press. Topstitch around three finished sides of the apron with a ⅛" allowance.

④ Place the Pocket

Center the pocket, right side up, on the right side of the apron, 1½" from the side edges. For the toddler size, place the pocket 2½" up from the bottom edge; for the child size, place the pocket 3½" up from the bottom edge. Topstitch three sides of the pocket to the apron at a ⅛" allowance, leaving the top edge open. (You will have two lines of stitching around the pocket edge.)

⑤ Make Crayon Pockets

Topstitch vertical lines through the pocket and apron starting on the left side of the pocket. Place the first line 1" from the pocket's left edge. For the toddler size, draw and stitch four more lines, each 1" away from the previous line; for the child size, draw and stitch six lines.

⑥ Attach the Waistband

Turn both short edges of the waistband under ½" to the wrong side and press. Turn one long side of the waistband under ½" to the wrong side and press. With right sides together, pin the raw edge of the waistband to the top raw edge of the apron front. Stitch in place. With wrong sides facing, fold the waistband in half lengthwise to the back of the apron and press. Topstitch ⅛" from the edge along the top and bottom edge of the waistband, making sure to catch the back fold of the waistband in the stitching line. Leave waistband ends open.

⑦ Make the Ties

Fold one apron tie in half lengthwise, with right sides together, aligning raw edges. Stitch along the long, raw edge and one short end, leaving the other short end open. Clip corners, turn right side out, and press. Topstitch around all three finished edges at a ⅛" allowance. Make a ½" pleat in the center of the open end of each tie. Tack pleat in place. Slip at least ½" of pleated end of tie into the waistband opening. Stitch through all layers close to the folded edge of the waistband and again ¼" away from the first stitching line. Repeat with the second tie.

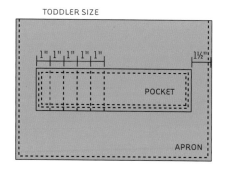

TODDLER SIZE

STEP 5

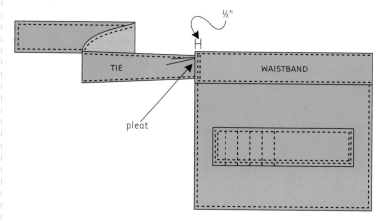

STEP 7

convertible craft apron

Designed by Roxanne Beauvais

What makes this apron especially unique is that it can easily be converted into a tote bag. It's perfect for the young on-the-go artist or an up-and-coming traveling baker!

MATERIALS

* ✳ Locate the pattern in the front pocket (sheet #3)
* ✳ 1 yard of 44/45" fabric (any weight will do, preferably cotton)
* ✳ 1 spool of coordinating thread
* ✳ 2½ yards of ⅝" grosgrain ribbon

Size – fits most up to a child's size 6
Seam allowance – ½" unless otherwise specified

① Measure, Mark, and Cut

Place your fabric in a single layer with wrong side facing up. Place the apron pattern piece, and measure and mark the other pieces as shown on the layout. Cut out the pieces, and transfer markings from all pattern pieces to the wrong side of the fabric.

* ✳ **Apron pattern** (cut 1)
* ✳ **Back panel** 13½" wide × 11½" tall (cut 1)
* ✳ **Front handle** 13½" wide × 2½" tall (cut 1)
* ✳ **Back handle** 11½" wide × 2½" tall (cut 1)
* ✳ **Pocket** 8" wide × 10" tall (cut 1)

NOTE: *Place pattern pieces and "tall" dimensions along the grainline of your fabric.*

② Make the Handles

Press under both short ends of the front handle ½". Fold and press handle as you would to make bias tape (*see page* 18). Topstitch around all four edges. Repeat to make the back handle. Pin the ends

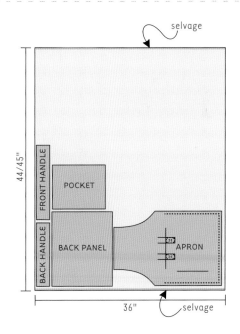

CUTTING LAYOUT

of the front handle to the right side of the apron at the placement marks. The loop of the handle should be toward the top of the apron. Make sure the handle is not twisted and secure the ends in place with a box stitch (*see page* 14).

❸ Make the Pocket

With right sides together, fold the pocket in half, aligning short raw edges. Stitch around three open sides, leaving a 2" opening for turning in the center of the bottom edge. Clip corners, turn right side out, and press. Center pocket along placement line on the right side of the apron, taking care to conceal the box stitches from the previous step. Topstitch three sides of the pocket to the apron, leaving the top edge open. The front strap should stow invisibly inside the pocket.

❹ Place the Back Handle

Fold the top edge of the back panel ¼" to the wrong side and press. Fold over another ½" and press. Position the back handle on wrong side of back panel using the same placement and spacing as the front handle, as shown on the pattern. Pin the short ends of the handle in place, tucking the handle ends under the ½" hem. (The loop of the handle will hang toward the bottom of the panel.) Topstitch across the top edge, close to the folded edge, as shown, catching the handle ends in the stitching line.

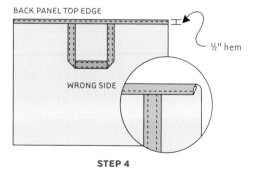

BACK PANEL TOP EDGE

½" hem

WRONG SIDE

STEP 4

❺ Attach the Back Panel

With right sides together, pin the back panel to the bottom of the apron, aligning the side and bottom raw edges. Stitch around the side and bottom edges. Clip corners, turn right side out, and press. Edgestitch around the two sides and bottom edge of the back panel and apron.

❻ Hem the Apron

On the top edge of the apron, fold the raw edge over ¼" to the wrong side and press. Fold over another ½" and press. Topstitch close to the folded edge. Fold and press ¼" on the remaining curved raw edges to the wrong side of the apron. Fold over another ¾" and press, creating a casing for the apron ties. Topstitch close to the folded edge.

❼ Add the Neck and Waist Ties

Insert the ribbon into the casing, starting at the waist of one side, exiting the top, leaving slack for the neck, entering the opposite casing, and exiting at the waist of the other side. Fold over the raw edges of the ribbon and topstitch to prevent fraying. When the apron is not in use, it neatly folds inside the bag until the next craft opportunity presents itself!

TODDLER ART SMOCK

Designed by Rachael Theis

Lightweight and stylish, this sleeveless art smock has been specially designed for your little one's artistic endeavors. With the wraparound style, the smock is well suited to projects that are a little messy up front.

MATERIALS

* ✳ Locate the pattern in the front pocket (sheet #4)
* ✳ 1 yard of 44/45" fabric (quilting-weight cotton)
* ✳ 1 spool of coordinating thread
* ✳ 2 packages of ¼" double-fold bias tape (4½ yards)

Size – fits most up to a toddler size 4T

Seam allowance – ½" unless otherwise specified

❶ Measure, Mark, and Cut

Fold your fabric in half lengthwise, with right sides together, aligning the selvages. Place pieces according to the cutting layout, and cut them out. Transfer markings to wrong side of the fabric.

* ✳ **Front** (cut 1 on fold)
* ✳ **Side panel** (cut 2)
* ✳ **Back** (cut 2)
* ✳ **Pocket** (cut 1 on fold)

NOTE: *Place pattern pieces along the grainline of your fabric.*

❷ Assemble the Pocket

Pin bias tape along the top edge of the pocket, fully encasing the raw edge. Stitch in place. With right sides facing up, pin the pocket to the lower portion of the front, aligning bottom and side raw edges. Baste along raw edges using a scant ¼" seam allowance. Stitch vertical lines on the pocket, through both layers, following the placement lines indicated on the pattern piece.

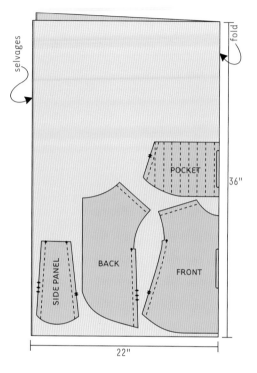

CUTTING LAYOUT

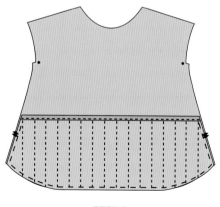

STEP 2

③ Attach the Front, Back, and Side Panels

With right sides together, stitch the front and back together at the shoulder seams. Press seams open. Pin bias tape along the top edge of one side panel, fully encasing the raw edge. Edgestitch in place. With wrong sides facing, stitch the front panel to this side panel, matching notches and dots. Trim seam allowance to ¼". With wrong sides together, stitch this side panel to the back, matching notches. Trim seam allowance to ¼". Repeat with other side panel on the opposite side.

④ Encase the Raw Edges

Starting at the bottom edge of the front/ side panel seam, pin bias tape along the raw edge, fully encasing the seam. Continue encasing the seam around the armhole, across the shoulder, and down the back/side panel seam. Edgestitch in place. Repeat on the opposite side of the smock, fully encasing all side seams. Starting at the top edge of the back, enclose the raw edge with bias tape, continuing around the bottom front edge of the smock and ending at the top of the other back edge. (The entire back and bottom edge of the smock should now be fully encased with bias tape.)

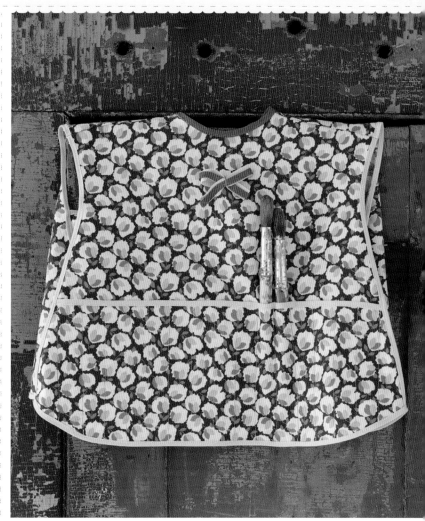

⑤ Finish the Neck Edge

Cut a 32" piece of bias tape and mark the halfway point. Pin the halfway point at the center front neck edge and pin it along the neckline, fully encasing the raw edge (it will extend off the smock on both ends to form ties). Edgestitch the entire length of the bias tape. Knot the ends to eliminate fraying. You may choose to add a bow on the front using the remaining bias tape.

FIREFIGHTER HAT

Designed by Caitlin Bell

Everyone knows little kids love to play dress-up, from sporting their favorite superhero attire to flinging on impressively full capes. Add a little headgear into the mix and your wee one can transform into the world's most heroic fire chief!

MATERIALS

* Locate the pattern in the front pocket (sheet #1)
* 1 yard of 44/45" red fabric (cotton broadcloth)
* 1 spool of coordinating thread
* 1 yard of medium-weight fusible interfacing
* 10" × 14" piece of plastic mesh canvas (like that used in needlepoint)
* ⅜ yard ½" elastic
* iron-on or sew-on patch for front of hat

Finished dimensions – will fit a child with 19½" head circumference or smaller

Seam allowance – ¼" unless otherwise specified

① Measure, Mark, and Cut

Fold your fabric in half lengthwise, with right sides together, aligning the selvages. Arrange hat pattern pieces and cut them out. Transfer all markings from the pattern pieces to the wrong side of the fabric.

* **Crown** (cut 12)
* **Brim** (cut 2)

Cut from fusible interfacing:

* **Crown** (cut 6)
* **Brim** (cut 2)

Cut from plastic canvas:

* **Brim support** (cut 1)

NOTE: *Place pattern pieces along the grainline of your fabric. Do not use fabric scissors to cut plastic canvas, or they will become dull.*

② Apply Interfacing

Fuse crown interfacing to the wrong side of six fabric crown pieces, following manufacturer's instructions. Fuse brim interfacing to both fabric brim pieces. On the wrong side of the brim pieces, mark circles for crown placement, but do not cut.

❸ Make the Crown Lining

With right sides facing, pin two interfaced crown pieces together. Stitch along one curved edge using ¼" seam allowance, stopping ¼" from top point. Press seam open. Stitch another interfaced crown piece to a raw curved edge in the same fashion. Repeat until all six interfaced pieces are stitched together and form a rounded hat crown. Clip curves. Turn and press bottom raw edge ¼" to the wrong side.

❹ Make the Crown Exterior

Repeat step 3 using the noninterfaced crown pieces. Turn right side out. Position iron- or sew-on patch at front of crown and attach.

❺ Form the Brim

With right sides together, align the raw edges of the brim and stitch together. Clip seam allowance along curves, being careful not to cut into the seam. Cut the hole where marked through both layers for crown placement, turn the brim right side out through the hole, and press. Topstitch ⅛" from the edge around the entire outside edge of brim. Align the brim fabric piece on top of the plastic canvas piece and mark crown placement hole on plastic canvas. Cut out the hole. Insert plastic canvas between the brim pieces through the hole.

❻ Finish the Hat

Slipstitch the crown exterior to the brim to conceal the raw edge of the crown placement hole. Turn the hat upside down and repeat, hand-stitching the crown lining in place. Determine a comfortable length for an elastic chinstrap, and hand-sew in place.

BABY GIFT SET

Designed by Nina Mayfield

Who knew you could make the perfect gift set for the new baby in your (or your friend's, or your sister's) life with just one yard of fabric? Of course you can! The most adorable booties, bib, and tactile blanket all in a little gift bag to go. The baby may not thank you, but Mommy sure will!

MATERIALS
* Locate the pattern in the front pocket (sheet #2)
* 1 yard of 44/45" fabric (quilting-weight cotton)
* 1 spool of coordinating thread
* ½ yard of cotton flannel
Size – up to 6 months

Infant Baby Booties

ADDITIONAL MATERIALS
* 6" of ¼" elastic, cut into 2 pieces, 3" long
* 1 package of ½" double-fold bias tape
Seam allowance – ¼" unless otherwise specified

1 Measure, Mark, and Cut

Placing the pattern pieces along the grainline of your fabric, cut the pattern pieces from the main fabric and then again from the flannel. Transfer all markings from the pattern pieces to the wrong side of the fabric. (Remember to position your pieces efficiently, so you will have enough room left in your yard and your flannel for the other projects.)
* <u>Bootie sole</u> (cut 2)
* <u>Bootie upper</u> (cut 2)
* <u>Bootie back</u> (cut 2)

2 Layer the Pieces

With wrong sides together, align the fabric upper and flannel upper. Baste together using a scant ⅛" seam allowance. Repeat the process with the sole and the back pieces. (The flannel side is the interior lining

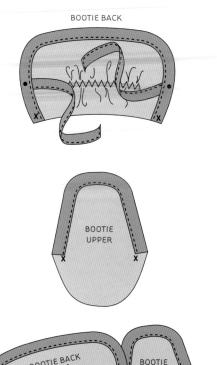

BOOTIE BACK

BOOTIE
UPPER

BOOTIE BACK

BOOTIE
UPPER

STEP 4
(ALL PIECES FLANNEL SIDE UP)

of the bootie.) Stitch elastic onto the wrong side of the back follow-ing the stitching lines. Use a zigzag stitch and stretch the elastic to fit as you stitch it in place.

③ Make the Ties

Cut four pieces of bias tape, each measuring 7", to be used for the ties. On one short end, open up tape and turn and press ½" to the wrong side. Refold tape and edgestitch the length of the tie and along the folded short end. Repeat with the three remaining tie pieces. Stitch ties in place at the placement marks on the flannel side of each back piece.

④ Encase the Back Edges

* Pin bias tape around the outer edge of the back piece, fully encasing the raw edge and concealing the unfinished edge of the ties. Stitch in place.
* Pin and stitch bias tape to the outer edge of the upper piece, fully encasing the raw edge between the Xs as marked on the pattern pieces.
* Join the back piece and the upper piece, just overlapping at the Xs, and baste together with a scant ⅛" seam allowance.

⑤ Attach the Sole

Cut two pieces of bias tape, each measuring 13", and press open to make 1" single-fold tape. On each piece, fold and press one short raw end under ½". With right sides together, stitch a piece of bias tape to the outer raw edge of the sole piece, overlapping the bias tape by 1" at the back of the sole and tucking the raw short end of tape inside the pressed end. With right sides together, pin the up-per and back to the sole, along the bias-tape edge. Stitch together and turn the bootie right side out. Repeat with the other bootie.

Bib

ADDITIONAL MATERIALS

* 1 set of snaps or 1" of Velcro

Seam allowance – ¼" unless otherwise specified

1 Measure, Mark, and Cut

Place the bib pattern piece along the grainline of your fabric, leaving enough uncut fabric for the projects that follow. Cut one from both the fabric and the flannel. Transfer the markings to the wrong side of the fabric.

2 Make the Bib

With right sides together, stitch around the bib, leaving a 3" opening in the bottom edge. Clip all curves, turn right side out, and press. Leave an opening to turn on the bottom. Top-stitch around the edge of the bib, closing the opening used for turning. Stitch either a snap closure or Velcro at the dots.

Tactile Blanket

ADDITIONAL MATERIALS

* Scraps of ribbon (any width) in a variety of textures (grosgrain, satin, velvet, etc.)

Seam allowance – ½" unless otherwise specified

1 Measure, Mark, and Cut

Measure and mark the following pieces along the grainline of your fabric, directly on the wrong side, and cut them out. (This will use up the flannel, but reserve some fabric for the gift bag that follows.)

* **Blanket front/back** 13" wide × 13" tall (cut 1 from the main fabric and 1 from the flannel)

2 Making the Blanket

Cut assorted ribbon into 3" and 4" lengths. Fold the ribbon pieces in half, creating loops, and pin them to the right side of the fabric square, aligning raw edges. Place the loops randomly, spacing them out so they go around all four sides. Stitch the loops in place with a scant ¼" seam allowance. With right sides together, pin the fabric and flannel squares together. Stitch, leaving a 4" opening for turning. Clip corners, turn right side out, and press. Topstitch around all four sides, closing the opening used for turning.

Gift Bag

ADDITIONAL MATERIALS

* 2 yards of ¼" to ⅜" ribbon for drawstring,
  cut into 2 pieces, each 36" long

Seam allowance – ½" unless otherwise specified

❶ Measure, Mark, and Cut

Measure and mark the following pieces along the grainline of your fabric, directly on the wrong side, and cut them out.

* <u>**Bag front/back**</u> 15" wide × 15" tall (cut 2)

❷ Make the Casing

Staystitch the side seams of both bag pieces. Clip to, but not through, the staystitch line, 2" from the top of the bag at each side seam. Above the clip line, press under the side raw edges ½". Along the top short edge of the bag pieces, press under ¼", then an additional ¾". Stitch in place close to the folded edge to make the drawstring casing.

❸ Stitch the Sides

With right sides together, align raw edges of the front and back pieces. Starting at the bottom edge of the casing, stitch around three sides of the bag. Clip corners, turn right side out, and press.

❹ Insert the Drawstrings

Thread one piece of ribbon through the casing on one side, around the entire top, and back out the same hole. Knot the ribbon ends. Do the same with the other piece of ribbon, through the opposite hole. You'll have knotted ends on both sides; when you pull on them, the bag will draw up tight — safely holding all the baby goodies you have made!

pirate growth chart

Designed by Tracy Parker

You don't need to track growth spurts on the wall anymore: this is the perfect portable chart, and it can track the height of one or many children. If pirates don't appeal to you, any whimsical print or theme will do. Get creative with the shapes you'd like to use in the appliqué as well as for the height markers.

MATERIALS

* ✳ Enlarge the appliqué pattern pieces on page 279
* ✳ 1 yard of 44/45" fabric (novelty-printed cotton, any weight)
* ✳ 1 spool of coordinating thread
* ✳ 8 craft felt squares (9" × 12") in a variety of colors (including 1 white, 1 black, 1 pink, 1 brown, and 1 skin tone)
* ✳ ½ yard of double-sided fusible web
* ✳ 1¼ yard ⅞" ribbon
* ✳ Superglue
* ✳ Two ¾" or smaller buttons
* ✳ One ¼" dowel, 12" long

Finished dimensions – 18" wide × 29" tall
Seam allowance – ½" unless otherwise specified

1 Measure, Mark, and Cut

Fold the fabric in half lengthwise along the grainline with right sides together, aligning selvages. Cut two pieces along the grainline that are 18" wide × 29" tall.

2 Interface the Felt Squares

Fuse double-sided fusible web to the back of all felt pieces, according to the manufacturer's instructions.

3 Cut Out the Appliqués

Cut all appliqué pieces from the felt squares. Make sure that you do not cut out your numbers backwards.

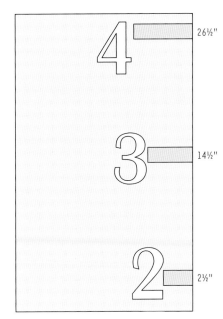

STEP 4

④ Appliqué the Growth Bars

* Measure 2½" from the bottom edge of the growth chart and fuse the shortest growth bar ½" from the right raw edge. Center the number 2 to the left of the rectangle, about ½" away, and fuse in place.
* Measure 14½" up from the bottom edge and fuse the second growth bar ½" from the right raw edge. Place the number 3 in the same way as number 2.
* Measure 26½" up from the bottom edge and fuse the last and longest growth bar in place, and center the number 4 as before.
* Zigzag around the edges of all felt pieces to hold them in place.

⑤ Appliqué the Face

Fuse the eye patch to the face shape. Using black thread, either machine-stitch or hand-sew a line from the top of one ear to the other, sewing over the top edge of the eye patch. Very carefully, using one or two stitches at a time, sew a small circle for the other eye. Fuse the pink circles to the face to make two rosy cheeks. Using red thread, sew a smile from the center of one pink circle to the other. Using thread that corresponds to the skin tone you have selected, sew a small line for the nose. Fuse the scull cap to the top of the head. Fuse the assembled pirate face to the desired location on the growth chart. Zigzag-stitch the completed face in place using coordinating thread. Add an earring to the left ear using a zigzag stitch and gold thread; you may have to go over the stitch a few times to fill it in.

⑥ Assemble the Growth Chart

With right sides together, align the raw edges of the front and back of the chart. Stitch around the side and bottom edges, leaving the top open. Clip corners, turn right side out, and press. Fold and press ½" at the top edge to the inside.

⑦ Make the Loops and the Hanger

* Cut ribbon into three 4" pieces and one 27" piece. Fold each of the short pieces in half, creating three loops. Position two loops on the top outside corners of the growth chart. Allow 1" of the loop to extend outside the project, while sandwiching the raw ends inside the growth chart. Pin in place. Pin the third loop in between the first two, centering it along the top of the growth chart. Topstitch around the entire edge of the growth chart, stitching the ribbon loops in place along the top edge.
* To make the hanger, tie a knot in the center of the 27" piece of ribbon. Make a 1¼" loop at each end of the ribbon and stitch it in place.
* Use superglue to stick one button to each end of the dowel rod. Allow to dry completely.

⑧ Hang the Chart

Insert the dowel through the various loops in the following order: left-side growth-chart loop, first hanger loop, middle chart loop, second hanger loop, right-side chart loop. Hang the chart so that the 2' marker on the chart is placed 2' from the floor. Topstitch the bottle stoppers to the bottle. Use a fabric marker to record your child's name and date on the message-in-a-bottle marker. Pin in place and wait for the next growth spurt!

NOTE: *Mitering (step 2) will be quicker and easier if you keep all squares from a single strip grouped together as you cut them.*

MITERED SQUARE BLANKIE

Designed by Patricia Hoskins

The mitered square has long been a favorite of knitters young and old; now, you can translate this bold, graphic design into patchwork! All you need is some striped fabric and a precise hand. One yard alone will make a little carry-along lovey; add some flannel for a separate backing to make a larger receiving blanket.

MATERIALS

* 1 yard of 44/45" vertically striped fabric (quilting-weight cotton)
* 1 spool of coordinating thread
* 27" × 33" piece of flannel (for receiving blanket)
* ¼" sewing-machine presser foot (optional) or masking tape to mark ¼" seam allowance on sewing-machine faceplate

Finished dimensions – "Lovey" is 20" × 20"; receiving blanket is 27" × 34".
Seam allowance – ½" unless otherwise specified

❶ Cut Squares

Fold fabric crosswise, right sides together, aligning stripes (fold will run perpendicular to selvage; each selvage edge will be folded in half). Press sharp crease along fold line, making sure all printed stripes are aligned. Remove selvage edges.

Cut ten 4¼" strips perpendicular to the fold and parallel to the selvage. Keep strips folded in half and trim short raw edges of strips to square off. Cut each folded strip into a total of eight 4¼" squares. With each cut, you will create two identical striped squares facing right sides together; keep these together. When done cutting, you should have a total of 40 pairs (80 squares total). Using a fabric marker or pencil, draw a diagonal line on the wrong side of the top square of each pair from the top left corner to the bottom right corner on each pair of squares. Pin each pair together, and again make sure the stripes are in alignment.

② **Miter the Squares**

Stitch a ¼" seam allowance on both sides of the diagonal line on every pair of squares. Cut along the marked diagonal line on every square to make two mitered squares from each sewn pair.

Press seam allowance open on each mitered square. Trim points on seam allowance to keep them flush with squares' raw edges. Press and trim each time you stitch a seam, before proceeding to the next pair of squares.

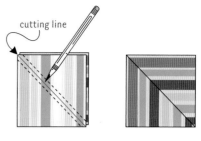

cutting line

STEP 2

③ **Piece the Blocks**

There should be 20 sets of four identical squares. Each set of four squares will become one block. For each block, arrange the squares one of two ways, depending on your personal preference.

To assemble squares, with right sides together, stitch the top two squares along the center raw edges. Repeat with the bottom two squares. Finish the block by stitching top and bottom rows, right sides together, aligning corners and center seam. Repeat with remaining pieces to make 20 blocks.

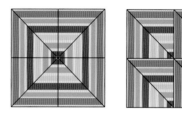

STEP 3
Arrange squares one of two ways

④ **Assemble the Pieces**

* **For the lovey.** Arrange nine blocks into three rows of three blocks each. With right sides facing, pin and stitch one row of blocks together, matching corners and center seams. Repeat for remaining rows, and finish by stitching all rows together. Repeat for back side of lovey. (You will have two extra blocks to do with as you please.)

* **For the receiving blanket.** Arrange 20 blocks into five rows of four blocks each. With right sides together, pin and stitch one row of blocks, matching corners and center seams. Repeat for remaining rows, and finish by stitching all rows together. Measure finished height and width of pieced top and cut flannel backing to fit.

* **For both the lovey and receiving blanket.** With right sides facing, pin front and back pieces together, aligning all raw edges. Stitch around all four sides, leaving a 6" opening on one side for turning. Trim corners, turn right side out, and press. Edgestitch all around, closing the opening used for turning. Try a fancy stitch, such as zigzag or shell: it looks great!

BIRD MOBILE

Designed by Oona Peterson

If you've been looking for the perfect mobile, this bird version is just for you! Hang it over the crib or mount it to the wall over the changing table. The circling bird family will bring cheer and enchantment to any child's room or baby's nursery!

MATERIALS

* Locate the pattern in the front pocket (sheet #3)
* 1 yard of 44/45" fabric (quilting weight)
* 1 spool of coordinating thread
* Small amount of fiberfill
* Small beads (or embroidery floss) for the eyes
* 1 yard of ¼" ribbon
* 6" plastic or metal ring
* 4 yards of ¼" ribbon to cover the ring
* Fabric glue (optional)
* Clear nylon thread or fishing line
* 1" plastic or metal ring

Finished dimensions – width of mobile ring is 6"
Seam allowance – ¼" unless otherwise specified

① Lay Out and Cut Pattern Pieces

To make seven birds, use the pattern pieces to cut the following.

Transfer the eye placement mark.

* **Body** (cut 2 per bird, for a total of 14)
* **Wings** (cut 4 per bird, for a total of 28)
* **Gusset** (cut 1 per bird, for a total of 7)

NOTE: *Grainline is not indicated on the pattern pieces, and you are free to position your pattern pieces to make the most of the print on your fabric.*

② Stitch the Body

With right sides together, pin the gusset to the body piece, aligning raw edges between marks on body, and stitch. Repeat for the other side of the gusset and the second body piece. At eye placement marks, make eyes by sewing small beads or embroidering French knots on the bird's head. Cut one 1½" piece of ribbon and fold in half to form a loop. Pin the ribbon to the center of the bird's back, aligning raw edges. Pin both body pieces together, right sides facing (gusset will be folded between body pieces), aligning all raw edges. Starting at the front end of the gusset, stitch around the body to the other end, leaving a 1" opening for turning and stuffing. Cut notches into curves, being careful not to cut into the seam. Turn the bird right side out and stuff as firmly as desired, taking care to get stuffing into all corners. Slipstitch the opening closed.

③ Make the Wings

Pin two wing pieces together, right sides facing, and stitch around, leaving a 1" opening for turning. Trim corners and notch curves, being careful not to cut into the seam. Turn right side out and slipstitch the opening closed. Repeat for the other wing. Hand-stitch wings to the bird (using slipstitch or other invisible stitch), centering one on each side.

Repeat steps 2 and 3 with remaining bird pieces, making seven birds total. Omit the ribbon loop for the last two birds, which will sit on top of the ring.

④ Finish the Mobile

Wrap the 6" ring with ribbon, sewing or gluing it in place. Sew two birds on opposite sides of the ring using clear nylon thread. Make the hanger for the ring by cutting four 16" pieces of clear thread or fishing line. Tie one piece every 90 degrees around the ring. Tie all four threads together in a knot about 8" above the ring. (Note that the length of all threads must be equal so the mobile will hang level.) Thread a 1" ring through all four threads and tie it in place close to the knot. Thread clear thread through the ribbon loops on each bird.

Tie birds at varying heights around the ring, spacing them evenly. Watch as the birds take flight!

Festive Flag Banners

Designed by Sue Ainsley

Create your own celebration with this fanciful flag banner. It's the perfect way to add the finishing touch to your child's living space. Looking for another festive idea? Try making a personalized banner for a party.

MATERIALS

* 1 yard of 44/45" fabric (any weight will do)
* 1 package of ½" double-fold bias tape (3½ yards)
* 1 spool of coordinating thread
* 3 craft felt squares (9" × 12")
* Fabric glue

Finished dimensions – one 6½" banner with 14 flags, each approximately 7" long.
Seam allowance – ½" unless otherwise specified

① Measure, Mark, and Cut

Make a pattern piece for your triangular flag banners. On a piece of paper, draw a 6" line. Find the center point of this line, and draw an 8" line perpendicular from this center mark. Draw two diagonal lines connecting the end of the 8" line to each end of the 6" line. To make 14 flags, use the pattern piece to cut the following.

* **Flag front/back** (cut 28)

NOTE: *Place the 8" measurement along the grainline of your fabric.*

② Make the Flags

With right sides together, align the raw edges of one set of flags and stitch along both long sides, leaving the top edge open. Neatly trim seam allowance at the point and turn the flag right side out. (You may wish to use a turning tool to aid in turning the point of the flag.) Press. Repeat with the remaining pieces to make 14 flags.

③ String the Flags

Fold one end of the bias tape under ½" to the wrong side, and stitch the end closed. Place and pin the first flag 12" from this finished end, sandwiching the raw edges in between the layers of the double-fold bias tape. Place and pin the second flag ½" from the first and continue until all remaining flags have been pinned to the bias tape. Cut the bias tape 12½" from the last flag, fold one end of the bias tape under ½" to the wrong side, and stitch the end closed. Beginning at one end of the bias tape, topstitch along the entire length of the banner, through all layers, securing your flags to the bias tape.

④ Personalize the Banner

Using your favorite bold and graphic font, print out the appropriate letters to personalize your banner, ensuring that each letter will fit within each flag. Cut the letters from the printer paper to use as patterns. Pin these patterns to felt and cut out the letters. Once cut, determine the placement of felt letters on the flags, and use fabric glue to adhere in place. Once dry, your banner is ready to hang!

BEANBAG BOOSTER SEAT

Designed by Ellen Baker

This is a great solution for the "big kid" who isn't interested in sitting in a booster seat but still doesn't quite reach the table. Made with your favorite oilcloth, coated cotton, or outdoor fabric, the seat is easy to clean and durable, not to mention comfy! This booster seat is recommended for children aged three to six, who can easily get in and out of a regular-sized chair. Easily portable, the seat works well for dining out or traveling with the kids.

MATERIALS

* 1 yard of water-repellant fabric (such as oilcloth or other coated cotton; any width will do)
* 1 spool of coordinating thread
* One 12" × 12" × 2" foam insert

* 3 pounds of buckwheat hulls
Finished dimensions – 12" × 12" × 5" (will fit any standard chair)
Seam allowance – ½" unless otherwise specified

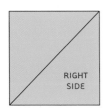

RIGHT SIDE

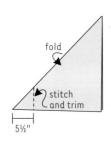

fold

stitch and trim

5½"

STEP 2

① Measure, Mark, and Cut

Measure and mark the following pattern pieces directly on the wrong side of your fabric, then cut them out:

* **Bag** 23½" wide × 23½" tall (cut 1)
* **Bottom** 12½" wide × 12½" tall (cut 1)

② Make the Body of the Seat

Fold the bag piece in half diagonally, with right sides together, creating a triangle. Mark a 5½" line along the edge and draw a line straight up to form a right-angled triangle as shown in the diagram. Stitch through this line. Repeat with the other point on the fold of the triangle. Then open the bag piece and refold the opposite way diagonally. Mark and sew two more right-angled triangles.

The triangles shape the bag piece into a basket shape with a square 12½" base and four sides measuring 5½" tall. Trim excess fabric. Do not turn right side out yet.

③ Attach the Pieces

With right sides together, stitch the bottom piece to the body piece on three sides, pivoting at the corners, leaving the fourth side open for stuffing. Turn right side out and gently push out all corners.

④ Fill the Seat

Insert foam through the opening and fill the cushion with buckwheat hulls. Pin together the opening and hand-sew it closed.

CHILD'S MESSENGER BAG

Designed by Lindsie Blair

This bag is great for preschoolers. It's easy for them to put on and roomy enough to store all their treasures (even an extra set of clothes during those potty-training years). This pattern is easily adjustable for a slightly older child as well.

MATERIALS

* 1 yard of 44/45" fabric (nondirectional home-decor weight)
* 1 spool of coordinating thread
* 2 pieces of Velcro, each 1" in length (any width will do)

Finished dimensions – bag is 10" wide × 12" tall, strap measures 29" long.

Seam allowance – ½" unless otherwise specified

1 Measure, Mark, and Cut

Place your fabric in a single layer with wrong side facing up. Measure and mark the following pattern pieces directly on the wrong side of your fabric following the layout at right, then cut them out:

* **Exterior** 12½" wide × 26" tall (cut 1)
* **Lining** 12½" wide × 26" tall (cut 1)
* **Flap** 10½" wide × 12" tall (cut 2)
* **Interior pocket** 9" wide × 5" tall (cut 2)
* **Strap** 5" wide × 30" tall (cut 1) (adjust accordingly for taller or shorter children)

2 Make the Interior Pocket

With right sides facing, pin pocket pieces together and stitch around all four edges, leaving a 2" opening in the center of the bottom edge for turning. Clip corners and turn right side out. Press. Edgestitch along the top edge of the pocket. Pin to the right side of bag lining, 2" from the top edge and 2¼" from each side, with the top edge of pocket closest to the top edge of bag. Stitch around three sides of the pocket, leaving top edge open.

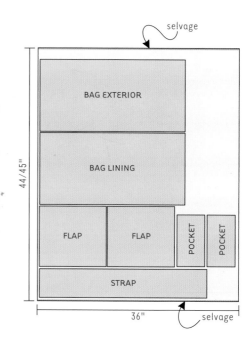

NOTE: *Place "tall" dimensions along the grainline of your fabric.*

CUTTING LAYOUT

❸ Make the Strap

Fold the strap in half lengthwise, right sides together. Stitch the long edge. Turn right side out and press flat. Edgestitch along both long edges of the strap.

❹ Make the Flap

With right sides together, stitch around two long sides and one short side of the flap, leaving the fourth (short) side open. This is the top of the flap. Clip corners and turn right side out. Press.

Edgestitch along the sides and bottom of the flap. Pin the hook pieces of Velcro 2" in from each side of the flap and 1½" up from the finished bottom edge of the flap. Stitch both Velcro pieces securely to the flap.

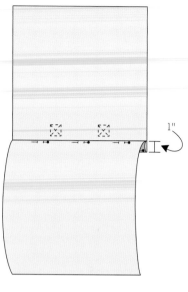

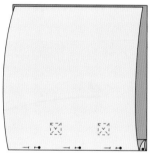

STEP 5

⑤ Make the Bag Exterior

Lay the exterior piece right side up. Pin the loop pieces of Velcro to the right side of the fabric 10½" from the top edge and 3½" in from each side. Stitch both Velcro pieces securely to the bag exterior.

Flip the exterior over so the wrong side is facing up. Fold it in half so that the top edges are aligned and wrong sides are together. Position the bag so that the fold is closest to you and the short raw edges are away from you. Pin along the folded edge to hold it in place. Fold the top layer down, 1" above the fold, creating a 1" overlapping fold. Pin the new folded edge.

Pick up all layers of fold; fold piece again so that the right sides are together and the top edges are aligned. Pin through all layers of fold. Stitch both side seams, through all folded layers. Press the side seam open and turn the bag right side out.

⑥ Make the Lining

Repeat step 5 using the bag lining piece. Turn lining inside out.

⑦ Assemble the Bag

Center the short end of the strap over the side seam of the exterior, aligning raw edges. Pin it in place. Pin the other end of the strap to the opposite side seam, making sure that the strap is not twisted. Baste in place. Pin the flap to the back of the exterior, between the straps, aligning the top raw edges (the Velcro on the flap should be away from the bag). Baste together. Place the bag exterior inside the lining, with right sides together, matching side seams. Stitch around the top of the bag, leaving a 4" opening. Turn the bag right side out, press, and topstitch around the top edge of the bag, closing the turning opening as you go.

CHAPTER 10

PLaYTime

Toys and games aren't just for kids anymore. In this chapter you will find an awesome selection of handmade toys and gifts for playful people, young and old. We love the same things you do: plushies, dollhouses, kites, and checkers. Escape the soulless toys offered at the malls and go make some high-quality fun; just be sure to make enough for everyone!

CUDDLY BEAR CUSHION

Designed by Becka Rahn

A cute bear friend and a cuddly cushion all in one! You or your little one will enjoy snuggling on the couch with this friendly pillow.

MATERIALS

- Locate the pattern in the front pocket (sheet #2)
- 1 yard of 44/45" fabric (corduroy, flannel, wools or furry felt work great)
- 4" × 10" scrap of contrasting fabric for ears and nose (cotton print)
- 2" × 3" scrap of felt (any color)
- 1 spool of coordinating thread

- One bag of fiberfill (12 ounces or more)
- Embroidery floss
- Two ⅝" to 1" buttons

Finished Dimensions – approximately 15" long × 10" high × 3" wide

Seam allowance – ½" unless otherwise specified

① Measure, Mark, and Cut

With right sides together, fold your fabric in half lengthwise, aligning the selvages. Cut out the pattern pieces and additional pieces listed. Transfer markings to the wrong side of the fabric.

- **Ears/tail** (cut 4)
- **Body sides** (cut 2)
- **Gusset A** 23" wide × 4" tall (cut 1)
- **Gusset B** 26" wide × 4" tall (cut 1)

Also cut from scrap fabric:

- **Ears/tail** (cut 2)

Also cut from felt:

- **Nose** (cut 1)

NOTE: *Place pattern pieces and "tall" dimensions along the grainline of your fabric.*

② Prepare the Gusset

- On gusset A, measure from one end and mark on the wrong side of both long edges at ½", 15¾", 20", and 22".
- On gusset B, measure from one end and mark on the wrong side of both long edges at ½", 7¾", 11¾", 16¾", 20¼", and 25¾".

③ Stitch and Attach Tail

With right sides facing, pin two main-fabric tail pieces together. Stitch the curved edge, leaving the straight edge open. Clip seam allowance around curves and corners. Turn right side out. Stuff lightly. Slipstitch closed.

With right sides facing, pin the gusset strips together, aligning the sides at ½" marks. Insert and center the tail in between the short ends of the two gussets, aligning the raw straight edge of the tail with the short raw edges of the gussets closest to the ½" mark. Stitch the gusset short ends at the ½" mark through all layers. Press the seam open. You now have one long body gusset piece with a tail sticking out at the seam. Staystitch along both long edges of the gusset and set aside.

④ Stitch and Attach Ears

With right sides facing, pin together two ear pieces (one from main fabric, one from contrasting fabric). Stitch the curved edge, leaving the straight edge open. Clip the seam allowance around curves and corners. Turn right side out. Press. Repeat for the second ear.

Cut along the center line of the ear dart on one body piece. Fold right sides together and match dart stitching lines. Insert one ear between layers, with contrasting fabric facing the bear's face. The straight edge of the ear should extend ½" beyond the dart stitching line (raw edges will not match). Stitch through all layers along the dart stitching line. Repeat with the second ear and body piece. Press dart seam allowances toward the bear's back.

⑤ Attach the Body Gusset

With right sides together, match the tail seam of the gusset to the tail mark on one body piece, with gusset A (the shorter gusset) lining up with the bear's back. Pin the gusset to the raw edges of one body piece; each mark along the gusset edge will correspond to a dot on the body. Clip the gusset seam allowance up to the staystitching line as needed to fit around curves and corners.

Gusset ends will meet at the bear's mouth. Stitch together, leaving the short edge at the mouth open for turning and future stuffing. Stitch again at a ¼" seam allowance to reinforce stitching.

Pin and stitch the gusset to other body pieces in the same fashion. Turn the bear right side out through the mouth opening.

⑥ Make the Nose

Place the felt nose piece on the wrong side of the remaining contrasting fabric scrap. Trim the fabric to about ¼" larger than the felt nose piece. Wrap edges of the fabric around the felt piece and press.

Pin the nose onto the bear cushion, fabric side out, centering it on the gusset with the lower nose edge about 1" from the open raw edge. Slipstitch or use other invisible hand stitching to attach. Use embroidery floss to backstitch a line from the bottom center of the nose to the raw edge of the mouth opening to make the bear's "lips."

⑦ Stuff and Finish

Fill the bear cushion with stuffing material, using a point turner (such as a chopstick) to push the fill into the small areas in the legs and nose. You can make the cushion as squishy or as firm as you like. Turn the raw edges of the gusset at the mouth opening to the inside. Slipstitch closed. Sew on buttons for the bear's eyes.

Leisure Suit Lapdog

Designed by Marlene Gaige

At a loss what to do with those cool vintage double-knit polyesters you stashed away (or inherited) way back when? Then this lap dog is your new best friend! You can whip up several from just one yard of fabric. Heck, repurpose those old dresses and leisure suits too!

MATERIALS

* Locate the pattern in the front pocket (sheet #2)
* 1 yard of 44/45" fabric (double-knit polyester, or see sidebar for other options)
* Scrap of contrasting fabric for ears
* 1 spool of coordinating thread
* Small amount of quilting thread, upholstery thread, or other strong thread (in color coordinating with eyes)
* Large glass eyes or buttons
* Size 5 pearl cotton or embroidery floss for nose (black suggested, or coordinate colors)
* Fiberfill
* 1 large fuzzy pipe cleaner
* Awl or small sharp scissors
* Long doll needles

Finished dimensions – approximately 6" wide × 8½" tall
Seam allowance – ¼" unless otherwise specified

❶ Measure, Mark, and Cut

With right sides together, fold your fabric in half lengthwise, aligning the selvages. Pin all pattern pieces in place and cut them out. Transfer all markings to the wrong side of the fabric.

* **Head/body** (cut 2)
* **Tail** (cut 2)
* **Ears** (cut 2)
* **Tummy** (cut 1)
* **Head gusset** (cut 1)

Cut from contrasting fabric:

* **Ears** (cut 2)

NOTE: *Place pattern pieces along the grainline of your fabric.*

FABRIC OPTIONS

If you don't want to use double-knit polyester, other fabrics may suit. If you choose a polyester knit with stretch, your dog may be taller or chubbier depending on which way you lay the stretch! If you choose to make the dog out of a woven fabric, he will be slightly slimmer.

② Make the Ears and Tail

With right sides facing, pin together one main-fabric ear and one contrasting ear; stitch around the curved sides, leaving the straight edge open. Clip the curves, turn right side out, and turn raw edges ¼" to wrong side. Press; do not stuff.

With right sides facing, pin the tail pieces together; stitch around the curved sides and leave the straight edge open. Clip the curves and turn right side out. Fold the pipe cleaner in half and insert it into the tail (some will hang out). Lightly stuff around the pipe cleaner. Set the ears and tail aside.

③ Assemble the Dog

Stitch darts on the tummy by folding the fabric, right sides together, where marked on the pattern. Align the curved lines and stitch along the curved dart lines. Trim the seam allowance.

With right sides facing, pin the body pieces together, and stitch the snout from A to C as indicated on the pattern.

With right sides facing, pin the head gusset piece to one body piece, matching points A and B, and stitch between the points. Clip to (but not through) the seam along the rounded corners to ease fullness. Repeat on the other side of the gusset to attach.

With right sides facing, pin the tummy piece to the body piece, matching points C and D. Stitch together between points C and D. Clip to (but not through) the seam along the rounded corners to ease fullness. Repeat on the other side of the tummy.

Stitch body pieces together from point B to about 1" down toward D, leaving the remaining seam open for turning and stuffing.

④ Fill the Dog

Turn the dog right side out and stuff firmly, pushing the fiberfill into all corners. Stuff the nose especially firmly for ease of embroidery in a later step. Slipstitch the opening closed, leaving approximately ¼" open on the back seam for inserting the tail.

⑤ Attach Tail and Ears

Slip the tail into the opening where marked, inserting the ends of the pipe cleaner into the body. Slipstitch the opening closed to attach the tail.

Position the ears on the head gusset as indicated on the pattern. Slipstitch to join the front and back ear pieces and to attach the ears. Fold over the ear tips and tack them to the head.

⑥ Attach the Eyes

Use rounded-head pins or small pieces of felt to experiment with eye placement, moving them around until you are happy with the way they look. Poke holes for eyes using an awl or the end of a small pair of scissors. Thread 24" of strong thread onto a long doll needle and knot the end. Go into the head from one eyehole and come out the other eyehole. Sew back and forth a few times, pulling thread tightly to indent the eye sockets. Come out an eyehole and thread an eye onto the needle. Pinch the eye wire slightly with pliers. Go back into the eyehole and out the opposite eyehole. Pull hard! Place your thumb over the eye and pinch the head as you tie a knot. Put the needle into the head and come out of the other eye and back again. Repeat for the second eye. When the eyes are completed, they should be sunk slightly into the head.

⑦ Attach the Nose

To make the nose, thread 18" of pearl cotton embroidery floss onto a long doll needle. Go into the dog's nose right in the middle of where his nose will be. Pick two points on each side of the center seam just slightly below the head gusset seam. Form the nose by going back and forth from left to right to build up thread in an overlapping satin stitch, using the same entry and exit points on both sides. Be careful to line up stitches next to each other.

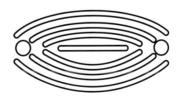

STEP 7
Stitching the nose

CHECKERS TO GO

Designed by Beth Walker

This set of checkers can follow you anywhere, with a board that doubles as a carrying bag! And what could be more fun than checkers with cute little critters or characters on them?

MATERIALS

* 1 yard of 44/45" quilting-weight cotton fabric
* 1 spool of coordinating thread
* Plastic pellets, rice, lentils, or similar filler material.
* 1 ounce of fabric paint
* Stencil brush or sponge
* Masking tape (optional)
* 1 yard of ¼" cording or ⅜" grosgrain ribbon (optional)

Finished dimensions – 19" × 19"
Seam allowance – ½" unless otherwise specified

1 Cut and Paint the Checkerboard

* Cut a 20" square of fabric.
* With fabric marker or pencil, draw a line 2" in from all four raw edges to form a 16" square in the middle. Draw lines every 2" within this square in both directions to form a checkerboard grid.
* Using fabric paint and a brush or sponge, paint alternating squares to complete the checkerboard design. (For a crisper edge, you may wish to tape off the squares before painting.)
* Paint the 2" border of the checkerboard, if desired.
* Press under the raw edge ¼", then press under another ¾". Stitch close to the folded edge, leaving a 1" opening at one corner to form the drawstring casing (*see page* 19). With a safety pin, thread cording or ribbon through the casing to create a pouch to store pieces when not in use. Knot the ends of the ribbon or cording together to keep them from getting lost inside the casing and to keep them from fraying.

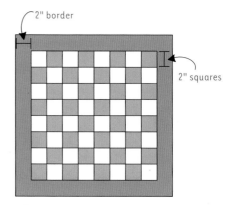

2" border

2" squares

2 Make the Checkers

* Cut a total of 48 circles, squares, or other basic shapes approximately 2" in size out of the remaining fabric: two pieces per checker, 12 checkers per side.
* With right sides facing, pin two pieces together and stitch around, leaving a small opening for turning and stuffing. Turn right side out and stuff with filler material. Slipstitch the opening closed.
* Repeat for the remaining pieces, making 12 checkers per side (24 total). If desired, use fabric paint to differentiate the two sides.

FABRIC OPTIONS

The pictured project uses a single fabric depicting both white and dark bunny figures, so look for a closely woven fabric with a small contrasting print. If no suitable single yard of fabric can be found to make two visibly different checker teams, use fabric paint or contrasting fabric scraps to mark one team.

Patches the Turtle

Designed by Erin Evans

Unlike some turtles, Patches won't hide away in his shell. He is ready to cuddle up with you and enjoy a good book or movie!

MATERIALS

* Locate the pattern in the front pocket (sheet #1)
* 1 yard of 44/45" fabric (quilting-weight or home-decor weight cotton or cotton blend)
* 1 spool of coordinating thread
* Embroidery floss
* Button, shank eyes, or felt (for eyes)
* Coordinating yarn for head hair (optional)
* ½ yard double-sided fusible web interfacing
* Fiberfill

Finished dimensions — 18" long × 11" wide × 6" deep
Seam allowance — ¼" unless otherwise specified

① Measure, Mark, and Cut

With right sides together, fold your fabric in half lengthwise, aligning the selvages. Pin all pattern pieces in place and cut them out. Transfer all markings to the wrong side of the fabric.

* **Top shell** (cut 1 on the fold and keep it folded)
* **Bottom shell** (cut 1 on fold)
* **Head** (cut 2)
* **Feet** (cut 8)
* **Tail** (cut 2)

NOTE: *Place pattern pieces along the grainline of your fabric.*

* Cut enough 3" squares, triangles, hexagons, or other shapes to cover and appliqué the top of the shell. Also cut identical 3" shapes out of the fusible interfacing for appliqué on top of the shell.
* Mark embroidery and eye placement lines on foot and head pieces as indicated, and embroider using floss color(s) of your choice. Attach eyes to head pieces.

❷ Make the Top Shell

With the top shell piece still folded in half, right sides together, stitch from each side of the fold to the shell point to form the dome shape. Turn right side out.

Following manufacturer's instructions, fuse each interfacing piece to the wrong side of each fabric appliqué piece and fuse to the top shell one at a time, overlapping shapes. Finish appliqué by using a zigzag stitch around the edge of each appliqué piece. Using a hand-sewing needle, bring loose thread ends to the wrong side of the top shell piece and tie off.

❸ Make Appendages

With right sides facing, pin head pieces together. If you want to add hair, cut yarn into several 3" lengths and insert it between the fabric layers at the top of the head, allowing one end of each yarn piece to extend slightly past the raw fabric edge. Stitch around the head (taking care not to stitch yarn into the seam except at the top), leaving the neck edge open. Clip the seam allowance at curves, being careful not to cut into the seam. Turn the head right side out and stuff with fiberfill.

With right sides facing, pin the foot pieces together, two at a time, and stitch around, leaving the straight edge open. Clip seam allowance at curves, being careful not to cut into seam. Turn the feet right side out and stuff with fiberfill.

With right sides facing, pin the tail pieces together, and stitch around, leaving the straight edge open. Clip seam allowance at curves and tip, being careful not to cut into seam. Turn the tail right side out and stuff with fiberfill.

❹ Finish the Turtle

With right sides together, pin and stitch top shell to bottom shell, inserting head, tail, and feet in between layers at desired spots. Let the appendages' raw edges extend slightly past shells' raw edges to make sure you stitch them into place. Leave a gap on one side between one pair of feet for turning and stuffing.

Turn right side out, press, and stuff to desired firmness. Slip-stitch the opening closed.

FaBRÎC DOLLHOUSE

Designed by Dawn Lewis

What little girl doesn't love to take her Polly Pockets or miniature animals everywhere she goes? This project, which can be made as a dollhouse or farmhouse, is a perfect carryall and toy, all in one!

MATERIALS

* 1 yard of 44/45" fabric (quilting-weight cotton)
* Two 10½" × 13½" sheets of plastic canvas (#7 ultra stiff or #10 mesh works well)
* 1 spool of coordinating thread
* Small package (34" × 45") of thin cotton batting
* Five buttons, at least ⅝" in diameter
* Elastic cording in coordinating color, cut into five 2" pieces
* Variety of 9" × 12" felt squares for appliqué decoration
* ⅔ yard of ⅝" grosgrain ribbon, cut into two 12" lengths
* Quilter's ruler (optional)

Finished dimensions – approximately 6" tall × 6" wide × 4" deep

Seam allowance – ½" unless otherwise specified

1 Measure, Mark, and Cut

With right sides together, fold your fabric in half lengthwise, aligning the selvages. Measure and mark the following pattern pieces directly on the wrong side of your fabric:

* **Small interior/exterior** 9" tall × 6" wide (cut 4)
* **Large interior/exterior** 22" tall × 8" wide (cut 1)

NOTE: *Place "tall" dimensions along the grainline of your fabric.*

Cut from plastic canvas:

* **Pieces A and E** 2¾" × 6" (cut 2)
* **Pieces B, C, and D** 4" × 6" (cut 3)
* **House-shaped pieces F and G** 4" × 5⅞" (cut 2)

2 Prepare Plastic Canvas Pieces

Wrap both sides of all plastic canvas pieces with batting. Secure batting with machine stitching or by hand just inside the plastic canvas edges, and trim the batting to size.

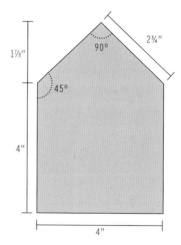

Cutting house-shaped pieces (see box on page 250 for directions)

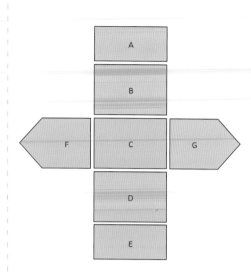

STEP 4
*The plastic canvas pieces will eventually
fit together like this.*

HOUSE-SHAPED PIECES

To make the house-shaped pieces,
start by drawing a 4" line for the base
and two 4" lines straight up on either
side — essentially a 4" square without a
top. Find the center of the bottom line,
2" from either side. Draw a line that is
5⅞" long, straight up from the center.
Connect the top line to the side lines to
make the roof; these lines will be about
2¾" long. You should have a 90-degree
angle at the center top. (See diagram
on previous page.)

③ Make House-Shaped Pieces

With right sides facing, align one small interior piece with one
small exterior fabric piece. Insert batting-wrapped plastic canvas
piece F between them, with the bottom edge of the plastic canvas
placed at least ½" above the bottom raw edge of fabric for seam
allowance. Mark a stitching line where fabrics meet snugly around
the sides and the top of plastic canvas piece. (This line may be
easier to draw accurately if you use the edge of a quilter's ruler to
determine exactly where fabrics meet.) Remove plastic canvas and
stitch along marked line, leaving bottom edge open.

Trim seam allowances, clip corners, and turn right side out.
Slide plastic canvas piece back between layers.

Repeat using second set of small interior and small exterior
fabric pieces and plastic canvas piece G.

④ Position the Canvas Pieces

With right sides facing, align one large interior piece and one
large exterior piece. Sandwich the remaining plastic canvas pieces
between the fabric layers in order from top to bottom (A-E).

When positioning canvas pieces, be sure to center the pieces,
leaving at least ½" free on all fabric raw edges for seam allowance
and a little room in between each plastic canvas piece for stitching. Also make sure that left and right sides of all pieces align with
each other vertically.

On the wrong side of the top fabric piece, mark stitching lines
around all four sides of each canvas piece as in step 3. Remove the
plastic canvas pieces.

⑤ Mark Handle and Closure Placement

Mark the placement of the button loops on the left and right marked stitching lines of plastic canvas piece E, just inside the top and bottom corners. Also mark the placement of one ribbon handle at the top raw edge, centering at least ½" in from the left and right stitching lines of plastic canvas piece A.

⑥ Assemble the House

Insert the fabric-covered piece F between the fabric layers where center piece C stitching lines are marked, aligning raw edges on one side and making sure the exterior side of the house-shaped piece faces the exterior fabric. Repeat on the right side with piece G. Pin into place. Insert one ribbon handle into place between layers on the top edge, aligning raw edges. Pin into place. Finally, insert four button loops between layers, aligning raw edges, and pin.

Stitch along the left, top, and right sides, following the outside stitching lines and catching all button loops, end pieces, and the ribbon handle as you go. Leave the bottom edge open.

Turn right side out and press. Insert the plastic canvas pieces one at a time, starting with piece A, and snugly topstitch each one into place before inserting the next piece. Finally, insert piece E, but do not stitch into place. Instead, turn the raw edges in, inserting the second ribbon handle and the center button loop into place. Slipstitch closed.

Hand-sew both sides of piece A and piece B to respective sides of house-shaped end pieces F and G, leaving piece D and piece E (with button loops) free.

Sew buttons onto the end and roof panels to match the button loops. Cut and hand-appliqué felt pieces onto fabric for decoration as desired (*see photo*).

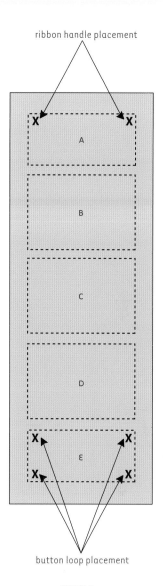

ribbon handle placement

button loop placement

STEP 5

PeG BeaR

Designed by Jhoanna Monte Aranez

Rub Peg's plush belly for luck! Bright, peppy prints really make this little toy pop, so put those cheery fabrics to work! If you have multiple children in your life and need more bears, you can easily make more than one from a yard of fabric.

MATERIALS

* Locate the pattern in the front pocket (sheet #2)
* 1 yard of 44/45" of fabric (quilting-weight cotton with small-to-medium scale print)
* 6" × 3" piece of linen or cotton (neutral color) for the face
* 11" × 4" piece of deep-pile polar fleece (cream or white) for the belly
* Scrap of black felt for the nose
* 1 pair of plastic safety eyes
* Black embroidery floss
* Embroidery needle
* Fiberfill
* ⅝" ribbon (optional)
* Pinking shears (optional)

Finished dimensions – approximately 5" wide × 24" tall

Seam allowance – ¼" unless otherwise specified

① Measure, Mark, and Cut

With right sides together, fold your fabric in half lengthwise, aligning the selvages. Pin all pattern pieces in place and cut them out. Transfer all markings to the wrong side of the fabric.

	Cut from linen:	Cut from fleece:	Cut from felt:
Body (cut 2)	**Face** (cut 1)	**Ears** (cut 2)	**Nose** (cut 1)
Ears (cut 2)		**Tummy** (cut 1)	
Arms (cut 4)			

NOTE: *Place pattern pieces along the grainline of your fabric.*

② Make the Arms

With right sides facing, pin one pair of arm pieces together; stitch around the curved edge, leaving the straight edge open. Repeat with the remaining arm pieces. Cut small notches around the curves, being sure not to cut into seam. Turn arms right side out, using a turning tool to gently push out the curves. Stuff each arm with fiberfill and edgestitch across the opening to close.

❸ Make the Ears

With right sides facing, stitch one fabric ear to one fleece ear. Stitch them together, leaving the straight edge open. Repeat with the remaining ear pieces. Cut small notches around curves, being sure not to cut into seam. Turn the ears right side out and set aside.

❹ Appliqué Features

As indicated on the pattern, appliqué the face onto one body piece: use a small, tight zigzag stitch around edges to secure. Appliqué the tummy to the same body piece in the same way. Machine-stitch or hand-sew the nose onto the face. Attach the eyes securely to the face, following manufacturer's instructions. Embroider the mouth and belly button.

❺ Assemble the Bear

* With right sides facing, pin the body pieces together, matching all raw edges. Insert the arms and ears into place as marked on the pattern, matching raw edges. Arms should be pointing inward and down and the fleece side of the ears should face the front body piece.

* Stitch around the body, leaving an opening as marked on the pattern. Cut small notches around all the edges, taking care not to cut into the seam. Gently turn the Peg Bear right side out through the opening. Use a turning tool to gently push out all the curves, particularly the feet.

* Stuff the bear with fiberfill, starting with the head and moving down to the tummy. Next, stuff the feet and legs, moving back up to the tummy. Use small amounts of stuffing at a time and try to stuff evenly across the body to avoid lumpiness. Dense, firm stuffing is preferable.

* Slipstitch opening closed.

* If desired, tie small piece of ⅝" ribbon around Peg Bear's neck for a jaunty flair.

GO FLY a KiTe

Designed by Joanna Teague

Kites mean pure enjoyment on those sunny, gusty days! You can use the leftover fabric to make a kite storage bag, which can be useful to prevent the kite strings from becoming tangled.

MATERIALS

* Locate the pattern in the front pocket (sheet #1)
* 1 yard of 44/45" fabric (strong, lightweight)
* 1 spool of coordinating thread
* 2 small brass rings
* Ball of string
* Ribbon or strips of fabric
* 2 kite sticks (wooden dowels), approximately 24" long
* 1 or more felt squares
* Small piece of cardboard
* 1 yard of ⅞" ribbon/braid
* ½ yard of ⅜" ribbon

Finished dimensions – kite is 24" × 24"; bag is 27" long × 4" wide
Seam allowance – ¼" unless otherwise specified

The Kite

① Measure, Mark, and Cut

Place your fabric in a single layer with the wrong side facing up. Follow the kite diagram to make a pattern for the kite. Add ¼" around all outside edges for seam allowance. Pin and cut out the pattern pieces, and measure and cut other pieces listed below. Remember to lay out and cut efficiently, so you'll have enough left over to make the storage bag.

* **Kite** measure and cut as shown from a 24" × 24" square (cut 2)
* **Stick guides** 2" wide × 14" tall (cut 2)
* **Top pockets** pattern pieces A and B (cut 1 each)
* **Bottom pockets** pattern pieces C and D (cut 1 each)
* **Reinforcement panels** pattern pieces E and F (cut 1 each)

NOTE: *The pattern pieces consist of three pairs of shapes that are identical but reversed, for right and left sides of the kite.*

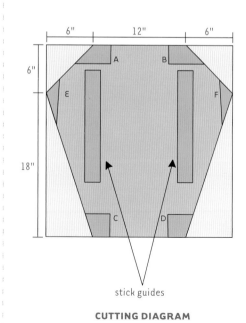

stick guides

CUTTING DIAGRAM

❷ Prepare Kite Fabric Pieces

Fold over and press ¼" seam allowance to wrong side all around kite, stick guides, and pocket edges. You may need to notch corners to make the seam allowance fold and press easily. Hem the pieces as follows:

* Edgestitch longest edge of pieces A, B, C, and D.
* Edgestitch the short ends of the stick guides.
* Edgestitch all edges of the kite.

❸ Attach the Pieces

With wrong sides together, pin pockets A and B at the top corners of the kite. Stitch around the three unhemmed pocket edges, leaving the long hemmed side open to hold sticks at a later step.

With wrong sides together, pin pockets C and D at the bottom corners of the kite. Stitch around the three unhemmed pocket edges, leaving the long hemmed side open to hold sticks at a later step.

With wrong sides together, pin reinforcement panels E and F onto the kite, as indicated on the pattern piece. Stitch around all three sides.

With wrong sides together, pin the long stick guides onto the kite, as indicated on the pattern piece. Stitch along the long sides, leaving top and bottom edges open to accommodate sticks.

❹ Finish the Kite

Hand-sew brass rings onto the reinforcement panels. Cut a 40" length of string for the bridle and tie each end onto the brass rings.

Wind at least 12 yards of string onto a small piece of cardboard. Tie the loose end of this string to the center of the bridle as indicated in the diagram.

Slide the kite sticks through the long guides and slip them into the top and bottom pockets. Cut lengths of ribbon for kite tails, and stitch to bottom stick pockets C and D on the wrong side of the kite. Varying the length of the tails will change the movement of the kite — try anything from 1 yard to 2 yards or more for the tails.

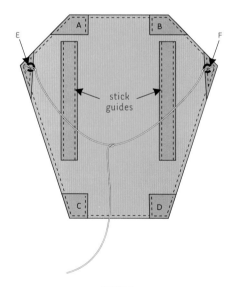

STEP 4
Attaching the bridle

The Storage Bag

① Measure, Mark, and Cut

Place your remaining fabric in a single layer with the wrong side facing up. Using a ruler and disappearing marker, washable fabric pen, or tailor's chalk, mark the dimensions on the wrong side of the fabric.

* ✳ **Bag** 10" tall × 28" wide (cut 1)

NOTE: *Place "tall" dimensions along the grainline of your fabric.*

② Add Letters

Cut "KITE" from felt using the appliqué pattern pieces provided on page 279, or you can draw your own. Sew letters into place by hand or machine, as desired.

③ Finish Bag

Fold the bag in half lengthwise, right sides together. Sandwich a ⅞" ribbon/braid between layers to make the strap. Position each ribbon end along the long bag edge, 1" from each end, aligning raw edges. Stitch along one short side and long raw edge (securing ribbon ends as you go), leaving the top short end open. Clip corners and turn right side out. Press under the raw edge ¼", then press under another ½". Stitch around the top, close to folded edge. Hand-sew two small pieces of ⅜" ribbon to the top for ties. Put your kite in the bag, tie up the top, sling it over your shoulder, and head to the park!

STEGGIE, THE PULL-ALONG DINO

Designed by Caitlin Bell

This cute plush stegosaurus is complete with a wheeled base for the child on the go. Steggie is also removable when it's time for some much-needed snuggling!

MATERIALS

* Locate the pattern in the front pocket (sheet #2)
* 1 yard of 44/45" fabric (flannel or quilter's cotton)
* 9" × 12" piece of felt
* Two ¼" or ½" buttons (for eyes)
* Four 1" squares of Velcro
* Fiberfill
* Piece of wood 5" × 7" × 1" (you can use wooden plaques found at craft stores)
* 4 wooden wheels
* 4 wooden axle pegs
* Acrylic paint
* Acrylic clear coat (optional)
* 1 screw eye
* 1 wooden bead
* ¼ yard of ⅝" ribbon
* Drill
* Craft glue

Finished dimensions – approximately 13" wide × 8" tall

Seam allowance – ¼" unless otherwise specified

❶ Measure, Mark, and Cut

Fold your fabric in half lengthwise, with right sides together, aligning the selvages. Pin all pattern pieces in place and cut them out. Transfer all markings to the wrong side of fabric.

* **Body** (cut 2)   *Cut from felt:*
* **Underbelly** (cut 1)   * **Spines** (cut 2)   * **Feet** (cut 4)

NOTE: *Place pattern pieces along the grainline of your fabric.*

❷ Stitch the Spines and Body

Pin the pieces for the spines together and stitch with a ¼" seam allowance along the spiky edge, leaving the straight edge open. Clip outer and inner points, being careful not to cut into the seam. Turn right side out and topstitch along the spiky edge. With body pieces aligned and right sides together, insert the spines between the layers, curving the straight edge to align with the curve of the body. Pin to secure, and stitch together from the dot at the neck to the dot at the base of the tail (as indicated by *dashed* lines on the pattern pieces). Leave an opening along the tail bottom for turning.

❸ Join the Underbelly

With right sides together, fold the underbelly piece along the dart stitching lines. Stitch the darts, trim excess dart seam allowances, and press open.

With right sides together, place the underbelly between the legs of the body pieces, aligning raw edges. Stitch with ¼" seam allowance as indicated by the dotted lines on the pattern pieces. Stitch each of the legs separately, leaving the bottom edges open. Clip all curves and corners.

❹ Add the Feet

Center and stitch the loop side of each Velcro square to each foot. With right sides together, pin each foot to each leg bottom, stitching them together with a ¼" seam allowance. Clip the leg seam allowances as necessary to fit the curve.

Turn the dino right side out through the tail opening and stuff with fiberfill, using a point turner (such as a chopstick) to push the fill into the pointy tail, head, legs, and other small areas. Slipstitch the opening closed and sew on buttons for eyes.

❺ Make Pull-Along Base

* Drill two holes into the longer 1"-thick sides of the wooden base 1½" from each corner, just large enough to fit the axles snugly.

* Paint the base, wheels, and bead with acrylic paint and allow them to dry. Follow with an acrylic clear coat if desired, for durability.

* Thread the axles through the wheels. Apply a small amount of glue to the drilled holes in the base and insert the axle pegs. Wheels should spin on the axles easily but not too loosely.

* Center Steggie on the base top and mark the Velcro placement. Glue the hook side of each Velcro piece where marked. If the base is clear-coated, superglue may be required.

* Install the screw eye into the center of one short side of the base. Thread ribbon through the screw eye and sew a loop to secure. Tie a knot approximately 1½" from the end, thread the end through the bead, and tie a second knot to secure the bead.

ELODIE THE ELEPHANT

Designed by Sarah Faix

*What's cuter than a baby elephant? Not a whole lot!
Sure to be loved by anyone who grew up, or is growing
up, watching Dumbo.*

MATERIALS

* Locate the pattern in the front pocket (sheet #2)
* 1 yard 44/45" of fabric (quilting weight)
* Scrap of contrasting/coordinating fabric (soft: flannel, chenille, or similar; optional)
* Two ½" (14mm) buttons for eyes (if for a young child less than 3 years old, embroider the eyes with floss instead)
* Embroidery floss for facial features
* Fiberfill
* Doll needle

Finished dimensions – approximately 6" wide × 10" tall

Seam allowance – ¼" unless otherwise specified

① Measure, Mark, and Cut

With right sides together, fold your fabric in half lengthwise, aligning the selvages. Pin all pattern pieces in place and cut them out. Transfer all markings to the wrong side of the fabric.

* **Body** (cut 2)
* **Head** (cut 2)
* **Legs** (cut 4)
* **Arms** (cut 4)
* **Ears** (cut 2)

Cut from contrasting fabric (optional; if not using, cut 2 more ears from main fabric):

* **Ears** (cut 2)

NOTE: *Place pattern pieces along the grainline of your fabric.*

② Stitch the Limbs, Ears, and Head

With right sides facing, pin two arm pieces together and stitch around the curved sides, leaving the straight edge open. Cut small notches around the curves without cutting into the seam. Turn right side out, using a turning tool to poke out curves and corners. Stuff with fiberfill, leaving 1" unstuffed, and edgestitch the opening closed. Repeat for the remaining arm and leg pieces.

With right sides facing, pin two ear pieces together (one main fabric and one contrasting), and stitch around the curved sides, leaving the straight edge open. Cut small notches around the curves without cutting into the seam. Turn right side out, using a turning tool to poke out curves and corners. Repeat for remaining ear pieces.

With right sides facing, pin two head pieces together, and stitch around the curves, leaving the neck open. Cut small notches around curves without cutting into the seam. Turn the head right side out, using a turning tool to poke out curves and corners, especially the skinny trunk. Embroider eyes or sew on buttons at desired locations. Embroider the mouth with a single stitch from one side of the face seam to the other.

❸ Assemble the Body

Position the arms on one body piece as indicated on the pattern, aligning raw edges. Edgestitch in place with a zigzag stitch.

With right sides facing, pin the body pieces together, and stitch both sides, leaving top and bottom edges open. Stitch again with a zigzag stitch within the seam allowance to reinforce a seam. Keep body turned wrong side out.

Insert the head into the body, right sides facing, aligning the neck raw edges and making sure the head front and back seams are centered on the body pieces. Stitch through all layers to attach the head, keeping raw edges aligned without creating tucks in the fabric. Stitch again at a ¼" seam allowance to reinforce this seam.

Turn right side out and stuff firmly, starting with trunk and head, working your way down to the body bottom. Push fiberfill up into the body slightly to make room for closing and attaching legs.

Turn the bottom raw edge under and insert the legs into the seam as indicated on the pattern. The elephant is pigeon-toed, so the toes point in. Slipstitch the opening closed, catching the legs as you sew.

❹ Finish the Elephant

Turn the raw edges of the ears in to the wrong side and press. Thread a needle with three strands of embroidery floss and sew a running stitch along this edge of each ear. Pull to gather, and tie knots at both ends to secure the gathers. Pin and slipstitch the ear in place on the head, making sure to catch the body fabric and both layers of the ear with each stitch. You may wish to add a second stitching line for extra strength. Knot and bury the ends when done.

ROCKET TO DREAMLAND

Designed by Jessica Bandelin

Your child will get a great night's sleep when this pillow blasts off to dreamland! The pocket can be used to stash lost teeth, a special toy, or any other object of his or her affection.

MATERIALS

* Locate the pattern in the front pocket (sheet #3)
* 1 yard of 44/45" fabric (quilting-weight cotton print)
* 1 spool of coordinating thread
* Three 9" × 12" rectangles felt (each in a different coordinating color)
* ¼ yard of ½" double-fold bias binding or ribbon in coordinating color
* Embroidery floss or yarn to match each felt color
* 1 large bag of fiberfill

Finished dimensions – 24" long × 15" wide × 15" deep

Seam allowance – ½" unless otherwise indicated

① Measure, Mark, and Cut

With right sides together, fold your fabric in half lengthwise, aligning the selvages. Pin all pattern pieces in place and cut them out. Transfer all markings to the wrong side of the fabric.

* **Rocket body** (cut 3)
* **Base** (cut 2)
* **Fins** (cut 6)
* **Pocket** (cut 1)

Cut from three different felt colors:

* **Small flame** (cut 2)
* **Medium flame** (cut 2)
* **Large flame** (cut 2)

NOTE: *Place pattern pieces along the grainline of your fabric.*

② Make the Flame

Use a running stitch and matching floss to hand-sew a small flame to a medium flame. In the same way, sew the medium flame to a large flame. Repeat for remaining flame pieces, creating a mirror image, then pin both large pieces back to back and stitch them together.

③ Assemble Rocket Base and Fins

With right sides facing, pin the base pieces together, inserting the completed flame between the layers and aligning the straight edge of the flame with the straight raw edge of the base. Stitch through all layers.

With right sides facing, pin two fin pieces together and stitch both sides up to the dot at the tip, leaving the straight edge open for turning and stuffing. Repeat for the remaining fin pieces. Clip the curves and point, being careful not to cut into the seam. Turn the fins right side out, using a turning tool to poke out the tips. Stuff the fins as firmly as desired, pushing fiberfill into the tip. Baste with an edgestitch at the opening to close.

④ Assemble Rocket Pocket and Body

Cut an 8½" piece of bias tape and encase the top edge of the pocket. Trim the edges of the bias tape.

Place the pocket, right side up, on the right side of one body piece, aligning the side and bottom edges. Baste in place close to the edges of the sides and bottom.

With right sides facing, pin two rocket body pieces together. Insert one fin between the layers, aligning raw edges at placement marks on one side. Stitch that side, from bottom to top of the rocket, stopping ½" from the rocket tip.

Repeat with the remaining rocket bodies and fins, ending by inserting the last fin between the first and last rocket body piece. Leave an opening on that last seam (where indicated on the pattern) for turning and stuffing.

Staystitch around the base piece ¼" from edge. With right sides together, stitch the base to the body, aligning the base seam with one body seam. Clip to ease where necessary. Turn the rocket right side out and stuff as firmly as desired. Slipstitch the opening closed.

CHAPTER 11

YOUR FURRY FRIENDS

How much do you love your pet? Well, surely enough that you won't forget about your favorite furry companions while crafting! There's something extra-special about the love they give you, so these projects are the perfect way to show them that you care (in addition to all the hugs, petting, and treats you already shower on them, of course)!

Pampered Pooch Walking Set

Designed by Jessica Roberts

You and your pet pooch will step out in style with this foursome. Best of all, all four projects can be made out of a single yard of fabric!

MATERIALS
* 1 yard of 44/45" fabric (quilting- or home-decor-weight cotton, woven)
* 1 spool of coordinating thread

Martingale Dog Collar

ADDITIONAL MATERIALS
* 2 welded or cast ¾" or 1" D-rings, depending on size of dog
* 1 welded or cast ¾" or 1" O-ring
* 2 yards of ½" or ¾" polyester ribbon, depending on size of hardware

Finished dimensions – varies by size of dog
Seam allowance – ½" unless otherwise specified

NOTE: *We suggest ¾" hardware for dogs under 40 lbs and 1" for dogs over 40 lbs.*

① Determine Collar Length

Measure your dog around the neck, going under the chin and up behind the ears. Hold the measuring tape tight, but don't choke the little guy! You should not be able to easily slip the measuring tape over the dog's head. This measurement is X. You may round up or down by up to ¼" to get a round number, if you like. Plug this measurement X into the following equation to find the length of the long collar piece: $X + 2 = \underline{\quad}(A)$.

② Measure, Mark, and Cut

Place your fabric in a single layer, wrong side up. Follow directions below, or see the table. (Remember to cut fabric as efficiently as possible to save room for the next three projects in this set.)

* For ¾" hardware, cut one long piece: A × 2⅜" and one short piece: 7" × 2⅜".
* For 1" hardware, cut one long piece: A × 3¼" and one short piece: 10" × 3¼".
* Cut two pieces of ribbon: cut one ½" shorter than the length of the long piece and cut the other ½" shorter than the length of the short piece (the ribbon provides extra strength to the collar and prevents stretching).

Piece dimensions	¾" Hardware wide × tall	1" Hardware wide × tall
Fabric long collar piece	A × 2⅜"	A × 3¼"
Fabric short collar piece	7" × 2⅜"	10" × 3¼"
Ribbon long piece	(A – ½") × 2⅜"	(A – ½") × 3¼"
Ribbon short piece	6½" × 2⅜"	9½" × 3¼"

❸ Fold and Stitch Collar Pieces

For both collar pieces, fold the short ends ¼" over to the wrong side and press. Fold in half lengthwise, wrong sides together, and press. Open the collar and press the raw edges toward the crease on the wrong side. Fold in half lengthwise again and press. Insert ribbon into the fold of each piece and topstitch all around.

❹ Attach the Hardware

* Fold each end of the long collar piece over the straight edge portion of each D-ring, overlapping fabric by ¾". Stitch each end with three lines of stitching, each parallel to the D-ring, going over the stitching at least twice for extra strength.
* Thread an O-ring onto the short piece (this is where you will attach the leash). Now, thread the short piece through both D-rings on the long piece and overlap the ends by ¾", creating a loop. Stitch the loop closed with three lines of stitching, each parallel to the D-ring, going over the stitching at least twice for extra strength.
* Attach tags to a D-ring and a leash to the O-ring.

Martingale Dog Leash

ADDITIONAL MATERIALS

* 1 metal swivel clasp
* 2½ yards of ½" or ¾" polyester ribbon, depending on size of hardware

Finished dimensions – approximately 42" long; width varies by size of dog

Seam allowance – ½" unless otherwise specified

❶ Measure, Mark, and Cut

Place your fabric in a single layer, wrong side up. Measure and mark the pieces below, and cut them out. (Remember to cut efficiently to save room for the rest of the projects in the set.)

* If you used ¾" hardware on the matching collar, cut two pieces 44" (or width of fabric) × 2⅜".
* If you used 1" hardware on the matching collar, cut two pieces 44" (or width of fabric) × 3¼".

❷ Make the Leash

* With right sides together, stitch both leash pieces along one short end and press the seam open. You should now have one long, narrow piece of fabric.
* Cut a length of ribbon ½" shorter than the length of leash piece (the ribbon provides extra strength and prevents stretching).
* Fold the short ends ¼" over to the wrong side and press. Fold in half lengthwise, wrong sides together, and press. Open the leash and press the raw edges toward the crease on the wrong side. Fold in half lengthwise again and press. Insert ribbon into the fold of each piece and topstitch all around.

❸ Make the Handle and Attach Hardware

* To make the loop for the handle, fold one end of the leash down by 8" and stitch three lines close to and parallel to the short end, going over the stitching at least twice for extra strength.
* Thread the other end of the leash through the hook and overlap it on the leash by ¾". Stitch three lines parallel to the short end, going over the stitching at least twice for extra strength.

Doggie Bandana

ADDITIONAL MATERIALS
* Snap or Velcro (optional)
Finished dimensions – varies by size of dog
Seam allowance – ½" unless otherwise
   specified

1 Measure, Mark, and Cut

Fold fabric in half, right sides together. Measure your dog's neck (follow instructions in collar pattern) and add 12" to determine bandana pattern piece length. Draw this line on the fabric, marking a center point. From the center measure a 10" line perpendicular to the first line and mark. This is the point of the bandana. (If your dog is shorter, you may wish to make this shorter.) Draw lines from each end of line to the bandana point, making a triangle. Cut two pieces. (Remember to mark and cut efficiently to save room for the following project.)

2 Make the Bandana

* With right sides together, stitch all three sides, leaving a 4" opening for turning along long edge. Clip corners, turn right side out, and press. Topstitch all around.

* If you prefer not to tie the bandana around your dog's neck, you could instead attach Velcro or a snap to both ends to fasten.

Dog Walk Bag

ADDITIONAL MATERIALS
* One 7" zipper
* Small snap
* Sewing-machine zipper foot

Finished dimensions – approximately 6" tall × 8" wide
Seam allowance – ½" unless otherwise specified

1 Measure, Mark, and Cut

Place your fabric in a single layer, wrong side up. Measure and mark the following pieces, then cut them out:
* **Attachment loop** 5" tall × 2" wide (cut 1)
* **Bag** 7" tall × 17" wide (cut 1)

2 Make the Attachment Loop

Press and stitch the attachment loop as you would to make double-fold bias tape (*see page* 18). Topstitch all around.

3 Attach the Zipper

Press under both short ends of the bag piece ½". Lay the zipper right side up and lay one folded short edge of the bag on top, close to the zipper teeth but far enough away so that zipper can open and close without catching fabric. Using a zipper foot, topstitch the fabric to one side of the zipper. Repeat for other side.

4 Make the Bag

Unzip the zipper halfway and turn the bag wrong side out. Position the zipper so that its center runs 2" below the top fold of fabric. On the side where the zipper is still closed, slip the attachment loop piece between the layers of fabric, above the zipper and along the top fold, aligning one end with the raw edge of the bag piece. Stitch the long edges, catching the attachment loop in the seam.

Clip corners and any zipper tape that extends past the seam line. Turn right side out through the zipper and press.

Stitch the snap halves to the upper back corner of the bag and the back of the attachment loop. Fill the bag with pooper-scooper bags, snap it around the leash handle or a belt loop, and head out!

COZY DOG BED

Designed by Mary Richmond

Give your dog some room to sprawl on this flat cushion with an extra-fashionable flair: piped edging. You might even be able to keep him off the couch. Imagine that!

MATERIALS

* ✳ 1 yard of 54"/60" fabric (medium- to heavyweight)
* ✳ 1 spool of coordinating thread
* ✳ 5½ yards of packaged piping with flange (optional)
* ✳ 3 pounds of polyester fiberfill
* ✳ Sewing-machine zipper foot

Finished dimensions – 30" long × 22" wide × 2½" deep, perfect for a small- to medium-size dog

Seam allowance – ½" unless otherwise indicated

① Measure, Mark, and Cut

With right sides together, fold the fabric in half lengthwise, aligning selvages. Measure and mark the following pieces directly on the wrong side of the fabric. On the wrong side of each piece, mark a dot ½" in from all four corners. Cut out the pieces.

* ✳ **Top and bottom panels** 23" × 31" (cut 2)
* ✳ **Side panels** 23" × 3½" (cut 2)
* ✳ **Front and back panels** 31" × 3½" (cut 2)

② Attach the Piping (Optional)

If using piping, starting at one corner, pin the piping to the right side of the top panel and baste using a zipper foot and a scant ¼" seam allowance, overlapping the ends. Repeat for the bottom panel.

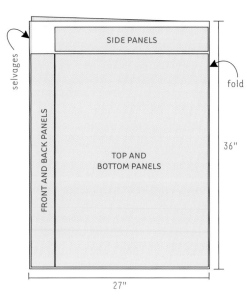

CUTTING LAYOUT

❸ Attach Front, Back, and Side Panels

With right sides together and matching raw edges, stitch the long edge of the top panel to the long edge of the front panel, beginning and ending at the marked dots. Stitch front panel to bottom panel in same fashion. Repeat for back panel and both side panels, leaving an 8" opening in the middle of one side for turning.

❹ Stitch the Side Seams

With right sides together and matching raw edges, stitch all four short side seams, beginning and ending at marked dots. Clip all corners, being careful not to cut through seams.

❺ Finish the Bed

Turn the bed right side out, pushing all corners out, and press. Stuff with the fiberfill, using small amounts at a time and filling the corners evenly. Slipstitch the opening closed. Now you have a cozy bed for your dog.

DOG WALKING COAT

Designed by Dorothy Grinolds

Keep your best friend warm and stylish with this doggie-style car coat. She'll be the talk of the town in these spanking new duds!

MATERIALS

* Locate the pattern in the front pocket (sheet #1)
* One yard of 44/45" or 54/60" fabric (heavyweight)
* 1 spool of coordinating thread
* ¼ yard of ¾" wide Velcro
* Two buttons (optional)

Finished dimensions – Varies depending on the size of dog (*see box*)

Seam allowance – ½" unless otherwise specified

❶ Measure, Mark, and Cut

With right sides together, fold the fabric in half, aligning the selvages. Use the pattern to cut the following pieces.

* <u>Coat body</u> (cut 2)
* <u>Collar</u> (cut 2)
* <u>Belt</u> (cut 2)

Also cut from Velcro:

* <u>2" pieces</u> (cut 4)

FABRIC AND SIZE OPTIONS

If you like, you could make the inner coat from flannel or fleece, or you could sandwich flannel or fleece between the coat layers for extra warmth. The pattern will fit XS-, S-, and M-sized dogs, as shown in the chart at right.

Larger sizes can be made by measuring your dog and enlarging the pattern on a copier as needed. For best results, transfer the pattern to a material such as muslin, cut it out, baste it, and try it on your dog before cutting your best fabric.

	XS	S	M
Dog neck	10"	14"	16"
Dog waist	16"	20"	22"

❷ Make the Belt

With right sides facing, pin the belt pieces together and stitch three sides, leaving one short end open to turn. Clip corners and turn right side out. Poke corners out with a turning tool. Turn raw edges under ½", press, and slipstitch opening closed. Pin to the top side of the coat, aligned with belt tabs, and topstitch in place. Add buttons at ends for embellishment if desired.

❸ Make the Collar

With right sides facing, pin the collar pieces together. Starting at one short end, stitch around three sides, leaving the inside curve open. Clip corners and cut small notches throughout outer curve, being careful not to cut through seam. Turn right side out and press. Topstitch around the three sewn sides of collar.

❹ Make the Coat Body

With right sides facing, pin the coat body pieces together. Sandwich the collar between body layers, centering along neckline and aligning the collar's inner curve raw edge with the neckline raw edge. Stitch around perimeter, leaving 3" open on the body bottom for turning. Clip corners on neck edges and waistband. Cut notches around the neck/collar and arms, being careful not to cut through seam. Turn right side out and press, turning raw edges at opening in to the wrong side. Edgestitch around the coat body, closing the opening and taking care not to catch the collar in the seam. Tack the collar down at the corners and center to hold it in place.

❺ Attach the Velcro

Stitch the hook half of each Velcro pair to the right side of the right neckband and waistband. Stitch the loop half to the wrong side of the left neck band and waistband. These stitches will show, so stitch carefully.

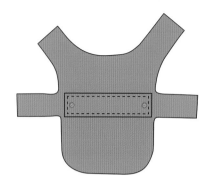

STEP 2

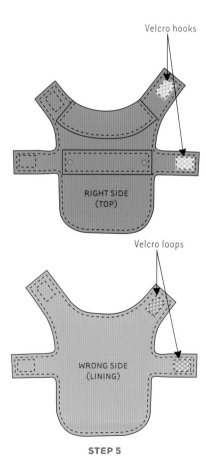

Velcro hooks

RIGHT SIDE
(TOP)

Velcro loops

WRONG SIDE
(LINING)

STEP 5

Better-Than-a-Box Pet Bed

Designed by Adrienne Lodico

This convex shape makes a cozier alternative to your small pet's favorite naptime box.

MATERIALS

* 1 yard of 44/45" fabric (nondirectional, machine washable)
* 1 spool of coordinating thread
* Fiberfill
* Stuffing stick or similar tool

Finished dimensions – fits any cat or small dog
Seam allowance – ½" unless otherwise specified

① Measure, Mark, and Cut

Cut out the pattern pieces in rows, as shown in the cutting layout. Trapezoid measurements represent the bottom length × top length × height.

* **Large trapezoids** 16" × 12" × 8" (cut 4)
* **Rim trapezoids** 16" × 12" × 4" (cut 4)
* **Small trapezoids** 12" × 8" × 6" (cut 4)
* **Large square** 12" × 12" (cut 1)
* **Small square** 8" × 8" (cut 1)

② Make the Bed Interior

With right sides facing, pin two small trapezoids together, with all raw edges aligned. Stitch along one diagonal side starting and stopping ½" from each corner; press seam allowance open. Continue stitching small trapezoids together end to end in the same way, ending by joining the first small trapezoid to the fourth small trapezoid to make a frame.

With right sides together, pin one side of a small square to one inside edge of the frame created above. Stitch together, making sure the seams meet at each corner of the square. Leaving sewing-machine needle in the down position ½" from the corner, pivot your work 90 degrees, and continue stitching each trapezoid piece to the respective side of the square. Finger-press the seams down while stitching. You will have a basket shape for the bed interior.

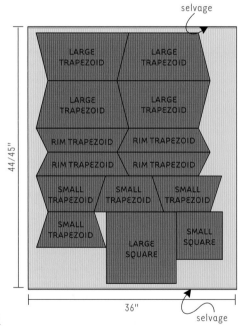

CUTTING LAYOUT

STEP 2

③ Make the Bed Exterior

Repeat step 2 using the large trapezoid and large square pieces, making a larger basket shape for the bed exterior. When stitching trapezoids to the square, leave a 4" to 5" opening in the middle of one side for turning and stuffing.

④ Stitch the Top Rim

* With right sides facing, pin two top rim trapezoids together, with all raw edges aligned. Stitch along one diagonal side starting and stopping stitching line ½" from each corner; press seam allowance open. Continue stitching top rim trapezoids together end to end the same way, ending by stitching the first trapezoid to the fourth trapezoid to make a complete frame.

* With right sides together, stitch the short side of each top rim trapezoid to the bed interior, matching the seams at corners as in step 3.

* With right sides together, stitch the long side of each top rim trapezoid to the bed exterior, matching seams at corners as in step 3. When finished, you should have what looks like a deflated, inside-out fabric balloon.

⑤ Stuff and Finish the Bed

Turn the bed right side out. Use fiberfill to stuff the bed. Start with putting the filling in each of the four sides, then continue by

filling in the bottom of the bed. Use a turning tool to push fiberfill down into the sides and all corners. Shape the bed as you stuff. Stuff the bed well but not too firmly, so that your pet can snuggle into the bed. Slipstitch the opening closed. Hand-tack the four corners of the smaller inside square through all four layers to help maintain shape. Place the bed in your lucky pet's favorite spot.

MILO'S FELINE-FRIENDLY TEPEE

Designed by Patricia Hoskins

Few cats can resist the allure of a box, bag, or small tent! This tepee can provide a cozy hideaway for your feline friend — or the perfect place to get ready for an ambush!

MATERIALS

* 1 yard of 44/45" fabric (nondirectional, home decor or heavyweight)
* 1 spool of coordinating thread
* 1 package of coordinating ½" double-fold bias tape
* Large, plastic, snap-in curtain grommets (optional)
* Four ½"-diameter dowels for sides, at least 27" long
* Four ½"-diameter dowels for base, 17½" long

Finished dimensions – 20" wide × 20" deep × 24" high

Seam allowance – ½" unless otherwise specified

① Measure, Mark, and Cut

Lay your fabric in a single layer, wrong side up. Trim selvages. Measure and mark the following pieces, then cut them out:

* **For tepee bottom.** Cut one 11½" piece across the width of the fabric, then cut this piece into two 11½" × 22" pieces.
* **For tepee sides.** With remaining piece, fold fabric lengthwise, selvage to selvage, and press the center crease. Fold lengthwise again, matching the crease to the selvage edges. Press all folds. Open the fabric and lay it wrong side up. Draw a diagonal line starting 2" down from top right corner to left raw edge, 1" up from the first crease. Draw a second diagonal line starting 1" below the first crease on the left edge, down to 1" above the center crease at the right edge. Draw a third diagonal line starting 1" below the center crease on the right edge, down to the left raw edge, 1" above the third crease. Draw a fourth and final diagonal line starting 1" below the third crease on the left edge, down to 2" above the bottom left corner.
* Cut along these lines to form three sides and two (half-sized) front flaps. The shortest (2") end of each side panel is the top edge.

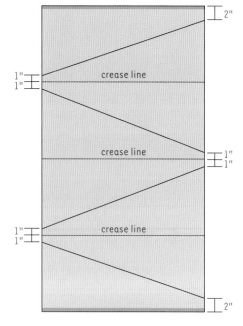

CUTTING LAYOUT
Tepee sides

STEP 2

② Form the Tepee Bottom

With right sides facing, pin the bottom pieces together, and stitch along one long edge. Press the seam open, then fold the seam allowances ¼" in to the wrong side and topstitch closed to make flat felled seams (*see page* 16). Cut out 2¼" squares in all four corners and mark a line parallel to and 1¼" away from each long raw edge, as in illustration.

❸ Bind the Edges

Bind the entire outer edge of the tepee bottom with bias tape. Fold long bound edges over to the wrong side along the marked lines. Topstitch to form a base dowel casing, ¾" from fold (stitch line should fall close to where bias tape edge meets fabric). Press the casing back toward the right side so that the bound edges face out away from the main bottom piece. Set aside.

❹ Install Grommets (Optional)

Grommets can be fun additions to the tepee, as you'll be able to dangle strings through the grommets for bonus fun! Install as many grommets as you'd like on the side panels, following manufacturer's instructions, making sure grommets are placed at least 2" away from all raw edges.

❺ Hem the Front Flaps and Sides

Make a narrow ¼" double-fold hem (*see page* 19) on the short top edge and long bottom edges of both front flaps and the remaining three side pieces. Do the same on the long straight side of each front flap. Leave all slanted sides unhemmed.

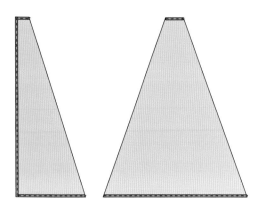

STEP 5

❻ Make Side Dowel Casings

* With right sides facing, pin two side panels together, and stitch along one long diagonal side with scant ¼" seam allowance. Attach the remaining side panel to a free diagonal raw edge of one of these side panels in the same fashion. With right sides facing, pin each front flap to its respective side panel, and stitch with scant ¼" seam allowance.

* Press seams open and turn tepee right side out. Topstitch panels together once more, ¾" in from each of these four side seams to form dowel casings.

❼ Attach Bottom and Base Dowel Casings

* With the right side of the base facing up toward the wrong side of the tepee, edgestitch each bound long edge of the base to the bottom of each of the three side panels, leaving the front flaps free.

* Starting at the back of the tepee, insert a base dowel into one edge of base casing. Insert two more base dowels in each of the remaining base casings. Finish the base by inserting the last base dowel into the front base casing.

* Insert side dowels into side dowel casings from top; you can let tops of dowels stick out and overlap like a traditional tepee; this will also help to keep the tepee sturdily upright.

APPLiQUÉ Pieces

Pirate Growth Chart
Page 223
Enlarge 300%

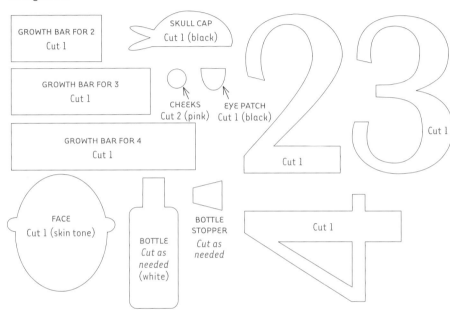

GROWTH BAR FOR 2
Cut 1

GROWTH BAR FOR 3
Cut 1

GROWTH BAR FOR 4
Cut 1

SKULL CAP
Cut 1 (black)

CHEEKS
Cut 2 (pink)

EYE PATCH
Cut 1 (black)

Cut 1

Cut 1

Cut 1

FACE
Cut 1 (skin tone)

BOTTLE
Cut as
needed
(white)

BOTTLE
STOPPER
Cut as
needed

Laptop Sleeve
Page 100
Enlarge 200%

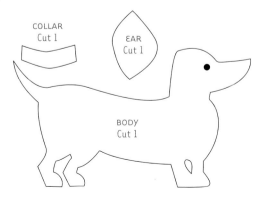

COLLAR
Cut 1

EAR
Cut 1

BODY
Cut 1

Go Fly a Kite
Page 254
Enlarge 200%

LETTERS
Cut 1 each from felt

GLOSSARY

Appliqué. Any technique of adhering one fabric piece on top of another in a decorative fashion. Appliqué may be applied with a double-sided fusible interfacing, a zigzag/satin topstitch along the edges of the top fabric, or a slipstitch with the top fabric's raw edges turned under, among other techniques. Hand embroidery is also often incorporated.

Backstitch. Used to secure and reinforce your stitching at the beginning and end of a seam to keep it from unraveling. (See page 13.)

Basting. Done by hand or by machine to hold your fabric sections in place until you are ready to complete your final stitches. This is done using the longest stitch on your sewing machine, so that you can easily remove these stitches later with a seam ripper.

Bias. The diagonal grain of the fabric; it accents the natural stretch of the fabric. True bias is found at an exact 45-degree angle from both the grainline and the crossgrain.

Bias tape. Made from a strip of fabric that has been cut along the bias grain of the fabric, usually with either a single or double fold along its length. (For more information, including how to make your own bias tape, see page 18.)

Binding. Encasing the raw edges of your project with another piece of fabric, often bias tape.

Blindstitch. Available on many sewing machines, this stitch is most commonly used for creating blind hems. For blindstitching by hand, see Slipstitch on page 14.

Bound edges. Using bias tape is a great way to finish edges. Always sew bias tape with the narrower side on top, as this will help ensure you catch the other folded edge of the bias tape in your stitching line (see page 18).

Casing. A channel sewn through two layers of fabric to allow elastic, cording, ribbon, or other material to pass through. Often used for elastic or drawstring waistbands. (For more on casings, see page 19.)

Center back. An unmarked line on a garment that corresponds to the center of the back of the body (often indicated on a pattern for placement and fitting purposes). Center back is not limited to clothing and can correspond to bags, toys, accessories, and other projects.

Center front. An unmarked line on a garment that corresponds to the center of the front of the body (often indicated on a pattern for placement and fitting purposes). Center front is not limited to clothing and can correspond to bags, toys, accessories, and other projects.

Crossgrain. The direction of the threads in a piece of fabric that run perpendicular to the selvage and parallel to the cut end of your fabric. It is the opposite of grainline, and there is a little bit of give when the fabric is pulled in this direction.

Darts. These are small seams that are most commonly used in clothing projects to take in fullness and add shaping. They are wide at the seam edge and taper to a point (see page 19).

Directional fabrics. Fabric prints may be unidirectional (one-way), bidirectional (two-way), or nondirectional (tossed) (see page 10). With a unidirectional print, there is a definite top and bottom to the print, most frequently because objects in the design all face the same direction, top to bottom. Bidirectional prints may be symmetrical top to bottom (if there are characters or objects, half face "up" and half face "down") but are not symmetrical side to side. Nondirectional prints allow you to place the fabric any direction without changing the look of the finished project.

Doll needle. A very long, thin needle that can completely pierce a three-dimensional stuffed sewn object such as a doll or plush animal.

Embroidery. A hand-sewing technique used to give your piece an extra-special touch. Some different types of embroidery stitches are French knots, stem stitch, chain stitch, satin stitch, and blanket stitch, to name a few.

Facing. A method to finish the edges of a shaped piece, such as at a neckline, an armhole, or a button placket. Facings are typically 2" to 3" wide, but the width can depend on the application, placement, and size of the garment.

Finger-press. To manually crease a seam allowance, fold, or other part of a fabric piece with your fingers. Frequently used when needing to press fabric out of the way during stitching, when it would be impractical or inconvenient to remove the fabric from the sewing machine in order to press with an iron before sewing the rest of the seam.

French curve. This sewing tool or template can be used to connect two (or more) points with a smooth curve. Especially useful for creating neck and armhole edges as well as trueing seams. Other similar tools include a fashion ruler, fashion curve, and curve ruler.

Grainline. The direction of the fabric that runs parallel to the selvage edge. Sewing patterns usually have a double-ended arrow printed on the pattern piece indicating grainline. When laying out your pattern pieces, make sure that the arrow lines up straight along the grainline.

Hand-sewing. A sewing machine can't do everything! Hand-sewing is often the only way to stitch a button or other closure onto a completed item or to ensure that you only go through one layer of fabric. A few other finishing techniques, such as slip-stitching and whipstitching, can only be accomplished by hand.

Interfacing. Used to provide shape, stiffness, and support in your projects, typically found in collars, cuffs, lapels, waistbands, and bags. Usually available in either iron-on/fusible or sew-in versions.

Lengthwise. This is the edge parallel to the selvage (see also Grainline). The opposite of "crosswise."

Markings. A variety of notations (typically found on pattern pieces) to help you with the construction of your finished project. Some examples of markings are darts, pleat lines, dots, notches, pocket placements. Be sure to transfer all markings to the wrong side of your fabric before removing your paper pattern pieces.

Nap. Certain fabrics have naps; corduroy, velvet, and faux fur are a few examples. When you rub your hand in one direction of the fabric, the color may appear to change. This is caused by the way the light hits the pile of the fabric. Treat nap fabrics as uni-directional and make sure to cut all pieces in the same direction.

Notches. Small triangles that appear along the edge of pattern pieces. During sewing assembly, notches are aligned on different pattern pieces to ensure that the project goes together correctly. Sometimes notches appear alone, other times in groups of two or three or more.

Notching. To make convex seams (outward curves) lie flat, notches are cut at regular intervals within the seam allowance to, but not through, the stitching line (see page 17).

Pinking. Cutting a zigzag raw edge using pinking shears or a pinking rotary cutter.

Pintucks. Often decorative and sometimes used for shaping, these folded tucks are formed by stitching together two lines, wrong sides together, that are about ⅛" apart (See page 19).

Pivot. A great way to turn a corner on a stitch line. Stop short of the fabric raw edge, the same width as your seam allowance. Leaving the needle down in the fabric, lift your presser foot up and turn the fabric 90 degrees to begin stitching the next seam.

Pleats. Folds in fabric that are either inverted or extroverted. They are common in skirts but also appear in a variety of other applications. Pleats provide both decorative and functional fullness. Pleats come in four different varieties: knife, box, inverted, and accordion.

Quilting. Quilted fabric generally has a piece of batting sandwiched in between two layers of fabric and then decoratively stitched through all layers. If you are quilting your own fabric, you should generally do so before cutting out your pattern pieces, as quilting draws fabric in and makes it smaller.

Right side. The side of the fabric on which the design is printed and almost always on the outside of your garment or accessory. If you are working with a solid piece of fabric where the right side is not readily obvious, determine which side you want to call the right side, and then try to be consistent. You may want to designate and mark the same side of each cut fabric piece as the wrong side to keep track.

Scant seam. To sew a scant ¼" seam, measure where you would place the fabric for a regular ¼" seam and move your fabric over just a teensy bit to sew a slightly smaller seam (somewhere between ¼" and ⅛").

Seam allowance. The distance between the seamline (stitching line) that joins two or more pieces of fabric together and the cut edge of the fabric. Standard seam allowances are frequently ⅝" wide, but it is becoming increasingly common for seam allowances to be ½" wide. Most projects in this book call for a ½" seam allowance.

Seamline. This is your basic stitching line for joining two (or more) pieces of fabric together.

Selvage. The selvage edge of the fabric is the edge that is often printed with the manufacturer's name and color information. This edge of the fabric is a finished edge and will not fray. The selvage edge runs in the same direction as the grainline. It is very important to know the selvage of your fabric. All cutting is done in relation to the selvage: grainline, crossgrain, bias are all designations that refer to the selvage edge.

Shank button. These buttons have no holes on the button itself but rather a shank on the back, which looks kind of like a stem. All sewing is done through the shank. Shank buttons stand out from the fabric, at the depth of the shank.

Smocking. Smocking is a decorative technique used to gather fullness. The width of the fabric required for a smocked project is often three times the width of the finished piece.

Staystitch. Typically sewn at a slightly longer stitch and just within the seam allowance, this stitch, which is sewn through a single layer of fabric, keeps a piece of fabric from stretching or distorting when sewn to another piece.

Tucks. Like darts, tucks are used to help eliminate fullness. They can be both functional and decorative. For a variation on a decorative tuck, see Pintucks.

Tufting needle. This is a heavier needle with a large eye, strong enough to go through thick fabrics and upholstery batting to create tufts in an upholstered object.

Wrong side. The side of the fabric on which the design is NOT printed and almost always on the inside of your garment or accessory. If you are working with a solid piece of fabric where the wrong side is not readily obvious, determine which side you want to call the wrong side, and then try to be consistent. You may want to designate and mark the same side of each cut fabric piece as the wrong side to keep track.

Zigzag. A basic sewing-machine stitch that looks like a zigzag. Typically, it can be varied in length and width. A very close zigzag stitch may be called a satin stitch and can be used for buttonholes (see page 14). The zigzag is also used for sewing stretch knits.

Resources

Fabric

Crafty Planet
612-788-1180
www.craftyplanet.com

Funky Fabrix
sales@funkyfabrix.com.au
www.funkyfabrix.com.au

Sew, Mama, Sew!
503-380-3584
www.sewmamasew.com

Spoonflower
919-321-2949
www.spoonflower.com

superbuzzy
805-644-4143
www.superbuzzy.com

Buttons

AccessoriesOfOld.com
301-760-7228
www.accessoriesofold.com

As Cute As a Button
619-223-2555
www.ascuteasabutton.com

Hushco Buttons
213-746-8555
www.hushcobuttons.com

Trims and Other Details

BeadWarehouse
802-775-3082
www.beadwarehouse.com

Cheeptrims.com
877-829-8746
www.cheeptrims.com

Les' Bon Ribbon
225-262-1921
http://lesbonribbon.chainreactionweb.com

JKM Ribbon & Trims
800-767-3635
www.jkmribbon.com

M&J Trimming
800-965-8746
www.mjtrim.com

Rochford Supply
866-681-7401
www.rochfordsupply.com

ZipperStop
212-226-3964
www.zipperstop.com

Inspiration and Other Forums

BurdaStyle
www.burdastyle.com

Craftster
www.craftster.org

Craft
www.craftzine.com

Etsy
www.etsy.com

getcrafty
www.getcrafty.com

ThreadBanger
www.threadbanger.com

CONTRIBUTOR BIOS

Adrienne Lodico

* *Better-than-a-Box Pet Bed, page 274*

From a very young age, Adrienne's supercrafty mama taught her to follow in her supercrafty footsteps. After a multiyear quest for the perfect green dress, she decided to create one of her own instead. Adrienne hasn't stopped stitching since! She blogs about sewing, knitting, pets, and other random bits of life at *http://hermionejschwartz.blogspot.com.*

Amanda Anderson

* *Organized Bed Pocket, page 34*

Amanda spends most of her time sharing her love of all things crafty with her patient husband and three children. She shares creative fun projects, ideas to bring the creative spirit into your home, links to neat stuff on the web, and ways to make daily life with your children more enjoyable on her blog *www.kiddio.org.*

Amanda Sasikirana

* *All-Ages Classic Jumper, page 191*

Amanda started sewing while she was pregnant with her daughter because she was unable to find the perfect baby girl clothes. You can find Amanda happily crafting away in Ohio, where she lives with her husband and toddler. She blogs about her sewing and knitting endeavors at *http://amandasasikirana.wordpress.com.*

Angie Knowles

* *Folding Chair Pinafore Slipcover, page 26*

Angie Knowles of ThreadNeedle Studio has been designing and sewing custom slipcovers in her home-based studio since 2000. Angie also teaches slipcover techniques to other professionals. Her work can be seen at *http://threadneedleinteriors.com.*

Anna Buchholz

* *Newborn Flyaway Jacket, page 186*

Anna began sewing at the age of five. After sewing countless outfits for her dolls, she moved on to sewing clothing and accessories for herself. In addition to sewing, Anna enjoys knitting, embroidery, and collecting vintage patterns. She currently resides in her native state of Ohio with her husband and adorable dog. See more of Anna's work at *http://sewsewetc.blogspot.com.*

Anne Lindholt Ottosen

* *Latte Changing Pad, page 182*

Sewing is Anne's favorite indoor hobby. Although she tends to get impatient with large involved projects, Anne always finds comfort in her sewing machine. Anne resides in Denmark with her patient husband and two children. Not a day passes without a sewing-related project, be it actual sewing, or reading sewing blogs and forums, or listening to podcasts. Anne hosts a sewing night with friends at least twice a month.

Becka Rahn

* *Laptop Sleeve, page 100*
* *Cuddly Bear Cushion, page 238*

Becka teaches and creates a little bit of everything fiber-art related: from sewing and dyeing clothing and creatures to beading and embroidering whimsical accessories and tiny art quilts. Becka lives with her husband and big blond dog in Minneapolis, where she works as the education manager and Web designer at the Textile Center of Minnesota. You can find her online at *http://beckarahn.com*, or her shop at *http://beckarahn.etsy.com.*

Beth Walker
* *Smock of All Ages, page 97*
* *Checkers to Go, page 244*

Beth taught herself how to sew so that she would face her fear of the sewing machine and satisfy her lifelong fascination with fabric. She also likes knitting, beads, other shiny things, and stencils of the cut-your-own variety. She writes, too. Some combination of all this has led to an essay in *KnitLit II*, an MFA in writing, and sewing patterns in some craft publications. Beth firmly believes that the world would be a much better place if everybody made something every day.

Bethany Nixon
* *Framed Tack Board, page 22*

Bethany is the proud owner of Reware Vintage (*http://reware vintage.com*), which sells both vintage and reconstructed goods. She is most known for (and especially enjoys upsetting record collectors by) cutting up vinyl and using it in her crafts. As the organizer of the Baar Bazaar in Detroit and a member of Handmade Detroit, she is inspired to help in the creation, networking, and promotion of the Detroit craft community.

Caitlin Bell
* *Firefighter Hat, page 216*
* *Steggie, the Pull-Along Dino, page 258*

Nifty Kidstuff (*http://niftykidstuff.etsy.com*) began when Caitlin was just 15 years old, as a way for her to make some cash without babysitting or working at a dreaded fast-food restaurant. She's been sewing as long as she can remember, from a 4-H quilting group as a toddler, to her first sewing machine at age six. Now Caitlin is a student at the Savannah College of Art and Design, studying fibers.

Cara Angelotta and Mark Cesarik
* *Mailbag Pocket Duo, page 32*

Sew Bettie was born in the summer of 2007 when Cara and Mark adopted the cutest puppy in the world, Miss Bettie Lou Sweet

Waters. As chief executive officer, Bettie inspires all of their urban whimsy fabric designs. The Sew Bettie limited edition fabric collection will inspire the crafty soul in you. Check it out at *www.sewbettie.com*.

Charlene Caruso
* *School Binder Cover, page 106*

Mother to three, Charlene started out making a formal maternity gown for a special event and from there went on to christening outfits, pillows, and so much more. She specializes in custom handbags and started her own company, Arm Candies (*http://armcandiesonline.com*). She then graduated to home décor and window treatments and is now a custom fabricator. Charlene is self-taught through books, DVDs, forums, and whatever other material she can read or watch.

Charlot Meyer
* *Cottage Apron, page 58*

Charlot is a full-time graphic designer and part-time enthusiast of all things handmade. Her current fascination is fashion pattern drafting and design. She is particularly intrigued by the link between clothing and memories. Mia Sorella Aprons was born from her belief that the things we wear are meaningful and telling artifacts of our lives. You can find her aprons online at *http://miasorellaaprons.etsy.com*.

Christine Haynes
* *The Mod Caper, page 151*

Christine is a Los Angeles–based designer and writer. You can learn to make more of her designs in her first book, *Chic & Simple Sewing*. Or pick up items from her eponymous clothing line at *www.christinehaynes.com* or in specialty boutiques around the world. Christine's work has been featured in the *New York Times*, the *Los Angeles Times*, People.com, *Venus Magazine*, *Daily Candy*, the *Today Show*, and more.

City Chic Country Mouse (Jamie Halleckson and Carmen Marti)

* *Tabletop Ironing-Board Cover, page 54*

Jamie (City Chic) and Carmen (Country Mouse) are a mother-daughter team. Jamie lives in the Twin Cities with her husband and three fur babies. She spends her free time coming up with new designs for City Chic Country Mouse (*http://citychiccountry mouse.etsy.com*). Carmen lives in northern Minnesota with her husband and rescue dog, Lady Bug. She has been sewing since she was a little girl and has tried many different crafts, but she always comes back to her first love — sewing!

Danielle Wilson

* *Lined Bookcase, page 24*

Thanks to the hard work and sacrifice of her husband, Danielle is able to stay home and care for their sweet baby daughter, Avery Jane — the inspiration for all of Danielle's projects! In between diaper changes, nursing, belly tickles, and baths, Danielle sews, crafts, paints, creates, and dreams — about all the things that make her sparkle. Visit Danielle at *http://my sparkle.blogspot.com*.

Dawn Lewis

* *Fabric Farmhouse, page 248*

Also known as the "UK Lass in the U.S.," Dawn is an English woman living in California with her American husband and two young children. Since having kids, Dawn has taught herself to sew, knit, and crochet, among other things. Read more about her crafty projects as well as her experiences since moving to the United States at *http://uklassinus.blogspot.com*.

Donna Pedaci

* *Toddler Pinafore Smock Top, page 188*

Donna lives with her husband and two daughters in Ohio. She enjoys creating simple, practical clothing with a whimsical touch, and nearly all her garments feature some sort of hand-sewn detail. Donna is inspired by old children's books, 1930s fashions, and Japanese craft books. You can find more about Donna and her creations at *http://purplekappa.typepad.com*.

Dorothy Grinolds

* *Dog Walking Coat, page 272*

Dorothy is an artist and animal lover. She has an MFA in photography and teaches photography at the local community college. She also designs dog coats and toys out of her home studio in Iowa. Her dog, Ladybug, a miniature dachshund, is her muse and model. Dorothy hopes to someday use the profits from her hand-made dog coats and accessories (*http://bugduds.etsy.com*) to support animal welfare.

Elizabeth Hartman

* *Dresser Organizer & Charging Station, page 29*

Elizabeth lives with her husband and two cats outside Portland, Oregon. She's been sewing and making things all her life. It's Elizabeth's goal to eventually quit her "day job" and design sewing/quilting patterns full time. She maintains and writes a sewing blog, Oh, Fransson! (*www.ohfransson.com*), and also sells her sewing patterns on Etsy (*http://ohfransson.etsy.com*).

Ellen Baker

* *Bohemian Banana Bag, page 162*
* *Beanbag Booster Seat, page 232*

Ellen lives in Atlanta with her husband and two young daughters. Ellen is the author of The Long Thread, a blog about handmade goods. She has always enjoyed making things, and being a stay-at-home mom provides creative inspiration and allows her to craft on a daily basis. Combining her love of graphic design and sewing, she sells original machine embroidery designs and sewing patterns at *http://thelongthread.etsy.com*.

Elorie Bechtel

* *Granny's Clothespin Apron, page 51*

Ellie fondly remembers her childhood in the Pacific Northwest — daydreaming while pinning clothes to her granny's wash line or lying under her grandpa's apple trees. Now living with her family in Missouri, Ellie brings her daydreams to life in a home they call "the Cabin," including, of course, sewing elaborate creations for her own little girls (from Granny's stash!). She writes about her life at *http://ellierichellie.blogspot.com*.

Erin Evans

* *All-You-Need Sewing Kit, page 76*
* *Patches the Turtle, page 246*

Erin is a fun-loving, mimosa-drinking girl from the South. She received her BA in art with an emphasis on textiles and fiber arts. Currently, Erin resides in Georgia with her husband and special-needs dog, Basil. You can find more of Erin's work at *http://erinmevans.com*.

Gene Pittman

* *Yoga Mat Bag, page 127*

Gene's appreciation for craft was instilled while he was an undergraduate in North Carolina. Constantly surrounded by makers of things, he grew to understand the "craft of craft" and apply it to his own work. Trained as a sculptor, he now spends most of his time behind a camera. Gene's work can be seen at *www.genepittman.com*.

Heidi Massengill

* *Quilted Circles Shoulder Bag, page 164*

Heidi is an experienced seamologist and fiber artist who resides in Ohio with her husband. She is co-owner of the fiber arts workspace and shop Stitch Cleveland (*http://stitchcleveland.com*), where she and her partners teach private lessons and classes. Heidi's creations fill the Stitch Cleveland shelves, and she has sewn for a wide variety of clients, including The Cleveland Ballet and the Cleveland Orchestra. She maintains a blog at *http://heidi.stitchcleveland.com*.

Helen Ringrose

* *Planner Sleeve, page 111*

Helen is a UK-based crafter and blogger who loves sewing, knitting, and crochet. She works as a design consultant for a craft company and blogs at *http://sewstylish.blogspot.com*.

Irene Rodegerdts

* *CD Pocket, page 103*

Irene is a stay-at-home mother of three with a very patient and loving husband. She loves to bake, sew, and knit. Irene creates to relieve stress. She sews nearly every day and is both awed and inspired by all the wonderful work of others. Irene always looks forward to trying new projects, which you can read about at *http://mushroomvillagers.wordpress.com*.

Isabelle Brasme

* *Bias Skirt, page 135*

Isabelle is a French woman living in Paris. She is a literature teacher and researcher by day and a self-taught seamstress by night. Isabelle began sewing in 2004 and has never looked back. Sewing has been a wonderful way for her to add balance to her busy life. Read more about Isabelle on her sewing blog *http://kittycouture.blogspot.com*.

Jana Nielson

* *Petite Diaper Tote, page 178*

Jana is a stay-at-home mother of six. She loves sewing, making up her own patterns, and doing all things crafty. Her motto is, "Sewing Keeps You Sane," and she says she has to do a lot of sewing because of all her children and their antics. See more of Jana's work at *http://lolaagain.blogspot.com*.

Jessica Bandelin

* *Rocket to Dreamland, page 263*

Jessica lives and works in Minnesota with her husband and their two lovely children. She enjoys sewing, knitting, and making music. Jessica learned to sew at the age of 10 on her mother's high school Spartan sewing machine, and it is still going strong 22 years later. Read more about Jessica at www.fifthlampdown.blogspot.com.

Jessica Roberts

* *Obi-Inspired Hot-&-Cold Pack, page 73*
* *Perfect-Fit Sleep Shorts, page 140*
* *Pampered Pooch Walking Set, page 266*

Jessica has been sewing and crafting for as long as she can remember. She currently crafts in Columbus, Ohio, under the tolerant eyes of her husband, bird, and dogs. You can see what she's currently up to at www.kusine.com.

Jessica Vaughan

* *Not-Ugly Car Trash Bag, page 113*

Jessica is known to many as Finny Knits (http://finnyknits. blogspot.com). Jessica wore many hand-sewn outfits as a child (thanks, Mom!) but went on to flunk Home Economics before finally learning to sew eight years ago from directions that came with her $100 Kenmore sewing machine, an obstinate little tart that answers to the name, "What the . . . ?!"

Jessie Senese

* *Grocery Tote, page 174*

Jessie loves to sew. She also loves thrift stores, old maps, children's books, flea markets, mod wallpaper, polka dots, costume jewelry, embroidery patterns, chocolate pudding, vintage fabric, and her darling family. Jessie sews to her heart's content in her home studio just outside of Chicago and invites you to follow along with her "misadventures in craft" at www.sweetjessie.com.

Jhoanna Monte Aranez

* *Peg Bear, page 252*

Despite excelling in arts and crafts in her school years, Jhoanna only began sewing following the birth of her first daughter. After failing to find a toy that was truly unique and one-of-a-kind for her daughter, Jhoanna taught herself to use a sewing machine. Her daughter immediately loved her first creation. Jhoanna began selling her creations, and One Red Robin (http://oneredrobin.com) was born. She creates original soft toys, dolls, kids' accessories, and artwork out of her small studio in her Melbourne, Australia, home.

Joanna Teague

* *Go Fly a Kite, page 254*

Joanna is a lifelong crafter from the United Kingdom who just loves making things. She mostly chooses to design with textiles, fitting her crafting around a busy family life. Be sure to check out Joanna's blog at http://thingshandmade.blogspot.com.

June Gilbank

* *Sewing Tools Trio (Pincushion and Needlebook Holder), page 83*

June is a crafter and crochet pattern designer in Ontario, Canada, where she lives with her husband and beloved cat. Her patterns, free tutorials, and craft blog are all available on her website www.planetjune.com.

June Scroggin

* *Bathroom Makeover, page 41*

June lives in Arizona with her husband. She has five children and eight grandchildren. June considers each day a magical gift and, as such, lives each day in a creative way. Her projects here have been designed to enhance a bathroom in an economical way as well as serve a practical need. This is also June's approach to daily life, which she dubs "Creative Functionality." You can follow June's blog at http://junie-moon.blogspot.com.

Katherine Donaldson

* *Origami Organizer, page 88*

Katherine is currently transitioning from being a computer scientist working in image processing to being a full-time play-at-home mom, and having a great time. Katherine has always been a geek and an artist, from sewing doll clothes in elementary school to majoring in computer science and mathematics while finding time for an art minor in sculpture. She loves everything tiny and boxes to hide it all in. You can see her current work at *http://oneinchworld.com/blog*.

Kevin Kosbab

* *Hanging Wall Pocket, page 79*

Kevin is a writer, editor, and craft designer with a midcentury aesthetic. His articles appear regularly in *Quilter's Home* magazine, with designs in other publications such as *American Patchwork & Quilting* and *Quilts & More*. Learn more about his midcentury-inspired quilts and other craft exploits at *www.feeddog.net*.

Lauren Booth

* *Folklore Bag, page 159*

Lauren is a molecular biology graduate student in California. She thanks her grandma for fostering a love of arts and crafts at an early age, and she's been crafting ever since!

Lelia Thell

* *Oven Mitt & Hot Pads, page 62*

A stay-at-home mom with two daughters, Lelia lives in Minnesota and sews whenever she gets the chance. She began quilting when her older daughter was a baby and now she sews aprons, bags, oven mitts, baby blankets, and whatever else she can think of. See her work at *http://lthell.etsy.com*.

Lindsie Blair

* *Child's Messenger Bag, page 234*

Lindsie and her husband live in Iowa with their two children. Lindsie enjoys all things creative; she loves to cook and write for her blog, This Abode (*http://thisabode.blogspot.com*), where she explores creative, frugal homemaking. She created the Child's Messenger Bag initially so her son with food allergies could carry his Epi-pens while away from home.

Lisa Powers

* *Mother-Daughter Halter Tops, page 142*

Lisa is a fiber artist with 30 years of jumbled experience! Sewing and teaching are two of the things that make her happy, as well as her husband and two awesome little girls. Lisa sells her wares through her two online shops: *http://infantile.etsy.com* and *http://onthesweeterside.etsy.com*.

Madeline Elizabeth Steimle

* *Simply Beautiful Sundress, page 144*

Madeline attends college in Illinois. She currently studies art and hopes to one day paint and design clothing for a living. Madeline's custom creations are available online at *http://lamadeleine.etsy.com*.

Maggie Bunch

* *Summer Fun Play Top, page 196*
* *"Twist & Shout" Twirl Skirt, page 199*

Maggie hails from the smocking and heirloom world. Her designs have been published in *Sew Beautiful* and *Creative Needle* magazines, and she teaches smocking through the Smocking Arts Guild of America. Mom to two young adults, and wife to a retired USAF pilot, she has used smocking as a means to meet new friends with each move. Smock with Maggie at *http://maggiebsmocks.typepad.com/smocking*.

Marlene Gaige

* *Leisure Suit Lapdog, page 241*

Marlene has been a textile addict practically from infancy! She learned to sew as a small child from her grandmother and she insists her boys learn to sew today. She has owned a store and has taught classes all over the world, but she enjoys creating patterns and playing with textiles the best. Marlene likes using vintage textiles because their history lends a unique vibe to any new piece created. Marlene's work is available for sale at *http://allmyown.etsy.com*.

Mary Richmond

* *Quilted Lunch Bag, page 108*
* *Cozy Dog Bed, page 270*

Mary has been in love with crafting ever since she can remember. After receiving a sewing machine as a gift in high school, the love of creating with fiber began. Mary enjoys sewing, cross-stitch, and rug hooking, and her latest passion is knitting. You can find her at *http://luckyknitter.blogspot.com*.

Matt DeVries

* *Matt's Map Bag, page 115*

Matt and his wife Patricia Hoskins are co-owners of Crafty Planet (*www.craftyplanet.com*), an independent craft shop in Minneapolis specializing in the hippest fabrics, patterns, knitting, and other needlework. In his far-too-infrequent spare time, Matt enjoys riding and working on vintage motorscooters, pinball, and skateboarding. Matt will have you know he can survive on a steady diet of breakfast cereal and peanut butter and jelly sandwiches.

Mellissa Abreu

* *Mini Craft & Tool Belt, page 208*

Mellissa, better known as "Wondermommy," is the work-at-home mom of two children. She has always loved to craft — her favorites are crocheting and sewing. More than crafting, she loves to share crafts with others and wants all moms to know that they have a Wondermommy inside. Find her at: *http://wondermommy. wordpress.com* and *www.wondermommy.biz*.

Michele Chisholm

* *Beach-Time Towel Tote, page 118*

Michele is a lifelong sewing enthusiast and crafter thanks to the craft talents of her parents. Now that her children are older and her new home includes an office and studio space, Michele has gotten right down to fulfilling a lifelong dream of running a sewing/crafting/embroidery business from home. Michele lives in South Carolina with her husband and children; keep up with her at *http://calicodaisy.blogspot.com*.

Mother's Apron Strings (Gwen, Stacey, and Lindsey Ross)

* *Kitschy Kitchen Apron, page 56*

Mother's Apron Strings is a mother/daughter trio who love to dabble in the craft room and kitchen. Mother's Apron Strings was born from a combination of these passions. With keen eyes for fresh fabrics and retro designs, their aprons are at the crossroads of kitsch and cute. Check out more of their goods at *http://mothersapronstrings.etsy.com*.

Natalya Kremenetskaya

* *Hey, Hot Dish, page 66*

Natalya spends countless hours in the kitchen concocting the most delicious savory taste sensations and holds a very impressive ribbon collection earned for her various casserole dishes. When she's not in the kitchen whipping up a cream soup-based hot dish, you can find Natalya busy with a card catalogue, as she is a head librarian in Moscow, Russia.

Nina Mayfield

* *Baby Gift Set, page 218*

Nina is a self-taught fiber artist who started sewing children's clothes and art dolls over 20 years ago. She has been published in *Altered Couture* magazine and has had her art in several local galleries and shops. She teaches classes in art to wear, doll making, and basic sewing skills. Nina has two sons and currently lives in Minnesota. Visit Nina at *http://audreysdaughter.etsy.com*.

Nina Perkins

* *Flouncy Bag, page 156*

The daughter of a seamstress and the sister of a costume designer, Nina grew up playing in fabric. She learned to design and sew without patterns from her sister, and got her inspiration from all the little girls in her life. She currently works as a photographer, delving into fabric design, and loving the life of a mother with young children. Nina is grateful for the gift of creativity and hopes to nurture this gift in as many fabric fanatics as she can.

Oona Peterson

* *Bird Mobile, page 228*

Oona runs her handmade business, RUN AMOK (*http://runamok.etsy.com*), out of a small, supercluttered craft room in Minnesota. She makes bags and purses from vintage kimono fabrics, screenprints fabric and paper, and loves to attach buttons to nearly every surface in sight. She blogs about her crafting endeavors at *http://_runamok.livejournal.com*.

Patricia Hoskins

* *Ruffled Café Curtain, page 36*
* *Wine-Lovers' Special (Coasters), page 71*
* *Mitered Square Blankie, page 226*
* *Milo's Feline-Friendly Tepee, page 276*

Patricia and her husband Matt are co-owners of Crafty Planet (*www.craftyplanet.com*), a retail fabric and needlework store plus craft workshop in Minneapolis, Minnesota. She dabbles in all manner of crafty things, especially those involving fabric and yarn, but has yet to keep many completed projects for herself (she has yet to complete many projects, for that matter).

Rachael Theis

* *Ballet-Neck Toddler Dress, page 201*
* *Toddler Art Smock, page 214*

Rachael began designing children's clothing and toys in 2003 after the birth of her daughter. Since that time she has pursued designing with fabrics, wool, wood, paper, and yarn. Each year Rachael participates in the Minnesota County and State Fairs — as a domestic goddess, Rachael finds these competitions very rewarding.

Rae Hoekstra

* *Hanging Laundry Bag, page 48*
* *Summer Nightie, page 137*

Rae would like to thank her mother for teaching her to sew at a very young age. Now temporarily retired from teaching high school physics to raise her baby boy, she takes every opportunity she can to sew. Rae resides in Michigan with her husband and son. Find her blog and Etsy store by visiting *http://madebyrae.blogspot.com* and *http://happygiraffe.etsy.com*.

Rebecca Jo Malmström

* *"Good Hat Day" Hat, page 153*

Becca Jo, of Minnesota, is a costume designer, spinner, knitter, beader, writer, and stuffed animal maker. Stories of her journey to become a "real" working "artist" can be found at *http://beccajo.blogspot.com*. You can find more of her lovely wares at *http://beccajo.etsy.com*. When Becca Jo isn't crafting, she's helping other crafters by organizing local craft shows with her friends.

Rebecca Yaker

* *Picnic-tastic Lunch Mats, page 60*
* *Craft or Garden Apron, page 94*
* *Spats, page 147*
* *Hands-Free Belt Bag, page 169*
* *Pleated Girly Skirt, page 204*

Rebecca began sewing at age five and is still chastised for breaking her mother's sewing machine! She creates unexpected luxuries of fun using all-American elements and icons in the most unpredictable ways. In 2005, Rebecca launched Hazel and Melvin's Room, for which she creates one-of-a-kind baby bedding and apparel. More of Rebecca's work can be seen at *www.hazelandmelvin.com* and *www.sockmonkeys.com*.

Regina Lord

* *Scrunchie Bag, page 166*

Regina is a married mother of two boys and a part-time registered nurse and lactation consultant. She spends every free moment sewing, painting, and crafting. Regina also loves to spend time with her family, hiking, and enjoying the Arizona sun. Learn more about Regina's creative goods and processes at *www.creativekismet.com*.

Robin Dodge

✳ *Pintucked Top, page 130*

Robin is a librarian at a design school and an insatiable crafter in her free time. She dabbles in as many crafts as the space in her tiny studio will allow, from sewing to metalwork, handspinning to screenprinting. Robin is currently focusing on fiber arts, primarily handspun yarn and handknit goodies (*http://onesheephill.com*). She just started a new knitting Web site at *http://metapostmodernknitting.com*. She occasionally finds time to make jewelry and is currently trying to expand her knowledge of metalwork.

Roxanne Beauvais

✳ *Convertible Craft Apron, page 211*

Roxanne lives in North Dakota with her husband and young daughter. She enjoys all kinds of creating, including knitting, paper crafts, and certainly sewing. Her latest creations can be seen on her blog at *http://craftaddictions.blogspot.com*.

Sarah Faix

✳ *Elodie the Elephant, page 261*

Sarah started sewing when she was a little girl and hasn't stopped since. When Sarah's daughter was born, she was disappointed not to be able to find a perfect "first doll." It took two years to gather the confidence to make the doll herself. That time also marked the birth of Bits of Whimsy Dolls. Her daughter still inspires all her creations; in fact, Elodie was a special request from her. You can find more of Sarah's creations at *www.bitofwhimsydolls.com*.

Sarah Hunter

✳ *Tea Cozy, page 69*

✳ *Wine-Lovers' Special (Wine-Bottle Holders), page 71*

✳ *Sewing Tools Trio (Sewing-Machine Cover), page 83*

Sarah loves to sew projects ranging from medieval dresses to wallets and pillows. She also designs imaginative play items for toddlers, which she sells through her business, Everyday May, in Georgia. You can find more about Sarah at *http://sewnbysarah.com*.

Sharon Madsen

✳ *Two-Drawer File Cabinet Cover, page 45*

✳ *Strapless Belted Tunic, page 132*

Sharon, a self-taught sewer since the age of 8, began selling her sewn creations at the age of 14 and has had several projects published. To this day her grown children claim they spent too much of their childhood in fabric stores. Sharon resides in Minnesota with her husband and two dogs, where she blogs about her sewing adventures at *http://sharonsews.blogspot.com*.

Shelley Crouch

✳ *Collapsible Shopping Tote, page 125*

Shelley has been sewing since she was big enough to grab bits and pieces from her mother's scrap basket, but she officially learned to use a sewing machine in middle school. Shelley has learned a lot through trial and error — she loves the tactile experience of sewing and enjoys creating things to make her homestead more comfortable. Shelley lives in northern Canada with her husband and cat. You can read Shelley's blog at *http://inapeanutshell.com*.

Stephanie Sterling

✳ *Strapless Bandeau Shorty Jumper, page 194*

Stephanie lives in Baltimore with her husband, young daughter, and dog, Teenie. A lawyer by day, she blogs at *http://neurosesgalore.com* about life, food, creavity, and, well, a little bit of everything!

Sue Ainsley

✳ *Festive Flag Banners, page 230*

While growing up in British Columbia, Canada, Sue and her twin sister were rather crafty and frequently toured local thrift shops for inspiration. Sue began sewing two years after the birth of her daughter and has not stopped since. She is inspired by everything sewing related, including her large stash of new and vintage fabric, patterns, books, finished projects, and knitting and sewing blogs.

Susan W. Schurz

* *Artist Brushes Case, page 92*

Susan owns a professional custom drapery workroom and is an instructor for the Custom Home Furnishings Academy in North Carolina. She is a nationally respected professional and educator, as well as publisher of educational videos and *Sketches for Home Decor,* a book of original window treatment designs. Visit Susan at *http://tavernhill.net.*

Tracy Parker

* *Pirate Growth Chart, page 223*

Tracy is a Midwestern mom who learned to sew at age five. After 20 years of perfecting her craft, she launched her own business called Pumpkin Girl (*http://pumpkingirl.etsy.com*). Her designs include kids' clothes and cards that are often made from recycled or sustainable materials. Her work has been featured on *www. inhabitots.com* and *http://coolmompicks.com,* and she won a red ribbon for infant sleepwear in the 2008 Minnesota State Fair.

Valerie Williams

* *Jewelry Roll, page 122*

Valerie is the designer and sewer behind Holland Cox (*http:// hollandcox.com*), the home of handcrafted handbags and accessories in unique silhouettes and bold fabric combinations. Every Holland Cox handbag is a limited edition or a one-of-a-kind piece. Valerie has a three-part belief system: sewing is the best hobby; everyone deserves to have nice things; and handmade is always better.

Welmoed Sisson

* *Smocked Pillow in the Round, page 39*

Welmoed is the owner of Bellwoods Interiors, a drapery workroom in Gaithersburg, Maryland. She created the pillow design for a display at the 2007 International Window Coverings Expo in Washington, D.C. Welmoed also teaches home dec classes for the PatternReview.com Web site, and runs the Creative Machine Yahoo group. She has been sewing since she was eight years old.

The photo stylist would like to thank:

MODELS

Ana Beinhart

Iris Larson

Nancy Lundy

Sasha Lunn

Austin Tondini

Aubrey Yokota

PETS

Jill Cornillon

Michelle Platt

Celia Bland

LOCATIONS

Jill Cornillon

Nancy Lundy

Tanya Marcuse

Kate Pfeffer

Tivoli Bread and Baking

PROPS

Jill Cornillon

Hunter Bee

Our Featured Fabrics

Most of the fabrics featured in this book come from the following manufacturers and/or designers. Visit their websites or your favorite fabric sources to view their current collections of fabric prints, which change regularly.

Rowan (Westminster Fibers)
www.westminsterfabrics.com

* **Amy Butler**
  www.amybutlerdesign.com

* **Joel Dewberry**
  www.joeldewberry.com

Free Spirit
www.freespiritfabric.com

* **Heather Bailey**
  www.heatherbaileystore.com

* **Heather Ross**
  www.heatherrossdesigns.com

* **Erin McMorris**
  www.erinmc.com

* **Denyse Schmidt**
  www.dsquilts.com

* **Valori Wells**
  http://valoriwells.com

Alexander Henry Fabrics
www.ahfabrics.com

Michael Miller Fabrics
www.michaelmillerfabrics.com

* **Sandi Henderson**
  http://sandihendersondesign.com

Timeless Treasures Fabrics
www.ttfabrics.com

Robert Kaufman Fabrics
www.robertkaufman.com

MODA
www.unitednotions.com

Jessica Jones for **J. Caroline Creative**
http://howaboutorange.blogspot.com (Jessica Jones)
www.jcarolinecreative.com (J. Caroline Creative)

Windham Fabrics
www.windhamfabrics.com

* **Jackie Shapiro**
  www.frenchbull.com

Sew Bettie Design
www.sewbettie.com

Henry Glass Fabrics
www.henryglassfabrics.com

* **Linda Lum deBono**
  www.lindalumdebono.com

Oilcloth International
http://oilcloth.com

JAPANESE IMPORTS:

Kokka
www.kokka.co.jp

* **Etsuko Furuya**
  www.f-echino.com

Junko Matsuda for **Daiwabo**
www.pinwheelstrading.com

Lecien
www.lecien.co.jp

INDEX

Page numbers in *italic* indicate illustrations.

Other Storey Titles You Will Enjoy

The Quilting Answer Book, *by Barbara Weiland Tolbert.*
Hundreds of solutions for every quilting quandary, guiding readers through
cutting, piecing, appliqué work, borders, and binding.
432 pages. Paper. ISBN 978-1-60342-144-7.

Sew & Stow, *by Betty Oppenheimer.*
Out with plastic bags and in with 30 practical and stylish totes of all types!
192 pages. Paper. ISBN 978-1-60342-027-3.

Sew What! Bags, *by Lexie Barnes.*
Totes, messenger bags, drawstring sacks, and handbags — 18 pattern-free
projects that can be customized into all shapes and sizes.
152 pages. Hardcover with concealed wire-o. ISBN 978-1-60342-092-1.

Sew What! Fleece, *by Carol Jessop & Chaila Sekora.*
More than 30 cozy projects crafted without patterns, easy to sew and
comfortable to wear.
160 pages. Hardcover with concealed wire-o. ISBN 978-1-58017-626-2.

Sew What! Skirts, *by Francesca DenHartog & Carole Ann Camp.*
A fast, straightforward method to sewing a variety of inspired skirts that fit
your body perfectly, without relying on store-bought patterns.
128 pages. Hardcover with concealed wire-o. ISBN 978-1-58017-625-5.

These and other books from Storey Publishing are available
wherever quality books are sold or by calling 1-800-441-5700.
Visit us at *www.storey.com.*